APPRECIATIVE INQUIRY
FOR CHANGE
MANAGEMENT

APPRECIATIVE INQUIRY FOR CHANGE MANAGEMENT

Using AI to Facilitate Organizational Development

Sarah Lewis, Jonathan Passmore, Stefan Cantore

KOGAN PAGE

London and Philadelphia

First published in Great Britain and the United States in 2008 by Kogan Page Limited

120 Pentonville Road	525 South 4th Street, #241
London N1 9JN	Philadelphia PA 19147
United Kingdom	USA
www.kogan-page.co.uk	

© Sarah Lewis, Jonathan Passmore and Stefan Cantore, 2008

The right of Sarah Lewis, Jonathan Passmore and Stefan Cantore to be identified as the authors of this work has been asserted by them in accordance with the Copyright, Designs and Patents Act 1988.

ISBN 978 0 7494 5071 7

British Library Cataloguing-in-Publication Data

A CIP record for this book is available from the British Library.

Library of Congress Cataloging-in-Publication Data

Lewis, Sarah, 1957–
   Appreciative inquiry for change management : using AI to facilitate organizational development / Sarah Lewis, Jonathan Passmore, and Stefan Cantore.
      p. cm.
   Includes bibliographical references and index.
   ISBN 978-0-7494-5071-7
  1. Organizational change–Management. 2. Appreciative inquiry. 3. Management–Employee participation. 4. Organizational effectiveness.
I. Passmore, Jonathan. II. Cantore, Stefan. III. Title.
   HD58.8.L494 2007
   658.4′063–dc22
2007032743

Typeset by JS Typesetting Ltd, Porthcawl, Mid Glamorgan
Printed and bound in India by Replika Press Pvt Ltd

Contents

About the authors

Sarah Lewis is a chartered occupational psychologist who specializes in individual and organizational change. After an early career in child protection and management she established Jemstone Consultancy in 1993. She is a regular conference presenter and has published occasional articles as well as her *Jemstone Tidbits* newsletter. An associate fellow of the British Psychological Society and a founder member of the Association of Business Psychologists, she can be contacted at sarahlewis@jemstoneconsultancy.co.uk.

Jonathan Passmore is a chartered occupational psychologist, and is a Fellow of the Chartered Institute of Personnel Development (CIPD). He works with OPM, a London-based consulting firm, and the University of East London. Jonathan has board-level experience as a chief executive and company chairman and is a regular contributor to conferences and journals, including the APA *Consulting Psychology* and the *International Coaching Psychological Review*. He is the author of the popular guide to coaching, *Excellence in coaching*, and has a second coaching book due out in spring 2008: *Psychometrics in Coaching*. He can be contacted at jonathancpassmore@yahoo.co.uk.

Stefan Cantore held a number of senior posts before joining OPM as a consultant. He has worked in health and social care, as a chief executive and Workforce Director. He now works with OPM in the areas of leadership and management development with an interest in whole systems change in public services using Appreciative Inquiry and World Café. He can be contacted at stefancantore2@tiscali.co.uk.

About the contributors

Paul E Borawski is Executive Director of the American Society for Quality (ASQ) and is responsible for the operation of ASQ headquarters with a staff of over 220 and a budget of over $46 million. As ASQ's Chief Strategic Officer, Paul leads their Living Strategy efforts and ensures the strategy is implemented, tracked, and kept responsive to changing environmental forces and member needs. Paul can be contacted at pborawski@asq.org.

Dr Juanita Brown is a co-founder of the World Café. She collaborates with senior leaders across sectors to create innovative forums for strategic dialogue on critical business and societal issues. She is a fellow of the World Business Academy, has served as a Research Affiliate with the Institute for the Future and is the co-author of *The World Café: Shaping Our Futures Through Conversations that Matter*, with David Isaacs and the World Café Community. She can be contacted at inquiry@theworldcafe.com.

Bruno Dalbiez has worked as an internal Organization Development and Change consultant for over 25 years in multinational, multicultural, high-technology companies in Europe and the United States. He is currently a senior Organizational Development and Change consultant with Nokia.

David Gilmour leads a marine lubricant business in BP plc and has held roles in sales and marketing. David became interested in Appreciative Inquiry in his role as the Strategy Director in the marine lubricants business: it gave him a new way of leading based on strength, continuity and hope for the future. He can be contacted at david.gilmour@bp.com.

Anne Radford guides consultants who want to more fully integrate strength-based approaches to change into their practice, and works with business leaders who need to change their leadership style to more fully involve others in delivering results. She can be contacted at www.aradford.co.uk, annelondon@aol.com. She also publishes and is editor-in-chief of the online publication *AI (Appreciative Inquiry) Practitioner*, which is available at www.aipractitioner.com, editor@aipractitioner.com.

Jacqueline M Stavros possesses 20 years of strategic planning, marketing, international and organizational change experience. Jackie is an Associate Professor for the College of Management, Lawrence Technological University, MI, USA, where she teaches and integrates Appreciative Inquiry in her coursework: Leading Organizational Change, Strategic Management, Organization Development, and Leadership. She uses Appreciative Inquiry to work with individuals, teams, divisions, and organizations to build dynamic relationships and co-create and facilitate strategic change initiatives. She has co-authored two books, several book chapters and articles. She can be contacted at jstavros@comcast.net.

Joseph R Sprangel Jr is an Instructor of Operations Management for Ithaca College, NY, USA. Joe previously taught courses as an adjunct professor for Lawrence Technological University and Spring Arbor University, teaching Operations Management, Leading Organizational Change, Organizational Development, Six Sigma for Managers, and Strategic Management. He has 28 years of industry experience in the areas of strategic planning, organizational development, leadership, and management in a variety of organizations. He is a student in the Doctorate of Business Administration programme at Lawrence Technological University. His research area of interest is the development of a framework to move an organization from status quo to sustainable development. His MBA is from Spring Arbor University and BBA from Eastern Michigan University. Contact: +1 (607) 274 3940 or jsprangel@ithaca.edu.

Caryn Vanstone is a Business Director with Ashridge Consulting. She works with UK and global companies and non-profits, and is Faculty on the Ashridge MSc in Organization Consulting. Caryn specializes in complex projects of change focusing on issues such as culture, values, engagement and performance, using high-participation, inquiry-based approaches. She can be contacted at caryn.vanstone@ashridge.org.uk.

Arian Ward is CEO and principal coach/consultant for Community Frontiers in Boulder Creek, CA. Arian has been working with ASQ since 2002 on the evolution of their Living Strategy, as well as on the organizational elements needed to support it, including ASQ's culture, business and communication processes, body of knowledge, communities, and membership model. Arian is a co-creator and one of the world's most experienced facilitators of World Cafés. He can be contacted at arian@communityfrontiers.com.

Acknowledgements

We would like to express our thanks to the many people who have contributed to this book or made it possible. To the Kogan Page team, particularly Viki and Charlotte for their support in developing the proposal and in getting the book to print. To our case study authors for their energy and dedication in telling their stories and dealing with our challenge that we did not just want the sunny-side-up version, but the whole picture of change including the difficult bits. To our families and friends who have lost us for periods while we wrote, met and talked about ideas, content and process. To our wide range of colleagues, especially those at the Office for Public Management (OPM) and Jemstone Consultancy, clients and friends who have helped in the development of our thinking and understanding of conversational approaches. We are particularly grateful to the Office for Public Management (OPM) and Jemstone Consultancy for their support and encouragement throughout this project.

In addition we would like to offer our appreciation to the faculty at Kensington Consultation Centre. Many of these ideas have been developed from their tuition over the years and it has not always proved possible to trace ideas back to their initial source, and so be able to adequately acknowledge individual faculty members. We would particularly like to mention Christine Oliver, who has been an inspiring colleague and teacher. We would also like to thank Debbie Barleggs,

David Lewis, Jordan Smith, Stewart Smith and Colin Brown for their willingness to comment on early drafts. The work is much improved as a result of their attention.

This book is dedicated to four special people who have influenced our lives and helped us in different ways:

To Charlie and May Green
To Jenny Lewis for helping me believe 'I can'.
To Zoe Nicholson for her inspiration and encouragement.

Introduction

How can we work with one of the most ubiquitous of human abilities to create the most profound change in our organizations?

This is the essential question we set out to answer by exploring the power of conversation to create new futures for people and organizations. Having a conversation with someone else is a process with which we are very familiar; however, its very familiarity can obscure its unique contribution to our ability to sustain, and change, our social relations. Recently, in different ways, some innovative practitioners have begun to explore the power and properties of conversation in an organizational context, developing such concepts as Appreciative Inquiry, Future Search, Open Space, World Café, and Circle. One common theme amongst their work is that they all highlight conversation as a key process for achieving organizational change. Our aim with this book is to offer an integrated perspective on these different practices by illuminating more clearly, and exploring in some depth, this common thread of conversation.

THE JOURNEY THROUGH THE BOOK

The first part of the book is devoted to making clear the difference between the conversational approaches to organizational change that we are presenting, and the mechanistic approach. We start, in Chapter 1, by bringing the mechanistic understanding of organizations clearly into the light. This allows us to see the contrast offered by our alternative characterization of organizations more clearly. We present this alternative view of organizations, 'organizations as living human systems', in Chapter 2. Having established the contrast, we use our third chapter to provide a historic account of the strands of theory and practice that support this second understanding of organizations. This chapter ends with a consideration of why it might be that, from different starting points, these sources are beginning to converge into clear patterns of practice. It also considers why the insights and understanding of human interaction that they offer might be of particular interest to us at the beginning of the 21st century. In the final chapter of this part we present an overview guide to the practice of Appreciative Inquiry. In this way we use Part 1 to introduce conversation-based practice as a genuinely alternative approach to organizations, based on a genuinely different understanding. We also demonstrate that this approach can be practically applied.

In Part 2 we offer further in-depth exploration of the specific skills that support integrated conversational practice, such as question creation (Chapter 5), learning to be a conversational practitioner (Chapter 6), and working with story in organizations (Chapter 7). In each of these chapters we also offer clear practice guidance. In Chapter 7, we also introduce further advanced conversational practice based on Maturana and Varela's (1987) idea of the domains of experience. In the second half of this chapter, we explore conversationally sympathetic ways of creating momentary snapshots of the ongoing organizational flow. Creating such temporary moments of clarity allows us to consider how to act purposefully to achieve change. In Chapter 8 we illuminate the practical relevance of this enhanced awareness of conversational skills by introducing four further specific approaches that have an understanding of the conversational life of the organization at their heart, namely World Café, Open Space, Future Search and Circle. In Chapter 9 we consider some underpinning conversational skills relevant to working in this way, such as being conscious of the spirit in which we work, and the need to develop appreciative eyes and ears.

In Part 3 we turn our attention to helping you pull together the skills, perspectives and approaches that we have introduced into a practical, conversation-based approach to organizational challenges. Chapter 10 specifically addresses some of the queries commonly encountered when people begin to practise in this way. We have chosen to frame this chapter around Appreciative Inquiry as the most prevalent of these approaches, and so the most likely to be familiar to our readers either through direct experience or through reading. The remainder of this part, Chapters 11–14, continues to develop the theme of putting skills into practice by presenting four case studies where the different authors give us their accounts of integrating these ways of thinking into their practice. These look at both Appreciative Inquiry and World Café in use in organizations as diverse as BP, Nokia, the American Quality Association and OTC.

SOME CHOICES WE MADE ALONG THE WAY

Writing this book has provided us with many challenges, not least those of how to present complex ideas simply, how to minimize the use of jargon while achieving precision where precision is needed, and how to avoid replicating good work that already exists. Our solution to the last-named challenge is to be explicit that we see this book as building on, and offering a companion to, existing works that explain in detail some of the approaches named. For instance, the *Appreciative Inquiry Handbook* by David Cooperrider and colleagues (2005) gives an excellent explanation of Appreciative Inquiry and fantastically detailed guidance on how to do it. Harrison Owen's (1997) text, *Open Space Technology*, again is an easy-to-read definitive guide to running an Open Space event. Similarly, Juanita Brown and colleagues (2005) have produced the definitive guide to the World Café. We see our text as sitting in close relationship to these, and also to one of the definitive texts in the organizational theory field, Burnes (2000) *Managing Change*. Burnes provides a very full account of the whole field of organizational change, of which we bring one corner into sharp relief. Should you wish to expand your field of view from our text to include a comprehensive overview of the many theories and approaches that have been advocated in the past 50 years, this is book is an excellent resource.

We have chosen to respond to the challenge of achieving both simplicity and precision as follows. We are clear that this book is built on and reflects an integration of: conversational approaches to organizational change; a systemic and relational understanding of organizations; a social constructionist perspective on social life and the nature of knowledge; a psychological appreciation of people's behaviour; and a pragmatic approach to the application of knowledge and skill. Each of these strands brings with it its own set of linguistic jargon and assumed understandings. For us these theoretical constructs are like the colour swatch supporting the design of a garment: we do not want to talk to you about the colour swatch, we want you to focus on the garment. However, the swatch is there, and we may occasionally want to call your attention to some particular aspect of it to highlight a feature of what we are describing. That said, our overall intention is to ensure that these strands, while consistently present, do not distract from our intention of providing an informed, easy-to-understand guide to what conversational practice is, what makes it work, and how to do it.

THE BOOK AS AN EMERGING AND UNFINISHED CONVERSATION

This book is offered as a contribution to an emerging and evolving conversation about creative conversations for change in organizations: why they are valuable, how they are effective, and how to promote, create and generate such conversations. It is born of an attempt to integrate our experiences of working in different, yet clearly related ways into a reasonably coherent resource for others. In this way it is a product of our particular histories, experiences, contexts, values and theories. These in turn are integrated with the work of many other practitioners and theorists, whose work we both make reference to and build upon. We believe our specific contribution with this book is to integrate this work in such a way as to place conversation centre stage when we begin to think about changing things in our organizations. Our hope is that we have brought existing strands of thought and practice together into an easy-to-understand framework for conversation-based practice.

Part 1

Understanding conversational approaches to change

In this first section we introduce the conversation-based approach to change. However, before we explain what it is, we explain what it isn't by reviewing the current dominant approach to organizational change. Chapter 1 explores the machine metaphor of organizations that is at the root of so much of our current change-directed behaviour. We consider how this metaphor for understanding organizations became so pre-eminent and how its influence can be detected in unspoken organizational beliefs about people at work, the role of management, and how to induce change.

In Chapter 2 we introduce an alternative view of organizations. We consider organizations as living human systems and look at how this different perspective encourages different beliefs about people at work, the role of management and how to effect organizational change. Specifically we consider the importance of patterns of relationship and communication within organizations for both organizational stability and change.

In Chapter 3 we consider how these conversational approaches to understanding organizations and organizational change have developed from different sources of thought. We notice how, from different origins, they are beginning to converge on some common ground. Particularly we note what they have to suggest about the nature and role of conversation in organizational life, and why this might be a particularly attractive way of understanding organizations at the beginning of the 21st century.

Finally, in Chapter 4, we examine one conversation-based approach to change in more detail: Appreciative Inquiry. This book is intended to be practical as well as theoretical and we have chosen Appreciative Inquiry as our practical example of a conversational process both because we know it well, and also because there is currently a ground-swell of interest in this approach. In this chapter we explain how to set up and run a standard Appreciative Inquiry summit as an example of conversation-based practice in action.

1

Organizations as machines, workers as cogs and management as a control process

INTRODUCTION

An important feature of the conversation-based approach to organizational change featured throughout this book is that it is based on an understanding of organizations as living human systems. This statement regarding the nature of organizations may seem as if it is stating the obvious. Yet it stands in stark contrast to the widespread if unacknowledged view of them as really just large machines with some human components. This mechanistic view of organizations is a legacy of the Industrial Revolution, and we have chosen to devote this first chapter to illuminating this view in order to throw the difference between these two perspectives into sharper relief.

We begin the chapter by observing the long history of human organization. We notice how the various forms of self-organization developed over time seemed inadequate to the task of meeting the organizational demands of the Industrial Revolution. We explore how the emergence of the large corporations, themselves a response to these challenges, acted as a trigger to questions about the nature of large organizations and to a desire for guidance. From here we single out Fredrick Taylor as the architect of the idea of the organization as a machine, an idea that spread through the development and dissemination of his *Principles of Scientific Management* (1912). Finally we examine the ongoing impact of Taylor's blueprint for the efficient organization on many aspects of organizational life. By illuminating the organization-as-machine view in some depth we hope to make it easier to see that the living-human-system view, presented in Chapter 2 and throughout the rest of the book, offers a genuinely alternative way to understand, and work within, organizations.

ORGANIZATION AS A GROUP SOCIAL SKILL

Ever since the bigger, better, higher-value coconuts were observed to be on the islands across the channel, interested individuals have found ways to organize themselves into groups to take the risks, and reap the rewards, of being the ones to venture forth. Often these individuals weren't related, which meant they weren't operating within the clear framework of obligation provided by family ties. This lack of family ties created the need for more formal agreements regarding the obligations between them. Such agreements had to meet the challenge of ensuring that the relationship between the degree of exposure to risk experienced by each individual, and their share of the rewards, was fair and could be upheld. Many forms of agreement were created to meet these challenges so that people could make the most of the opportunities available for wealth generation. These agreements took such forms as: partnerships, guilds, joint venture companies, joint stock companies, state sponsored companies, and companies by Royal Charter.

While all of these organizational structures had their virtues, they also had limitations. Many of these arrangements were time limited, or were for a specific purpose only, and so had to be constructed anew for each new venture. Longer-term agreements ran into difficulties if a founder died or wanted to leave the arrangement, as inheritance issues were difficult to resolve. No agreement was able to solve the problem of unlimited liability for those involved. These various difficulties conspired to ensure that any particular organization rarely lasted any length of time or outlived the founders' active involvement. Once the

Industrial Revolution was under way, requiring huge investment to build canals and railways, these limitations became more pressing (Micklethwait and Wooldridge, 2003).

Fortunately for would-be investors and entrepreneurs, The Companies Act of 1862 provided an answer to the challenges outlined above by making possible the development of the limited liability joint stock company. It is difficult now, since it is such an accepted part of our economic and commercial landscape, to appreciate the revolutionary nature of this piece of legislation. The Act encapsulated three ideas which, put together and enshrined in legal form, changed the organizational environment in an unprecedented way. These ideas were: that a company could be an artificial person; that it could issue tradable shares to any number of individuals; and that the individual investors could all be offered limited liability. The Act facilitated the creation of an entity that had a life of its own, a construction that endured as individuals joined and left. This acted to free the organization from its founders and from reliance on the financial resources of a few socially cohesive people. It also freed organizations from an obligation to have a specific limited purpose such as building a canal, or opening up trading opportunities in India. Now a company could be formed for the general purpose of 'doing business', meaning that it could live for ever. The modern corporation now dominates the economic and consumer experience, influencing both how we work and how we consume. The preponderance of big corporations (5.5 million in the United States in 2001; Micklethwait and Wooldridge, 2003), combined with the prevalence of organizations in the spheres of education, religion and state, ensures that we live our lives within the inescapable context of organizations. No wonder we are interested in how they work and how to improve them.

TAYLORISM AND SCIENTIFIC MANAGEMENT

One of the first people to engage with the challenge of the modern corporation was the American Fredrick Taylor. Born into a Quaker family in 1865, Taylor displayed some interesting personal characteristics from an early age. For example, it is recorded that he was fairly compulsive as a young adolescent, always counting and measuring things with the object of improving how things could be done. He also invented a harness for himself to wear in bed when he was about 12, to stop him turning on his back and so prevent the nightmares from which he suffered. He was very bright and his family had hopes that he would become a lawyer, but he chose instead to study engineering and started in employment as a low-ranking machinist and pattern maker at the Midvale Steel Company. He rose up the organization quickly, becoming chief engineer within 6 years. During this time he introduced piece-rate working to the organization, and displayed a general interest in studying how jobs were done and how they could be done more efficiently (Burnes, 2000; Papesh, 2006).

These interests in efficiency and innovation are evident throughout Taylor's career. In 1897 he became a consulting engineer, working to help organizations become more productive and profitable. He noted some of the problems in organizations, such as work-shirking or foot-dragging, and what he called 'soldiering', that is, doing the least necessary. He was keen to help organizations reduce this unproductive approach to work. However, his early proposals of how to solve these problems involved a certain amount of what Rose calls 'managerial thuggery' (Rose, 1988), such as victimization, sacking and blacklisting of workers he found inadequate. He also introduced very effective time- and motion-based improvements in ways of working and so productivity. His ruthless focus on efficiency gains and cost-cutting (including cutting labour costs) made him many enemies, to the extent that he was removed from his most lucrative and successful assignment at Bethlehem Iron Works in 1901. Following this he devoted his time to developing his comprehensive theory of Scientific Management (Figure 1.1) (Papesh, 2006).

Fredrick Taylor is extremely important to our understanding of organizations and organizational theory. In 1912 he published *The Principles of Scientific Management,* and in the same year he was called to attend a Governmental Special Committee established to investigate the Taylor and Other Systems of Shop Management. Off the back of this exposure he toured and lectured extensively, effectively becoming the first management guru or consultant. His advice and guidance were well received by the managers and owners of these new industrial organizations who were meeting the challenges of management with recourse to only their own personal experience and rules of thumb. The organizations of which they were nominally in charge were proving to be a battleground for the relative power of labour and capital. This power battle was frequently expressed through disputes over the attempted reduction of the status of the craft workers by the dismantling of their expertise, or over the imposition of disciplined ways of working. Taylor's work offered a rationalization of managers'

A Summary of the Principles of Scientific Management

- Shift all responsibility for the organization of the work from the worker to the manager. Managers should do all the thinking relating to the planning and design of work, leaving workers with the task of implementation.
- Use scientific methods to determine the most efficient way of doing work. Design the worker's task accordingly, specifying the precise way in which the work is to be done.
- Select the best person to perform the job thus designed.
- Train the worker to do the work efficiently.
- Monitor worker performance to ensure that appropriate work procedures are followed and that appropriate results are achieved.

Morgan (1997)

A summary of the assumptions underpinning the Principles

We might note the assumptions inherent in his work, as spelt out in his testimony to the House of Representatives Committee in 1912, or identified by Collins, that:

- there is one *scientifically* verifiable best way to organize work;
- staff can be *scientifically* selected;
- workers and managers share a *mutuality of interest* because of the unitary nature of the organization;
- organizations are *rational entities*;
- people are *rational, economic actors*;
- there are scientific laws of administration from which human values and *emotions can be excluded*;
- these laws are *universal*, applicable to all and any organizations;
- organizations should be designed *scientifically*.

Collins (1998), Taylor (1912)

Figure 1.1   A summary of the principles of Scientific Management

right to manage, guidance on how to organize the business and advice on how to manage workers. His comprehensive and 'science'-based theory legitimized both the reduction of the power of skilled workers and the increase in power of the managerial class. Effectively it gave managers a story of 'righteousness' that supported their right to run the business in the most productive and profitable way regardless of the views of the employees. It did this by making it possible for managers to refer to a higher-order authority or power than their own personal whim, in this case the power of science as expressed through the authority of logic and reason.

Looking at Taylor's work, we can see an underlying story of the nature of this new organization, the corporation. Existing as an entity in its own right, and drawing down authority from the gods of science and technology, the corporation was looking less and less like a human construction. For Taylor, an engineer by trade, it began instead to look more and more like a machine. Imbued as he was with an awareness of the value of efficiency in all things, he began to conceptualize the organization as a machine in need of efficiency improvements. For Taylor the way forward to a more peaceful and productive organizational environment was through engineering the organization. His whole blueprint for how an organization should be successfully managed is based on the understanding of the organization as a vast machine. Calling on a contemporary understanding of organizational metaphor (Morgan, 1997), we can say that his underlying metaphor is of the organization-as-machine. This metaphor has proved to be extremely durable and extremely powerful in influencing our understanding of, and behaviour within, organizations. The majority of managers and workers, whether they realize it or not, carry this idea of an organization into their every organizational interaction. Many of Taylor's specific principles, as well as his underlying assumptions, appear to have penetrated the very ether of organizational belief, being present as unspoken and widely accepted truisms (Figure 1.2).

It is important that we examine the beliefs that follow from this idea of the organization-as-machine as they act as highly influential, yet usually unarticulated, rationales for change-orientated behaviours. Below we select a few of these beliefs to examine in more depth, looking at their relationship to the mechanistic understanding of organizations and their influence on organizational behaviour.

BELIEF IN THE POWER OF PROBLEM SOLVING TO CHANGE ORGANIZATIONS

Human beings are great problem solvers. Not only do we have a natural ability to improve our environment, that is, to solve all manner of problems that are pertinent to us, but we also hone this natural ability during our years at school into highly developed logic-based reasoning skills. Having these skills, we then tend to see all problems as being solvable by their application. The organization-as-machine metaphor only encourages this tendency, leading us to see all problems as problems of logic. These are familiar from our school days, for

Taylor's legacy still evident today

- Efficiency being regarded as an unquestioned organizational virtue, often at the expense of other organizational virtues, such as effectiveness.
- The science of job design with its emphasis on simplification and specialization is still present, for instance in service industry assembly lines.
- The importance of management and organizational studies.
- The process of business planning and strategy, and the industry around it.
- The command and control organizational structure.
- Job measurement, job evaluation and job equivalence.
- The emphasis on one best way of organizing.
- The unitary view of organizations, and the concomitant concept of 'resistance to change'.
- The understanding of organizations as rational machines.
- Management as control.
- Target setting and standardization.
- The emphasis on productivity.

Taylor's legacy regarding our understanding of organizations in change

- The understanding of leaders as the head and the organization as the body, with all that that assumption entails.
- The premise of predictable and controllable change.
- An assumption of cascading intention.

Figure 1.2 Taylor's legacy evident today

example, 'If train A leaves Edinburgh at 6.20, and train B leaves London at 6.50 and both are travelling at 100 mph, when and where will they pass?' Reading this, you will immediately have noticed that we don't have all the information necessary to solve the problem, yet you will also likely be of the view that with appropriate information we could. It is this conviction, that with the right information we could solve the problem, which is at the heart of logic-based problem solving. So when we say that we believe a problem to be a problem of logic, we are saying that we believe that if we can find, create or generate sufficient data and analyse it against a set of criteria then the right (and indeed the best) answer to our problem will emerge. We can have faith on this being the best answer to our problem as it will be based on rational thinking, free from distortion by such contaminating factors as feelings, beliefs, values or prejudice.

This basic data analysis process works for many problems, and we use it all the time. If I want to know what time to catch a train I gather data about train times and journey lengths, weigh them against my criteria of quality of journey and 'contingency time' and decide on the particular train for me: problem solved. It also works for some categories of organizational change, and organizational theory abounds with more or less sophisticated models of this process. Pascal *et al* (2000) suggest that this form of problem solving is appropriate when the desired end state is known in advance, and the skills and motivation exist to achieve it. For instance, if the desired change is an increase in the ratio of the production of widget A to widget B, and the workers are multi-skilled and quite used to adjusting the production ratio, then treating this as a problem of logic might well result in the development of a successful change plan. This will then be communicated and implemented through the creation and implementation of a more or less formal project plan. In the case of larger-scale organizational change the application of logical problem-solving methods tends in practice to result in a series of project plans. Project plans work well as a route to change when, as stated above, the desired end state is known, the skills to achieve it already exist and the workers are motivated to achieve it; however, these conditions are frequently not present when organizations need to change. In this case, a different approach is required.

Problems arise when organizations make a category error and fail to recognize that they are now dealing with a qualitatively different challenge. This failure of distinction arises as the logic-based problem-solving model is so pervasive that there is a tendency to perceive all issues of organizational change as issues of logical problem solving; and to treat them as such. Even change plan failure is taken not as evidence that the approach is at fault, but rather as evidence that the selected process has not been applied rigorously enough. In this instance it is assumed that to rectify the problem more of the same is needed. In this way organizations can get caught in a vicious circle of ever more planning, relentlessly increasing levels of plan-adherence monitoring, and escalating demands on those involved to supply ever more data. Organizations show this persistence in applying logical problem-solving methods despite a lack of any evidence of success because it's their default mode and because they have little awareness of alternatives. Yet however expertly or determinedly a change process is applied, if there has been a category error, then the process can't deliver the desired change. Working within the metaphor of organization-as-machine makes it easy to see every issue as a problem, and every problem as a problem of logic. It makes it hard to see people as fully rounded human beings living in a world where the force of logic is only a small and partial determinant of their actions. It makes it hard to see change as being embedded in patterns of human communication and relationship.

BELIEF IN THE POWER OF NAMING PROBLEMS
TO PRODUCE CHANGE

In the same way that organizations often act as if they believe that creating an action plan is the key to implementing change, so they can often act as if naming a problem is the key to initiating change. Believing this, organizations can devote considerable resources to determining the answer to the question 'What is the problem?' Those charged with initiating change will draw in outsiders to help them answer this question and related ones such as 'What is the real problem', 'What is the main problem?' or 'What is the underlying problem?' Meetings are convened to devote time to these questions. The reward for these endeavours is worth the effort as once an issue is named as a problem, a process exists for dealing with it: the problem-solving process. When they are thinking like this, organizations can make everything into a problem. For instance, something might start off as an opportunity, or a challenge or an unexpected event, but it becomes, through the unconscious application of the problem-solving model, a problem as in 'The problem is how we are going to make the most of this opportunity' or 'The problem is how we are going to meet the challenge'. Sometimes it's almost as if we can't see issues in organizations until we can see them as a problem, that we can't think about things until we can think about them as a problem. Clearly, though, if you get the problem wrong then the solution will be wrong, hence the emphasis on getting the problem right.

Thinking of organizations as machines that sometimes develop problems that need fixing makes it hard for organizations to embrace change as a positive activity to be engaged in when nothing is wrong. The majority of us display this attitude to the machines in our lives; take, for instance, our attitude to our cars. For most of us, if our car is working well, then, apart from maintaining it, we leave it alone. When it draws our attention to itself, by going wrong, then we work to fix it. Many managers and leaders see their organizations the same way. Change is seen as an interruption to the normal smooth running of the organization, by its very nature disruptive. It is only to be encouraged if there is a problem to fix. This means that when someone wants to introduce some innovative change, they have first to create an awareness of a problem. Once the organization's attention has been drawn to the problem, then they might be interested in the proposed solution. Cooperrider notes that this way of thinking eventually results in organizations being seen as problems, and organization being seen as being inherently problematic. 'It's not so much that organizations have problems, they are problems' (Cooperrider and Whitney, 2001: 25). The organization becomes focused on finding and fixing problems. So if you want to draw the organization's attention to something you have to identify it as a problem. In many organizations one of the most powerful attention-grabbing phrases is 'We've got a problem here', which often leads straight into the naming game, as in 'What type of a problem?'

BELIEF IN THE POWER OF INSTRUCTION TO ACHIEVE CHANGE

Organizations are beset by the belief that telling people what to do or what is needed is a sure-fire way to achieve the desired change – despite daily evidence that telling people what to do, or what you want, doesn't work. Evidence of the hopeless optimism of this belief is present in every aspect of our lives. If telling people what to do made them adapt or change their behaviour we would all have perfectly behaved children, and gum-free pavements, yet we don't. People rarely do what they are told unless some specific conditions exist, namely: that they have specifically asked for guidance on what to do (and even then they don't always follow the advice given); that they are in dire straits and need someone to do their thinking for them (if you offer the drowning man the proverbial straw and tell him to clutch it he probably will); or that they can be coerced by the application of unpleasant consequences for non-compliance. Fortunately for those in organizations who wish to produce change by instruction, this last condition is often present. Many workplaces are very coercive environments and there are unpleasant penalties for not doing what you are told. You are expected to comply with organizational requests regardless of your own feelings about the matter, and should you feel disinclined to do so then various coercive measures, such as informal 'dressing-downs' or formal disciplinary procedures, can be brought into play. In such an environment, telling people what to do may well produce compliance. However, when people do things because they have to, rather than because they want to, over time unintended consequences become apparent. Coercive environments can contribute to poor morale, work avoidance and work absence (Sidman, 1989).

THE BELIEF THAT EMOTIONS ARE PROBLEMATIC

The organization-as-machine metaphor has no place for emotions. Emotions and emotional displays are seen as problematic and are as much as possible to be factored out of organizational functioning. Effective workers in organizations are desired to act as if they have no other role in life, as if they have no life outside work, and as if they don't experience emotional reactions to life. When people do display strong emotions at work, this is often seen as problematic, and the behaviour acquires a problem label. In the context of organizational change, a strong negative emotional reaction to the suggested change is usually labelled 'resistance' or 'lack of understanding' or 'a communication problem', all of which are seen as problems, more or less amenable to fixing. Rarely is such a reaction labelled as a legitimate reaction to unpleasant news, or as useful information about an aspect of the change that may have been overlooked. In the same way that patients get in the way of a smoothly run hospital, and schools are disrupted by noisy and inattentive pupils, so people, when they start behaving like people, can be a thorn in the side of a smooth-running organizational machine.

BELIEF IN THE POWER OF CRITICISM AND FEAR TO MOTIVATE CHANGE

For all that organizations may operate within the belief that telling people what they need to change will do the trick, they do not rely on the power of instruction alone. A lot of organizational energy is devoted to the vexed question of motivation, and its first cousin, performance management. When managers are considering how to help staff improve their performance, criticism, usually called feedback, is often the first port of call. Giving feedback is motivated by, among other things, a belief that illuminating the logical argument for change will be sufficient to induce change. The logic assumption runs along the lines of: 'If I tell you what the problem is with what you are doing (how it's wrong), and what you need to do about it (to put it right), then you will understand the logic of the situation and the need for change and so will change.' Emotions, therefore, needn't come into it. However, it is not uncommon to experience strong negative reactions when 'given feedback'. Specifically, people often feel fearful, upset, criticized and attacked. It is these very emotions that act as the motivation for change as people work to avoid a repeat of the unpleasant experience or to regain the regard of their manager. Without this emotional component the 'feedback' would be a lot less effective in achieving behavioural change. However, organizations find this emotional fallout problematic (after all, emotions have no place in a machine), and so they spend a fair amount of time attempting to work out how this 'feedback' can be given 'constructively', that is, in a manner that doesn't cause an adverse emotional reaction. This desire to produce behaviour change without producing an emotional reaction ties the organization into an unrealized paradox as they rely on the emotional impact to achieve the motivation for change, while simultaneously working to ensure that no emotional impact is felt.

The emotional fallout for the individual and ultimately the organization of an over-reliance on this form of motivation can be severe and long-term. A particular danger of too much 'constructive feedback', that is, criticism, is the withdrawal of a willingness to innovate, volunteer or take risks. And, in tandem, there can be an increase in the energy put into self-preservation and blame avoidance (Sidman, 1989). Of interest to us is the contrast between a predominant organizational story of organization-as-machine, where emotions are counterproductive to the smooth running of the machine, and a reliance on emotions to achieve motivation for change. This confusion is frequently expressed in the metaphors used about raising motivation during organizational change, many of which contain violent images of pain and fear. We are thinking particularly of such popular motivating images as 'the burning platform' and 'holding their feet to the fire' (Welch and Byrne, 2001).

BELIEF IN THE HEAD AND BODY ORGANIZATIONAL SPLIT

Machines need controlling mechanisms. Therefore, if organizations are machines, so do organizations. Within the organization-as-machine metaphor organizations can be seen to consist of control processes and performance processes. In Taylor's model the separate and complementary roles of manager and worker reflect this division: the managers provide the controlling mind while the workers perform. This clear distinction between the two roles also owes a lot to the 17th-century philosopher René Descartes and his work on the relationship between the physical body and the Godly soul.

Descartes introduced the idea of the mind/body split as a way of 'solving' the question of the relationship between the ethereal mind (or soul) and the physical body. He suggested that the body was essentially like a machine, while the mind possessed the controlling processes. Understanding the relationship this way means that to make my arm move I must first think of moving my arm. The body cannot move independently of a controlling process (a thought) in the mind (Wikipedia, 2007). This understanding of the distinct and different nature of the two entities has been highly influential in Western thinking. The mind is seen as the seat of all that is rational and logical, while the body's true role is to obey the mind like a machine. Incidentally, the bodily 'passions' are seen as temporary dysfunctions that can have a disruptive effect on the mind. It is this understanding of the body as a machine that links Cartesian thinking to organizational functioning.

We don't have to look at organizational functioning too hard to see how this Cartesian dualism thinking continues to influence relationships in the workplace between those who see themselves as the organizational 'mind', licensed to direct and control the body, and those in the body of the organization, who are expected to do no more or less than they are directed. This understanding of the two roles is often left unchallenged during organizational change. It is taken as read that the managers will do the thinking and will design the new control processes, while the workers are expected, like the body of the machine, to perform as directed. This duality is further reflected in the belief in the linear sequencing of thinking and doing, these activities being seen as separate, mutually exclusive, and to follow each other sequentially. So first the managers do the thinking about, and planning of, what to do, then the workers implement the plan.

BELIEF IN THE POWER OF SEPARATING ELEMENTS TO ENHANCE CLARITY AND SO THE ABILITY TO ACT EFFICIENTLY

Organizations are keen to reduce complex phenomena to more manageable elements in the belief that this will help them act more efficiently. To this end a complex change project is broken down into a sequence of manageable activities. A typical change sequence might start: establish the nature of the problem; gather data about the problem and some current state information; agree what change is required and how it will be measured; discuss the success criteria; decide what to do; draw up an implementation plan; and communicate said plan. To some extent this separating out and sequencing of the elements can be seen as a way of trying to impose some simplicity, some order, upon a chaotic world. It offers a way to concentrate on one thing at a time. As a way of introducing order and reducing complexity, this approach has merit. The trouble is that the idea of thinking about one thing at a time slides imperceptibly into a belief that only one thing is happening at a time, the thing we are thinking about.

So while helpful for introducing order, these beliefs can also become a hindrance as they direct our attention towards one thing at the expense of our awareness of another. Looking only at the thing we are doing we miss the other things that are happening simultaneously. For instance, focused on the data we are gathering, we fail to observe that the very issue about which we are gathering data is changed by our data-gathering activity. Sending out staff surveys isn't just data collection; the very activity impacts on the engagement, satisfaction and expectations of individuals. Making an appointment to see a coaching client is not just something that we do 'before' we meet the client, it is part of the relationship-building and contracting process. In our quest to make the world understandable, and specifically to make change manageable, we have a tendency to make the issue small enough, and simple enough, to fit the resource (the brains) brought to the task. In a complex situation it might be more productive to find a way to bring sufficient brains together to encompass the complexity of the task.

BELIEF IN A 'RIGHT ANSWER' TO THE PROBLEM OF DESIGN

An understanding of the organization-as-machine carries with it the idea of 'perfectibility' or ultimate design. In other words, there is an inherent suggestion in this way of thinking that there will be a 'right answer' to the question of 'how best to organize ourselves'. It is this, often unspoken, belief that prompts leaders and managers to adopt one organizational design after another. They do this in the hope that this one will be 'the answer' and that they can then cease the quest for 'the answer' and all the change that entails and just 'get on' with running their organization. Even as they acknowledge that change is now an organizational constant, people can continue their search for the ultimately adaptive design, not appreciating that by definition this is unachievable.

SUMMARY

In this chapter we have presented an analysis of some of the assumptions about organizational change that follow from the conceptualization of the organization as a machine. We have suggested that the emergence of the story of organization-as-machine is connected to the creation of the limited liability joint stock company as a legal entity. We have noted that this story had terrific resonance at the time of the Industrial Revolution, when the power of science, machine and technology was in the ascendant. Our interest has been in the observation that this metaphor of organization-as-machine continues to be a powerful, if frequently unacknowledged, story in organizational life. We have also noted that some of the puzzling and sometimes paradoxical things that organizations do can be related to this prevalent belief about the nature of organizations. We have spelt this out in some detail so that the alternative understanding offered by a view of organizations as living human systems, as explored in the rest of this book, can be seen more clearly. The next chapter will follow the same process of introducing the perspective, identifying its underlying beliefs, and then identifying the assumptions about organizational change that follow from it.

2

An alternative approach: organizations as living human systems

INTRODUCTION

In the first chapter we considered the prevalent view of the organization as a machine. Among other things we noted that this view had its origins in the Industrial Revolution, and that Fredrick Taylor, himself an engineer, had codified this view into a set of principles offering guidance on how to manage organizations. It is sometimes assumed that since this perspective is now over a hundred years old, it must be of only historic interest. On the contrary, we find that this view is remarkably durable, and that its influence is evident throughout organizational life and activity. One of the reasons this view has had such a long shelf life is that it chimes very well with our sense of ourselves as logical, rational beings with great problem-solving abilities. We like to emphasize our abilities in these areas as they are seen to be key differentiators between ourselves and animals. However, to view ourselves exclusively this way is to overlook our many emotional, social and creative abilities. Similarly, to view organizations as machines is to overlook their emotional, relational and creative life. It is to this that we now wish to turn your attention. To be able to see these aspects of organizational life more clearly we need to view organizations from a different perspective to that of organization-as-machine. Viewing organizations instead as living human systems encourages us to focus on the relational and conversational features of organizations.

The organization-as-living-human-system perspective recognizes that people, in relationship with each other, create organization; and that without people working together organizations would not exist. The phrase 'living human system' draws our attention to three specific attributes of organizations. First, they are alive rather than, as the machine metaphor might suggest, inert. Second, that they are human, that is, they are made up of people. And third, that they are systems composed of related elements. Each of these attributes, signalled by the phrase 'living human system', has important implications for our understanding of organizations and organizational life.

In this chapter we shall examine the meaning of the phase 'living human system' and then consider the implications for understanding organizations and organizational life that follow from this perspective.

THE ORGANIZATION AS LIVING

An organization can be viewed as 'living' in two distinct ways. First, there is the idea that it is made up of living organisms, that is, people. Second, there is the idea that the joint creation of the people involved, 'the organization', itself is alive. This is the idea that we want to examine further here. To talk about an organization as 'living' suggests that potential exists for both growth and renewal. It also suggests that the organization will have a need for sustenance, something that gives it life. If we can gain an understanding of what, within all the organizational activity, are the things that give it life, then we can achieve change through nurturing and growing the life-giving aspects of the organization. Viewing the organization as 'alive' reminds us that living systems are located within, and are responsive to, their environment. In this way we can recognize organizations as being part of the bigger environment, not sealed units within it. We might also note that to be alive is to be dynamic in our behaviour, not static in our form. Viewing the organization this way, we can experience the constant adaptation and change and the lack of a finite state within organizations as to be expected, maybe even as an important resource for growth and renewal, rather than as problematic.

ORGANIZATIONS AS HUMAN

Organizations only exist because of people. Organizations are made up of people. People create organization. People create organizations. Organizations are a human phenomenon. Where people are present, all human life is present. Organizations contain all aspects of human life. Human life is disorderly, at times chaotic, emotion ridden, illogical, irrational, a mystery and exceedingly common. Where there are people there will be confusion, misunderstanding, enlightenment, common cause, conflict and harmony. Where there are people there will be behaviour driven by logic, desire, emotion, imagination, tiredness, righteousness, habit, mischief, good intentions, and misjudgement. Human beings are, on the whole, in the main, without a doubt, essentially, messy. Organizations, being made up of messy people, are messy. Organizations are not tidy. They do not run on orderly lines. They can't, as they are human in nature. This might seem obvious, but it is easily overlooked when the organization-as-machine perspective encourages us to regard the people in organizations primarily as either control processes or cogs.

ORGANIZATIONS AS SYSTEMS

And finally, an organization is a system. A definition of a system is that it is made up of parts that are interdependent, inter-reliant, and interconnected (French and Bell, 1999). It is increasing becoming apparent that the whole world is one big system. However, our mechanistic conceptualization of organizations as being made up of many discrete elements: marketing, production, sales, planning, finance etc, can lead us to believe that we can affect parts of the system in isolation. We may believe, for instance, that outsourcing the customer care function will leave the rest of the organization unaffected, or that computerizing human resources (HR) systems is a purely technical matter. The living-human-system understanding of organizations encourages us to look at organizations differently.

Essentially it is the pattern of the system that interests us rather than the individual elements. The system patterns are expressive of the relationships between the elements. And because it is a human system the patterns we are interested in are patterns of belief, patterns of communication, patterns of action and reaction, patterns of sense making, and patterns of emotion. Because we view the organization as a living human system, we are interested in understanding what amongst all of these patterns are the aspects and elements that give life to the system.

Viewing organizations as living human systems leads us to focus on particular features of organizational life when we are working to achieve organizational change. The interactions we have with others to this end are influenced by our beliefs about how to achieve growth and renewal of this living entity, of how to work with all that is human within the organization, and of how to work with the interconnectedness of the organizational system. Below we examine some of the specific beliefs about what supports continuity and change in organizational life that stem from this way of understanding organizations.

BELIEF IN THE POWER OF APPRECIATION TO PROMOTE GROWTH

A belief in the power of appreciation to achieve change is particularly highlighted within Appreciative Inquiry. The more we've worked with Appreciative Inquiry and similar approaches the more fascinating the idea of appreciation, and the power of appreciation to achieve change, has become. When someone is appreciated, when what they do is appreciated, they grow towards that appreciation.

One of us recently experienced the power of appreciation. Arriving to deliver training at a conference centre we were greeted with a few problems: missing light bulbs, tables laid out incorrectly, no flipchart stands in the room, a lack of response by anyone to our needs until 'Janice the conference person arrives', and delegates due in half an hour. However, once we managed to get on the conference centre manager's radar these things were quickly sorted. As this was happening, we made sure we spent our time appreciating those who responded quickly to our needs rather than criticizing those who had allowed them to occur in the first place. Our clients then arrived and some of them commented to us that the biscuit ration at the pre-session coffee had been a bit mean. When our conference host reappeared, we asked if it might be possible to have some fruit with the first break. Doubt appeared on our host's face: it wasn't usually done, but she would ask Chef. At the break fruit appeared, not a lot but some. We took the next opportunity to express our appreciation of the efforts made, and we also commented positively on the lunch which, containing salad, was a very welcome improvement on the usual brown buffet. We explained how, as people who spent far too much of our time facing buffet lunches, we really appreciated the thought and variety that had gone into this one. This time a stunned look appeared on our host's face; you'd think no one ever said anything positive to her. She glowed briefly and said she would pass our comments on to Chef. At our next chance encounter she said how pleased Chef had been with our feedback. And so it went on, the lunches got better and better over the three days, and we made sure to convey our recognition and appreciation. Our host couldn't do enough for us, and we made sure to let her know we appreciated her efforts. We had, from a potentially very irritating and niggling start, a great three days' course and service.

We include this account as just a small demonstration of the power of appreciation. Of course we had some initial concerns to deal with, and we got our needs met by making known what we needed, but from then on we picked out and commented on the positive things that were happening and in this way we grew better service for ourselves. Over years of practice we have developed an appreciative eye and ear to balance our very well-developed critical eye and ear, and the more we practise using our appreciative skills the more aware we become of the power of appreciation to achieve growth and change.

The belief in the power of appreciation to achieve change stands in contrast to the belief in the power of criticism to produce change. Growing behaviour and producing change through appreciation doesn't involve threat or coercion or humiliation or fear or any of the other negative emotions associated with achieving behaviour change through criticism. This tends to mean that the behaviour change produced is freely given, rather than a product of reluctant compliance. It is this recognition of the vastly under-utilized power of appreciation that is at the heart of Appreciative Inquiry. In practical terms this means that, when considering an organizational assignment from an appreciative perspective, one of the first challenges is to identify 'What is the behaviour that we want to grow?' and not 'What is the behaviour that we want to stop?'

BELIEF IN THE POWER OF INQUIRY

You will remember that we talked in Chapter 1 of the prevalent belief that action is linearly sequenced. This is the idea that we first do one thing, then another. It also suggests that we need to do things in a linear sequence. One way this is expressed in organizational life is through a belief in the necessity of an investigation of the issue (to establish cause and current state) that must take place before any action is taken. This is then followed by the development and implementation of a plan (to change things). Hidden in this understanding of an effective sequence of events to achieve change is the belief that the first phase, investigation, doesn't actually change anything. However, once we recognize organizations as living entities rather than inert objects, we can see that if we prod them (that is, ask questions of them), we are likely to get a reaction. In other words, by our very interaction with the organization we are likely to produce a change in the organization. Recognition that an organization, like any living entity, will react to stimulation suggests that a belief that the 'inquiry' phase has no impact is misplaced. Rather we can anticipate that the living organization will 'respond' to the questioning process in some way, will indeed be affected and changed by it. All the conversation-based processes we consider in this book recognize the power of inquiry, of itself, to change things.

With this understanding we can begin to appreciate that the act of asking a question about, or inquiring into, an aspect of our lives is not consequence-free. It leaves neither the people involved nor their understanding of the world unchanged. In general terms, questions direct attention towards particular aspects of life and produce accounts about that area of life. This means the more we inquire into a particular area, the more accounts or information we will generate. This acts to 'grow' that area of our life. As the particular aspect grows, so it will loom larger in our world. For example, the more we enquire into examples of team-working in an organization, the more accounts of team-working we generate. The greater the quantity of examples of team-working we generate, the more of it we can see. This realization leads to two important points from a living-human-system point of view. First, there is a recognition that to inquire is not a precursor to doing something – it is doing something. And second, that since we are likely to produce more of what we ask about, we should take care selecting that into which we choose to inquire, as it will change our lives.

THE POWER OF TALK TO CHANGE THINGS

In the organization-as-machine understanding of organizational life it is taken as understood that talk happens before change. Talking is the process by which you plan the changes you are going to make, or the process by which you gather data. There is little appreciation that talk itself might change anything, rather change is something that happens after the talk. Consequently, talk often holds little value in organizations, certainly in contrast to some other behaviour known as 'doing something' or 'taking action'. We can see this reflected in the way meetings are frequently seen as 'talking shops' (not a commendation), 'wasting time (when we could be getting on with doing something)' and 'pointless'. From a conversation-based perspective, how we talk about the world affects how we see, experience, make sense of and understand the world, and hence the way we act in the world. From this perspective both continuity and change are inherently contained and expressed in patterns of conversation. It's not so much that we talk about the world as we see it, it's more that we see the world as we talk about it. When we change the patterns of talk or conversation, we change the world. Consequently, these methodologies focus on people talking together in various ways to produce a change in their experience and understanding of the world, and so in the way they are inclined to act together.

THE POWER OF IMAGINATION TO PRODUCE CHANGE

The view of organizations-as-a-logical-problem-to-be-solved tends not to put too much store by imagination as a force for change, preferring to rely on the workhorses of analysis and logical deduction. Imagination as a process is seen to belong more to the domain of 'the creatives' than the average organizational worker. Imagination is not expected to have much effect on things in the organizational world because it is a mental activity that, of itself, won't cause anything to happen. We have a strong belief that we have to 'do' something before anything will happen; just 'thinking about things' or 'imagining things' isn't going to change anything really, not unless some intervening variable such as 'will' or 'forming a plan' is put into effect.

Increasingly, however, it is becoming appreciated that imagination can have a powerful effect on motivation and belief in and of itself. Imagination can have a direct effect on behaviour. Sports psychologists use imagination in the form of visualizations to help increase their clients' abilities and motivations. Within Appreciative Inquiry imagination is similarly used to create desirable images of the future, desirable images of how things could be, that act to pull people towards them. People become excited by their imagination, they become motivated to achieve desirable objectives, and their behaviour becomes more organized to achieving the desired state. The important point to note is that for this process to work we don't necessarily have to put anything into 'action'. Rather, as self-organizing organisms, we are attracted towards positive things and will organize our behaviour to seek out experiences that we find rewarding. A 'positive thing' that we might organize our behaviour towards could be a picture of the future, of how things could be, that we find attractive. Importantly, within Appreciative Inquiry methodology this attractive image of the future doesn't come from just anywhere; it is built on the foundations of what we know we can do, meaning that the imagined future state is essentially both desirable and achievable.

THE POWER OF POSITIVE EMOTIONAL ENERGY TO ACHIEVE CHANGE

One of the key tenets of Appreciative Inquiry and related approaches is that people are motivated differently by the experience of positive and negative emotional states. This observation, suggested initially by experience, is increasingly being supported by the research within the field of Positive Psychology looking at the different effects of positive and negative emotion. The work of Barbara Fredrickson (Fredrickson and Branigan, 2005) particularly suggests that while the experience of negative emotion (fear, anger) certainly focuses our attention, it also tends to reduce our ability to be creative, socialize, deal with complexity or take risks. Experiences of positive emotion, on the other hand, don't have the same effect of narrowly focusing our attention. Rather they encourage us to look and think broadly, to interact with others, to try new things, to be creative. Many organizations consider the production of negative emotions to be the appropriate driver for change. They want their people to feel anxious or fearful or insecure, in the belief that this will focus their attention on the threat (correct) and motivate them to change their behaviour (also correct). However, what will also happen is that they will be more concerned for themselves and less interested in working with others, will be less able to be flexible or creative in their thinking, and will be more likely to reduce the complexity down to one or two key things. Importantly also, once the threat is removed, so is the motivation. Most obviously we run from danger, but once the danger is past, most of us quickly stop running.

In their efforts to motivate their staff, organizations can get caught in a cycle of having to produce one 'crisis' after another, while at the same time people become more and more adept at assessing the 'real' level of danger and so more selective in their reaction. Ultimately, when a real and present threat exists, the organization that has cried 'wolf' too often struggles to motivate their staff to change their behaviour. The idea of producing change both organizational and behavioural by making people feel good is a little alien to many managers. However, combined with a powerful vision of a goal, positive emotions such as passion, hope and confidence increase our ability to find a way past difficulties, to work together with others, and to be resilient in the face of difficulties, stress or dangers. All of these are attributes that many organizations exhort their managers to demonstrate during times of change, yet inadvertently do little to encourage.

Both positive and negative emotional states are related to feelings of energy. Being in great danger can be very energizing, while feeling powerless or depressed can act to reduce energy levels. Superhuman feats can be produced during times of terrific danger when the body is infused with adrenaline, and is protected from the sensation of pain or exhaustion. This state cannot be maintained over the long term. For sustainable change, as opposed to an emergency reaction to an unexpected crisis or threat, the energy that is associated with a positive emotional state is much more appropriate, being both durable and renewable. Morale makes all the difference to people's ability to make the most of what the world offers them. Change takes energy, and positive emotion-based energy is a powerful resource for change. Many people are energized by exciting conversation, and conversation-based change processes recognize and utilize this source of energy generation. Add in the effect of talking about experiences or ideas that make us feel hopeful, competent, special, happy, confident, excited, passionate, 'fired up' or some other such positive emotional state, and the energy effect can be tremendous.

THE BELIEF THAT LANGUAGE IS CREATIVE

The conversation-based approaches to change that we explore in this book all recognize that conversation, with its use of language and words, is a fluid and influential tool that can create and generate new meaning between people. This understanding stands in contrast to a widespread yet hidden view of language as being made up of words of fixed meaning. From this perspective language is just a tool to carry fixed static meaning encoded in words between people, like a container ship carrying cargo. From a living-human-system perspective we see that in the river of language words mix to create new meaning between people. Meaning is emergent in language, not encoded by it. This makes language and conversation an important source of organizational change and renewal.

BELIEF IN THE PLACE AND POWER OF STORIES IN ORGANIZATIONAL LIFE

One of the things we use language for is to create accounts of our lives and our world. We tell stories about ourselves to ourselves, and to each other. Organizations also tell stories about themselves. Stories that the organization tells about itself hold behaviour patterns in place. Behaviour makes sense in the context of the stories about how things are and so what it is sensible to do. For different behaviour to 'make sense' the stories about life must themselves be different. In this way the stories an organization tells about itself are key to its potential for change. However, organizational stories are not always readily accessible to the organization, being embedded in complex patterns of behaviour and belief. To make them accessible requires particular skills in both inquiry and conversation, both of which we examine in more detail throughout the later parts of this book. Once they become accessible, however, through being told, they can change and patterns of behaviour can change. Appreciative Inquiry recognizes this very explicitly in its emphasis on discovering stories in the organization about what gives the organization life, so increasing organizational resource.

SUMMARY

In this chapter we have introduced an alternative way of viewing and understanding organizations, that is, as living human systems, which we will be exploring in greater detail throughout the rest of this book. We have noted how, when we view organizations as living human systems rather than as machines, our beliefs about how to achieve effective organizational change are different. From a living-human-system perspective we can begin to recognize conversational processes as powerful and creative sources of energy, renewal and change. We can see that the organization-as-machine perspective directs our attention away from human resources such as imagination, storytelling, emotional capacity and responsiveness to the environment, making it hard to access these as resources for change. The living-human-system perspective embraces all that is human within organizations. In this way it offers a genuinely different way to access and develop the capability of an organization to self-renew and to grow; in other words, to change.

3

The development of conversational approaches to organizational change

WHERE DOES THE STORY BEGIN?

In one sense it begins at the start of human civilization when the need to connect with one another and to organize first became apparent. Conversations, which brought people together around questions vital to their survival, formed the heart of community life. To understand the recent resurgence of interest in conversation as an approach to organizational change we will skip a few millennia and use the emergence of Appreciative Inquiry during the past three decades as a lens through which to view the history of conversational approaches to change. We have chosen Appreciative Inquiry because in our view it offers a good example of a well-thought-through philosophical and practical approach to using the power of conversation in organizational contexts.

WHAT IS THE HISTORY OF APPRECIATIVE INQUIRY?

Looking at the history of Appreciative Inquiry can be like researching a family tree. David Cooperrider is rightly considered the father of Appreciative Inquiry. He is currently Professor and Chairman of the Department of Organizational Behaviour at the Weatherhead School of Management, Case Western Reserve University.

The term Appreciative Inquiry first appeared in Cooperrider's feedback report to the Cleveland Clinic's Board of Governors following an organizational diagnostic exercise he had been undertaking there. At the time, in 1980, he was a 24-year-old student on the doctoral programme at the university. In his work at the clinic Cooperrider noticed the level of positive collaboration in the organization and began to study the life-giving factors which gave rise to this. Everything else was ignored. As a result of the learning from this experience he began work on his seminal doctoral dissertation 'Appreciative Inquiry: Towards a methodology for understanding and enhancing organizational innovation'. His doctorate was conferred in 1985.

Looking further back up the family tree, the name of Kenneth Gergen appears. Gergen is a prominent American psychologist and university professor. He fulfils something of a grandfatherly role in the life and development of Appreciative Inquiry. His groundbreaking work on developing the notion of social constructionism since the 1970s has played a major part in supporting Appreciative Inquiry with strong theoretical underpinnings.

Social constructionism is a school of thought within the postmodern 'movement' which engages with other bodies of knowledge, from a perspective that meaning and power are all that we really can claim to know about. Some authors suggest that it is a primary source of postmodern thinking. It is called social constructionism because it aims to account for the ways in which phenomena are socially constructed. Social constructionism takes a relativist position, as opposed to a realist one, in that it believes that an external world (including organizations) does not exist independently of our perceptions, thoughts, language, beliefs and desires. A convinced social constructionist would argue that we only truly exist when we are in relationships with others.

Before Gergen, in 1966 Peter L Berger and Thomas Luckmann published their seminal treatise, *The Social Construction of Reality*, and laid the ground for this new approach to understanding the nature of knowledge. Given the profound impact of their writing they can be considered the great-grandfathers of Appreciative Inquiry. As we develop Appreciative Inquiry and practise conversational approaches to change, so it becomes clear how profoundly the social constructionist school of thought continues to influence all of us engaged in this type of work.

Further up the Appreciative Inquiry family tree the name of Kurt Lewin, the father of social psychology, appears. Social psychology is the study of how human thought and self-awareness are social in origin and made possible by language and social interaction. Lewin is credited with the early development of Action Research during the 1940s. At the heart of Action Research is a spirit of inquiry rather than a mechanistic analytical study. Of vital significance is the recognition that such research is not an abstract disconnected exercise by observers searching for findings but will itself bring about change in whatever is being explored as the research proceeds. This belief has become an important principle underpinning Appreciative Inquiry processes.

More recently a new cousin has appeared on the Appreciative Inquiry family tree. Positive Psychology first came to widespread prominence as a result of a speech in 1998 by Martin Seligman, a professor of psychology and at the time President of the American Psychological Association. He proposed that psychology be just as concerned with what is right with people as it is with what is wrong. Positive Psychology focuses on what works with a person, rather than what doesn't.

Positive Psychology takes a deeply appreciative approach to people's lives, their communities and the institutions that they create. Given its relatively recent appearance it cannot be said to have influenced the early development of Appreciative Inquiry. However, we would argue that Appreciative Inquiry is a positive psychological method.

With the advent of Positive Psychology, and Appreciative Inquiry as its corresponding philosophy in organizational theory, we can perceive a growing movement across psychology, sociology and organizational behaviour to look at what actually happens successfully in life rather than looking at life only as a problem to be solved or an illness to be treated.

WHY IS APPRECIATIVE INQUIRY BECOMING POPULAR?

The Appreciative Inquiry family tree offers some understanding of its history but it does not explain the growth of interest in it during the past few years both in America and increasingly across the globe. Some answers to our question 'Why is Appreciative Inquiry becoming so popular?' can be found if we reflect on the influence of a number of global trends and developing schools of thought. These take us beyond the fields of conventional psychology, sociology and organization development and into new paradigms, particularly postmodernism. Inevitably there will be conjecture about the relative importance of these ideas and trends and you may feel that some are more relevant to the growth in popularity of Appreciative Inquiry than others. In the spirit of a postmodern approach we respect your perspective and offer ours as one story among many. And it is to postmodernism that we turn first of all to find an answer to our question about the rising popularity of Appreciative Inquiry, needing to understand something of the nature of postmodernism before we can appreciate its influence on the development of interest in Appreciative Inquiry and related approaches.

POSTMODERNISM

Mentioning the phrase 'postmodern' can result in wide range of responses. Some say that there is no such thing as postmodernity; others will want to engage in an extended conversation about how you define it. It's a contentious philosophical subject made even more so by the absence of any real consensus on what it may be and how it impacts on our world and us as individuals. Space precludes going into depth but we suggest that it can't be ignored, certainly in the fields of organizational theory, psychology and change. The fact that it is talked about, written about and is increasingly reflected in recent organization theory means that we need some understanding of how postmodernism is impacting on us.

At its most basic, postmodernism is what comes after modernism (Table 3.1). Modernism is said to have begun with what is termed the 18th-century Age of Enlightenment. In that century, and those that followed, reason and rationality reigned supreme. Knowledge was something that could be sought and found. The scientific mindset gained supremacy and objective truth was something that could be determined through investigation and then clearly stated for all to accept. Technological advances and the industrial age emphasized control through knowledge as opposed to the earlier feudal way of life that had been based on control through position of power. Hierarchy in factories and systems of control combined with a relentless search for efficiency gave rise to the notion of scientific management propounded by Fredrick Taylor in the early years of the 20th century. The image

Table 3.1 How does postmodernism contrast with modernism?

Postmodernist Perspective	Modernist Perspective
There is no one right way of doing things in organizing human activity.	It is possible to identify and implement the best way to organize in any given activity.
Differences between perspectives and ways of doing things are inevitable and welcome.	If it is possible to reduce variation then that is to be welcome in the interests of efficiency.
There is no definitive history of anything. All history is composed of stories we tell each other to make sense of our experience of the world.	It is possible to ascertain clear indisputable facts of historical events.
We construct our selves through a multiplicity of stories told by us and by others.	We have a fixed identity, which is our real selves and can be known as such.
Knowledge is created though conversations between us all.	Knowledge can be found out through rational research and is independent of any view people might hold about it.

of the organization as a machine became the dominant organizational metaphor and the accepted way of thinking about organizational behaviour.

How does postmodernism impact on our thinking about organization development?

Postmodernistic thinking radically challenges conventional organizational theory. Rather than clear command and control organization structures to define the organization, everyone brings their own perspectives and images of what the organization represents to them. The organization shifts from being perceived as a solid machine to one of a shapeless organism constantly in a state of development. No longer can actions be 'controlled' from the top; rather systems moderate and adapt themselves to their environment. People respond to external and internal organizational influences and they influence the nature of reality through their behaviour and particularly through the language they use. Reality in organizational life becomes something that is constructed by people in the course of their conversations. Everything is relative – what is truth for you is not necessarily truth for me. My story may not fit with your outlook on the world but nonetheless it is my story and is true for me. Organizations themselves can be considered to be socially constructed images. There is nothing concrete about them. They are what we make and remake and again remake them to be! Similarly, there is an alteration in our understanding of what 'change' actually means. Rather than relying on some fixed 'scientific' measurement of change, people tend to agree between themselves that change has happened because they can describe it to one another. This description may be in terms of perceptions, supportive measures and feelings. In any case, the postmodern mindset is not that concerned with an historic perspective but rather it is 'here and now' personal experience that counts.

The supporters of this postmodern worldview have argued strongly in recent years against the prevailing modern, rationalistic mindset that has characterized organization development theory. In 1986, Gareth Morgan with his work on Images of Organizations opened up the debate about what we actually conceive an organization to be and just how powerful the words and pictures we use are in shaping our understandings. Margaret Wheatley in her groundbreaking work during the 1990s takes us into the paradoxes of self-organizing systems, both changing and stabilizing. Her rebuttal of old-style Newtonian thinking as applied to organizations leads us to consider the interconnectedness of life and the organic nature of the universe as highly relevant to shaping how we are as people in 'organizations'. Karl Weick offers insights into collective sense-making whilst Peter Senge emphasizes dialogue, teamwork and the learning organization. His more recent work focuses on deep listening or 'presencing' and makes reference to a range of spiritual traditions as the source for some of his thinking. Ralph Stacey has linked the world of complexity sciences with organizational and systems development, whilst his colleague Patricia Shaw developed her organizational consulting practice and research around the idea of 'conversing as organizing' and 'organizing as conversing'. These are just a few of the thinkers and practitioners who in the past couple of decades, along with David Cooperrider himself, have created a body of thought which resolutely rejects the machine metaphor and seeks actively to replace it in our minds and hearts with a new way of viewing the world and the organizations which exist within it.

Postmodernism and the growth of the popularity of Appreciative Inquiry

In the context of postmodern thinking Appreciative Inquiry offers important new perspectives. Instead of an overarching theory of how organizations work, the focus of Appreciative Inquiry is on co-constructing new theory based on our experiences. We explore our experiences together as we tell each other our stories, giving subjectivity priority over objectivity. The role of the 'expert' is diminished and power shifts to the wider community. We accept uncertainty as a way of life and that planning cannot be undertaken by any one individual but is a shared responsibility. All of these are hallmarks of a postmodern mindset and are clearly seen in Appreciative Inquiry with its focus on bringing people together to explore what works through story, its dreaming of a future state, its valuing of all people and its assertion that organizations and associated organizational theories are social constructions which together we can choose to change.

Beyond its practical application Cooperrider and colleagues see both Appreciative Inquiry and its postmodern roots as 'an invitation to re-vitalize the practice of social science'. The implication is that old truths need new life, new perspectives and new relevance. It's a broad challenge to the whole sphere of organizational theory as it has developed during the past 100 years. We leave it to you to judge whether or not you think the challenge will succeed or just be a passing 'blip' in an organizational theory world dominated by certainties, structures and the best way to organize. If Cooperrider and others like him succeed in their challenge then the implication for all of us working with organizations and systems will be huge. Not only will we need to develop new mindsets but our skills and behaviours will also have to change. Indeed it will be for us with others to construct new roles and ways of 'being' which enable us to contribute, not as 'experts' but as fellow travellers, storytellers and co-creators.

The answer to the question 'Is Appreciative Inquiry becoming popular because it offers postmodern perspectives on organization development in the 21st century?' is in our view both yes and no. Yes, because Appreciative Inquiry really does tap into the desire to approach organization development in new ways, which fit with, and have themselves been influenced by, postmodern thought. And no, because Appreciative Inquiry itself contains some very modernist elements, such as the design phase of the Appreciative Inquiry process. This very much appeals to the modernist desire for an ordered linear process and solutions to well-defined problems. The growing popularity of Appreciative Inquiry cannot be ascribed to postmodern thought alone. There are the other factors at play which have stimulated the growing interest in it as a philosophy and organization development process.

APPRECIATIVE INQUIRY AND THE INFORMATION REVOLUTION

With the advent of the internet our access to the latest information has never been more rapid. With this huge array of perspectives comes the challenge of making sense of them, a process that arguably is more satisfying when undertaken with others. Appreciative Inquiry offers such a way. The Appreciative Inquiry process means that it is not just your perspectives that count but that there is also the possibility of a shared understanding which becomes clearer as you explore the questions you have in a community of fellow explorers. The Appreciative Inquiry philosophy also means that you focus your interests not so much on history or on problems but rather on the things that work. This cuts out a lot of material written by many organizational development experts. An Appreciative Inquiry mindset will also encourage you not to spend time seeking the right answer. Instead you will perceive a wide variety of questions leading you to new avenues of inquiry. Given the challenges we face trying to live in the age of nanotechnology, Appreciative Inquiry seems to offer a new paradigm which sits more comfortably with both our desire to understand deeply and the satisfaction gained from sense making in the context of a community.

APPRECIATIVE INQUIRY AND GLOBALIZATION

As we receive more information about the world so we become more aware of global issues and concerns. Apparent global challenges call us to consider innovative ways of responding. The underlying philosophy of Appreciative Inquiry offers a degree of hope that often feels absent from other ways of thinking about the world's problems. We are encouraged to consider what is working in our world and then explore together how we can have more of that. The search becomes a shared search and not a solitary one. In this shared process we can find a sense of security and a common bond. The burdens no longer rest only on our shoulders. The Appreciative Inquiry process brings people together in a search for a better world in a way that old diplomatic processes don't seem able to do. The old ways remain focused on mediation and compromise, whilst Appreciative Inquiry offers a different path.

One of the critical differences is Appreciative Inquiry's emphasis on getting as many people in the room as possible. The old ways rely on the power brokers huddling in smoke-filled rooms. Appreciative Inquiry argues that that is not good enough. To handle the complexities of today's world more involvement is needed. Neither is involvement to be interpreted simply as a form of tokenistic consultation but rather as a place where co-creation occurs. Appreciative Inquiry argues that we are all involved and as such all have a powerful voice and contribution to creating the new reality.

APPRECIATIVE INQUIRY AND THE HUMAN SEARCH FOR HOPE

Just as globalization has the potential to stir up anxiety in us about the world and its future, so the scenarios we face in our own lives and the systems which support us have the potential to do the same. Many people are experiencing high levels of stress and anxiety. Evidence of this may well be the growing interest in spiritualities of many different varieties. People seem to be looking for reassurance and a sense of belonging in an increasingly complex and disorientating world. Appreciative Inquiry speaks right into this. Appreciative Inquiry is not a religion in the conventional sense. But in its focus on the notion of a 'positive core' at the heart of organizations and, by implication, individuals, Appreciative Inquiry offers what all religions offer, which is hope. In offering hope, Appreciative Inquiry engages the souls of searching men and women with its optimistic outlook. The bringing together of people in a community as part of the Appreciative Inquiry process offers connectedness to a higher purpose, also a characteristic of many religions. It's not in our view any coincidence that some of the most successful applications of Appreciative Inquiry have been in church or religious organizations. Appreciative Inquiry finds a very natural home in these places. However, in the temples of commerce Appreciative Inquiry tends to have a much rougher reception, with accusations that it is naïve and ignores realities.

Appreciative Inquiry sometimes provokes such a strong response because it holds up a mirror and shows us aspects of our ways of doing things that are no longer working. Our belief in 'command and control', for example, is directly challenged by one of Appreciative Inquiry's underlying assumptions that knowledge and power are not vested in the few at the top of the organization but rather are created between all of us as we interact together. We have all in some way bought into a set of ideas about who we are and what organizations are. Appreciative Inquiry pulls us up and asks us questions about these fundamental issues. At a time of uncertainty in our environment Appreciative Inquiry and other conversationally based approaches only add to our discomfort and underlying anxiety. But, whilst all this may be true, for many people Appreciative Inquiry and other conversational approaches to change have an irresistible draw. That is because they offer the possibility of real honest connection with other people in the midst of turbulent times.

APPRECIATIVE INQUIRY MEETS A NEED FOR CONNECTION IN ORGANIZATIONS

With increasing numbers of people working on short-term contracts, people needing to move more frequently with their jobs, home working, and flatter organizational structures and increased matrix working, relationships in the workplace are under strain. Rarely is there now time at work to stop and have a conversation. People need to press on constantly to the next project. Human contact at a meaningful level is often relegated to something seen as a luxury which people don't seem to have time for in their hectic schedules. As a consequence, people at work often experience a profound sense of disconnection. The pressure is on them as individuals to perform but the tasks they are called to undertake require engaging with others. As a result of organizational and wider societal culture, what happens is the human equivalent of a pool game. People knock into one another, bounce off and move on to the next interaction. It looks like a lot is happening but actually there is no meaningful connection. This leaves people dissatisfied.

Appreciative Inquiry offers a better way. It draws people into deeper relationship with one another. The Appreciative Inquiry philosophy and processes value people and seek to draw them together in a creative relationship. The outcome is intended to be positive for all of the organization, system or community. In offering a new way of engaging with one another, Appreciative Inquiry meets a deep-seated need in each one of us, to be respected, to be listened to and to have the opportunity to shape the future.

Appreciative Inquiry brings humanity and relationship back into an organizational world that has long sought to suppress these in the interests of productivity. Appreciative Inquiry challenges us to reject the view of organizations, and by implication people, as machines and to begin to value them as human communities with the potential not just to enhance our material world but also to bring us back into deep relationship with one another.

SUMMARY

We have used this brief history of Appreciative Inquiry as a lens through which both to view its origins and to look at some of the more recent trends which are prompting a growing interest in it. Whilst we have concentrated on some key individuals, schools of thought and domains of knowledge like psychology and sociology, there is no doubt that a determined historian could discover many more links and enrich the detail on the Appreciative Inquiry family tree. What is evident to us is that there is a growing desire to build a future for our world based on what works well. The trends indicate that change practitioners are increasingly adopting conversational approaches like Appreciative Inquiry as a response to this desire. As more people offer Appreciative Inquiry and other conversational approaches in their practice, so the sheer variety of processes and applications is likely to multiply many fold across the globe and the Appreciative Inquiry family tree in the next decade will include many 'children' who demonstrate the diversity of thought and practice stimulated by the work of the founding fathers.

4

Appreciative Inquiry: how do you do it?

INTRODUCTION

So far we have talked about the nature of conversation-based change processes such as Appreciative Inquiry, and how they differ from other change interventions, particularly those based on a mechanistic understanding of organizations. For us, Appreciative Inquiry along with other processes such as World Café, Future Search and Open Space can be grouped within this emerging field. To help us understand the difference between these approaches better, we want to explain one particular approach, Appreciative Inquiry, in some depth.

This chapter aims to provide an introduction to the core Appreciative Inquiry method. We make the point throughout this book that Appreciative Inquiry is less a process and more of a way of being which guides the practitioner. However, we also recognize that the journey towards this state of being an Appreciative Inquiry practitioner involves doing Appreciative Inquiry processes. In this chapter we aim to describe the Appreciative Inquiry model under its familiar four D headings: Discovery, Dream, Design and Destiny. We will review each of the four elements in turn and offer action steps for each stage. Prior to this we will review the selection of topics and consider how the inquiry question can be phrased.

PREPARING FOR CHANGE

Before embarking on any change programme we would advocate that the organization needs to answer for itself a series of questions. This is not an exhaustive list but these are the types of questions we ask when invited to talk with clients about a change plan.

(a) Is Appreciative Inquiry right for us?

Appreciative Inquiry invites a different way of thinking about change. It replaces the model of undertaking an organizational analysis, implementing a plan and then managing resistance, with a focus on identifying and growing what is already giving life to the organization. While more traditional methodologies call for stakeholder mapping, risk registers and benefits realization plans, Appreciative Inquiry focuses on the language, discourse and stories within the organization. Such a change in style and focus can feel unsettling for the organization by virtue of its unfamiliarity. It can also have an effect on the existing patterns of interaction and discourse, which is again unsettling for the organization. For these reasons an organization needs to consider carefully the benefits of this approach against the capacity of the organization to accept, tolerate or work with significant difference.

(b) What are we trying to do?

In many change plans there is a lack of clarity about what the board or top team wants to get out of the process of change. Change has come to be seen as a sign of good management, sometimes without adequate thought as to what the process of change will deliver. This has most frequently been seen in structural changes, and emanates from a belief that changing lines of accountability and areas of responsibility will lead to fundamentally different outcomes. Rarely is this the case. We would advocate that in any change process those commissioning the change are clear about what outcomes they are seeking. This can be expressed as a list of measurable outcomes in the benefits realization plan or can be more intangibly expressed as a vision for the new organization or new state.

(c) What new skills or knowledge do we need to do this?

Change in all forms often demands new skills. This may be new skills in project management, or new skills in spreadsheets to manage the risk register. Appreciative Inquiry is no different. For Appreciative Inquiry the skills required are more in understanding the process and in undertaking some of the technical components such as writing interview questions and undertaking the interviews in a way which stimulates new thinking rather than one which produces only well-rehearsed stories. We will explore these skills more in the next section.

(d) Will we do this in-house or work with an external facilitator?

There is an assumption often made by clients that change always requires an external facilitator. We don't hold that view. What we do say is that organizations need to have thought through the implications of managing a process in-house as well as of commissioning outside help. Both have their advantages and disadvantages.

We have summarized some of our thinking on the advantages and disadvantages in Table 4.1.

(e) How urgent is this?

The top team also need to give thought to how urgent is the change plan. Is the organization facing a crisis which needs to be addressed within weeks or months? Or is the change plan part of a continual process of changing and evolving as the organization adapts and responds to wider changes in its environments; from customers, competitors and regulators? The answer to this question will have a direct impact on the steps involved in the process. It will also impact on who and how many will be involved in the process and on the resources which the organization aims to commit.

(f) How will we introduce Appreciative Inquiry to our organization?

The commissioning team also need to give thought to how they will introduce the process. The context in which the process is introduced can

Table 4.1 In-house and external managed change

Method	In-house	External advice/assistance
Advantages	• Understand the organization. • Lower cost. • Are building in-house skills for the future. • Can be there around the clock. • Take a long-term view of change. • Ensure change fits with other organization needs. • Build relationships through the process.	• Understand the process and have done it several times before. • Can call upon more resources as needed during peaks and troughs of change. • Can link project team into wider network. • Bring an external perspective.
Disadvantages	• Opportunity cost in using staff on change rather than on their core tasks. • Can lack a balanced perspective. • Takes more time as learn mistakes as going along and time is shared with other tasks.	• More costly than in-house. • Can be short-term focused. • If problems occur after have left can be difficult to resolve as skills have walked out the door. • Can miss internal tricks as don't see the connections between plans outside scope of project.

have a significant effect on how people across the organization respond to it. The introduction of the process thus needs clear communication both around what Appreciative Inquiry is, and why the organization wants to begin a process or change initiative.

In particular, the name Appreciative Inquiry has led us in some projects with clients to re-title Appreciative Inquiry as 'Re-motivate' or 'Imagine'. This reflects our own wish to respond to the needs of the client and a desire to reflect local language, rather than stay pure in our use of the model.

DEFINE

Before the change process can start, the organization needs to define the focus of the inquiry or the type of change required. We would argue first that Appreciative Inquiry as a strategy for change is well suited to emergent change, where the answer and possibly the future state is unclear. Second, it is more suited to longer-term change where there is time for whole system involvement, rather than in a turn-round situation requiring emergency management and radical action. In such situations plans are often driven by the change agent, with limited consultation and with decision making on financial and operational issues controlled by the centre of the organization (Slater and Lovett, 1999).

Defining the change is a key component of the process and could be seen as stage one of assignment. The commissioning team may wish to focus on six criteria in drafting the definition for change:

1. Keep it open: the process needs to let the issues unfold as the inquiry proceeds, so high-level objectives at this stage are better than SMART goals set by the management team.

2. Be open minded: the team needs to retain an open mind about the actions which can follow.

3. Outcome focused: the process needs to focus on an outcome, even though this may be vaguely defined, and thus allow room for development and refinement during the process.

4. Positive phrasing: the outcome needs to be positively orientated, or at least be capable of being positive for all involved in the change process.

5. Involvement from the start: involve stakeholders from across the system in defining the focus of the inquiry.

6. Exciting: lastly we would advocate that the topic selection should excite stakeholders. It should be provocative and encourage people to want to talk about it. Sometimes this can be down to phrasing.

Clients tend to think in terms of problems and so present their issues in terms of problems. A key skill for an Appreciative Inquiry practitioner is to be able to 'recast' their initial labelling of the issue into one more appreciatively phrased. For example, in one case the organization wanted to address sickness and absenteeism. These are both important issues for organizations, and in the case of this organization the problems were threatening the organization's future, as long-term sickness in one team meant the whole team was off sick! Rather than focusing on 'reducing work absence', the focus of the inquiry was cast as 'creating a work environment where what we do every day matters to our clients'. In this case the organization was working with disabled and disadvantaged people, but this focus on the clients' needs had been lost in disputes between groups within the organization (Passmore, 2003).

Careful thought and reflection needs to go into the framing of the final topic and of the initial question. As Cooperrider, Whitney and Stravos (2005) note, 'the seeds of change are implicit in the first question asked'.

DISCOVERY

The discovery phase is about discovering the organization's key strengths and appreciating the 'best of what is'. This phase is about understanding what gives life to the organization and what has brought it this far or to this point in its history. The discovery phase is about exploring and uncovering the unique qualities of the organization: its leadership, history, reasons for existing, or values, which have contributed to its life and success. During this phase the members of the organization have the opportunity to come to know the history of their organization as a history of positive possibilities rather than problematic past events, crises and forgotten or irrelevant events. In this way it is about connecting today to the history which is the life blood of the organization.

The phase revolves around the capturing of this information initially through conducting interviews, then mapping the elements that emerge from the interviews to identify common themes and stories and from here communicating these stories and their meta-themes back to the wider group.

The discovery phase can be planned over weeks or months. It can equally be undertaken in a single day if all of the key stakeholders can be brought together in a room. If all of the stakeholders are not present, or if the initiative is being undertaken in a large system, involving hundreds or thousands of people, decisions will need to be made over the timing of the interview process and the logistics of collating and communicating stories. We suggest a six-step process based on our experience, which typically involves working with a group in a single

Table 4.2   AI Summit: discovery

Day	Phase	Activities
1	Discovery	• Agreeing the focus for the inquiry – introduction to context, purpose of meeting and how to undertake interviews. • Planning the interview – small group activity to write the interview questions. • AI interviews – all participants engage in 1:1 interviews organized around the topic. • Collecting – small group collect key stories discovered during process which demonstrate organization when it is at its best. • Mapping – large group process to map the findings around themes which may include resources, capabilities, relationships, partnerships and positive hopes. • Enduring factors – large group process to identify factors that have sustained the organization over time from the larger map above.

room for a single day. This is summarized in Table 4.2. It forms the first day of the four-day process that we use to explain our approach throughout this chapter.

Our six key elements are not the only way to do this but we have found this works for us with groups of a dozen to 200 people.

Agreeing the focus for the inquiry

The starting point, assuming pre-event communications have taken place about the day or series of days, is to welcome people to the event and communicate some key elements. This scene-setting communication is likely to pick up and build upon the earlier communications. It is an opportunity to explain the background in more detail, particularly why change is felt to be needed and why Appreciative Inquiry is an appropriate way forward. We also find it useful to tell a few stories about interviews, which communicate to the group how to do an interview. Stories seem to work better than a full set of slides with dos and don'ts. In storytelling about interviewing the main themes to communicate are: preparing, selecting a good place to have the conversation, giving

Table 4.3 Defining the topic: moving to the positive

Change agenda suggested by the Board	Positive focus to the topic
Addressing poor quality customer service	Delighting customers each and every time
Tacking poor staff attendance and high turnover	Creating a happy and rewarding place to work
Building strategic advantage	Being simply the best
Increasing profit margins	Retaining existing customers and finding new customers

people time to talk so they feel listened to and respected, using active listening skills of nodding, verbal attentions and summarizing to check understanding, and feeding back the best bits you heard (Table 4.3).

Planning the interview

The core element to planning the discovery phase is getting the questions focused on the agreed topic. The planning process may take place before the day, with a small group drawn from across the organization invited to undertake some preparation work. Doing it in this way reduces the risk of interviewers not knowing what to ask or stimulating problem–solution-focused conversations. It also ensures better designed questions. Groups sometimes pilot the interviews, reducing the final number of questions from their original pool of 12 to 6 or 8.

In designing the interview thought needs to be given to two parts: the overall structure and the questions within the structure. The structure of the interview needs to provide space at the beginning to get the person talking. For some people this is not a problem and they will happily start telling stories and sharing their views from the first question. Other people need time to warm up and develop a relationship with the person they are talking to. No two people are alike and the interviewer needs to make a judgement about when to move from relationship questions to process questions. Typically three or five relationship questions are useful to have in an interview guide, but the interviewer does not need to use all of them. The relationship questions are likely to be about the person's role in the organization and what they value about the organization or their role. As the interview moves into exploring the organizational process, the focus shifts to the organization as people experience it. The aim in this part is to draw out stories and experiences about the organization and the person at their best. As the person talks, the interview should aim to crystallize the stories. The aim is to get to the heart of the story, what factors made the difference or created the feeling. This process involves skills in questioning, and we discuss question form and style later.

When at a loss about the questions to ask there are a couple of very helpful guides worth consulting. The most useful is *Encyclopaedia of Positive Question* (Whitney *et al*, 2001). The other useful guide in the area is the *Appreciative Inquiry Handbook* (Cooperrider, Whitney and Stravos, 2005). We have drafted some sample questions to give an example of what the Interview guide might look like (Table 4.4).

Table 4.4 Sample interview questions

Topic introduction	At *Advocacy for Health* we offer a wide range of services to people who find it difficult to speak up for themselves. Our experiences of working over the past 10 years have contributed to advocacy becoming an important part of health care. The topic we are looking at today is how we make the organization a great place to work as well as one that does great work for others.
Relationship questions	What have you been looking forward to about the day? Tell me what your role is at *Advocacy for Health*. What is the best part of your role?
Process questions	Describe a time when you have found working at *Advocacy for Health* exciting and uplifting. When the organization is at its best, why do people come and work for *Advocacy for Health*?
Possible probe questions to be used alongside process questions as required	What was it that made a difference? Tell me more about X. What did it feel like? Who else was involved? What happened next?

Appreciative Inquiry interviews

The aim for the interview phase is to ensure that all participants are engaged in 1:1 interviews. During the course of the session it's helpful to get everyone both to be interviewed and to interview someone. This means during a whole system event allocating time, maybe 30 minutes for each interview, before people change partners. While it is possible to get people to interview each other, we believe that moving to a new pairing works best, and ensures the pairs stay focused on the task and start afresh with the relationship and process, rather than skipping bits having done them before in the first interview.

Collecting

Once the 1:1 interviews have been completed there is a mass of data and this stage aims to collect the key stories before starting to group them. Inevitably in all group discussions people go off task, or tell two or three stories which cover the same theme. An activity which draws out the main themes is helpful at this stage. This can be undertaken in small groups of 4–8 people, with the groups reviewing the stories told and identifying collectively which ones should go forward to a mapping stage.

The key skill involved at this stage is for the facilitators to set up an exercise which encourages the group to focus on the stories which will contribute towards the heart of the inquiry. The larger the group the longer the exercise will take.

Mapping

Once the small groups have reviewed at their tables the stories from 4–8 people, the task is to bring these together in some way to capture the wider themes in the room. One way of doing this is to start by trying to identify 6–12 high-level themes through a facilitated discussion and to map these on the wall using Post-It notes and a long roll of paper. Our experience is that people can tend to handle 6–12 themes; fewer than 6 means that items don't get separated out sufficiently, more than 12 and people struggle to remember what the themes were.

What's important is that the group identify these themes rather than the facilitators having a set of themes which they have prepared earlier. This process may mean that the themes emerge during the exercise. If groups experience difficulties in identifying themes, we might offer as a starting point some high-level themes like financial resources, staffing capacity, staff capabilities or skills, internal relationships, external partnerships, regulation and inspection, positive feelings, positive hopes and use of technology.

With the themes established the large group can move to the process of mapping the stories against the high-level themes.

Enduring factors

The final part of the discovery phase is to identify the enduring themes. These are the factors that have sustained the organization over time. The activity can be done in a large group as an open discussion with the key themes emerging. Another method is to have an open discussion and at the close of this to allow people to vote for the enduring factors through putting ticks or stars next to the themes which they consider to have been most important. The voting process both brings energy into the room as people need to stand and walk round the room to the maps on the walls, and also gives a sense of democracy in action with clear outcomes emerging in real time.

As people leave for the day or at the close of the session there is a clear sense that everyone had a chance to have a say and that even those who are quiet and less openly engaging in a large forum equally influenced the outcome. The outcome of this phase is an extensive collection of stories of what gives life to the organization and the identification of common themes.

DREAM

The dream phase is about bringing out the dreams people have for their future within the organization and also their dreams about the organization's future. The research evidence from positive psychology (Martin, 2006; Seligman, 2006) shows how talk affects behaviour and outcomes. The research evidence has shown that the more positive the language used by the individual, in terms of its personal, pervasive and persistent elements (Table 4.5), the more likely it is that successful outcomes are achieved. This external use of language reflects the inner dialogue that all humans have, and the positive or helpless view which they hold of themselves in the world. Affecting the way people talk can affect the way they feel. By encouraging people to talk about positive

Table 4.5 Personal, pervasive and persistent

Heading	Definition	Example
Personal	Relates to the individual	'I am so skilled'
Pervasive	Relates to different situations	'Whether it's writing, presenting or just talking it goes well'
Persistent	Relates to past, present and future	'I know that tomorrow's presentation is going to be as successful as the one I did last week'

experiences and dreams, Appreciative Inquiry encourages people to feel more hopeful and optimistic about the future.

The Appreciative Inquiry process seeks to make use of the human tendency for dialogue. It seeks to create a positive belief in the future through the discovery of past successes. As we do so, this recognizing of past success in turn facilitates a belief in our future potential. However, for organization change to be successful stakeholders need to have the ability and the confidence to expand their horizons beyond their day-to-day or month-to-month plans and strategies, and to dream – dreams which are not about who does what and when, but are about why they and the organization are there. It's for this reason that we advocate using playful and creative processes during this phase, even more than at the discovery phase.

The dream phase is highly practical as it is grounded in the organization's history, rather than being unbounded thinking. It is also generative as it seeks to explore potential. The dreaming phase involves building on what people have discovered about the organization at its best and projecting this into their wishes, hopes and aspirations for the organization's future. The aim of the process is to amplify the positive core of the organization and to stimulate a more energized and inspirational future. Such a process can be expressed in numerous ways, from a rewriting of the organization's mission to enacting the future of the organization in a play or devising a story about what the people in the organization will be doing when it achieves its dream.

As with the discovery phase, this can be managed over time and can involve large numbers of stakeholders from the organization and beyond. It can equally be undertaken in a single day and we have set out our process for managing it in this way.

We suggest a five-step process. This is summarized in Table 4.6.

Table 4.6 AI Summit: dream

Day	Phase	Activities
2	Dream	• From discovery to dream – 1:1 interviews reconnecting to outcome and discussing future. • Dream sharing – a small group activity to talk about future dreams. • Bringing dreams to life – a small group activity to discuss specific dreams for the organization. • Building a dream map – mapping the outputs from the small group activity through series of larger groups. • Enacting dreams – groups act out the dreams.

From discovery to dream

One way to start the day is to reconnect people with the stories and excitement from day 1. This can be achieved through 1:1 conversations. The conversations can be based on pre-designed schedules, or could simply invite people to ask questions around three themes; 'What stories most resonated with them from the previous day about the organization at its best?'; 'Reconnecting to outcome and discussing future'; and 'What three wishes do they have for the future?' This last question acts to generate accounts of dreams of the future. If the organization has performed well and been praised, such as through a regulator visit or high annual profits report, then an additional question specific to their circumstances, such as what led to this happening, might also be appropriate.

Dream sharing

Following the re-engagement at a 1:1 level, the next stage which we use is to encourage people to share these dreams with the wider group at their table. As they do so, we ask them to informally identify common dreams. This phase is helpful as the process helps individuals to shape and refine their own dreams as they listen to the dreams of others at their table.

Bringing dreams to life

These two processes so far have helped people to generate, refine and clarify their dreams. They also help people move their dreams towards a consensus position. The next stage is to invite the table groups to talk about the dreams with attention to specific details. These details might be around the culture of the organization, the ways people would behave towards each other, resources and technology available and the customers. These can be fed back to the larger group, if the numbers allow, or can be left within the small groups. We talk more in Chapter 10 about different ways of working in the dream phase.

Building a dream map

A map of the dreams can be the outcome from the small group feedback, alternatively the map can be produced through several smaller groups joining together to build a common map of the dreams. The latter of these processes can help facilitators to ease the process of combining the dreams from multiple groups.

One mapping technique which we have used is to invite people to produce a montage of the organization dream using pictures, stories and words cut out from old magazines. These visual representations taken from the magazines can then be posted on the wall for the groups to wander round like an art exhibition. To help others understand the dream maps created by each group, an interpreter placed by each map can help those viewing it to get a better understanding of the contents and its meaning.

Enacting dreams

This last activity can be fun and acts as a good close for the afternoon event. Groups are invited to take their own dream maps and to produce a short play. These can all be performed in an hour if the groups have used the art exhibition technique or can run over two hours as a major activity that leaves the group with a sense of energy to take into day 3. One of the most entertaining we have seen was based around the walking scene in *Reservoir Dogs*! The outcome of this phase is a shared exciting vision or dream of how the future could be for the organization, based on what we know we can already do, when we are at our best.

DESIGN

The design phase is concerned with making decisions about the high-level actions which need to be taken to support the delivery of the dream. This involves moving to agree a common future dream and the actions to support this.

As with the previous phases, this can be done initially with task groups, and then with engagement with the wider system over time through mini-workshops or an online discussion group. Again our approach is based around the four-day systems-wide event. Our experience offers one way to bring to life the design phase, but it is only one way, and we encourage variety and diversity in applying the process. As we have said, Appreciative Inquiry is not a process but a way of engaging with others to bring about change. We suggest four steps which we have summarized in Table 4.7.

From dream to design

The first part of day 3 can be used to again reconnect to the activities from the previous day. We prefer to keep these as small group activities with the goal of enabling people both to reconnect to the past day's discussions and to start the process of turning the aspirations and blue-

Table 4.7 AI Summit: design

Day	Phase	Activities
3	Design	• From dream to design – small group discussions on the outcome from the dreams. • Organization design – large group discussion to identify what groupings in the organization are needed to bring the dream to life. • High-level plans – large group discussions drawing on interview results to identify key themes. • Provocative propositions – small group activity to write design statements about what it is going to happen.

sky dreams into specific actions. They can use this early time to start to think about what needs to happen to enable the dream to become a reality for them and the organization. This is done by an open-table discussion without a requirement to feed back to the wider group, as the goal is more for the individual to reconnect to their process rather than an output to share with the whole group.

Organization design

One of the common themes to emerge from most group discussions is questions about organization design; what does the organization need in terms of organization structure, style, collaborative working and communication, to deliver the dream? We tend to work at answering these questions through a further round of 1:1 interviews, with the core question framed as: 'What groupings in the organization are needed to bring the dream to life?' Within this we encourage the 1:1 interviews both to add to the core question and to probe it further, so more detail can be added to the dream.

High-level plans

The third step in the process is to draw the host of 1:1 interviews into the room and to cluster common themes to produce a high-level plan. This involves a facilitated discussion in a large group, drawing on the interview results. The facilitators then work to capture, cluster and map the outcomes from this full-room discussion. This can be captured as a parallel map next to the organizational dreams. So by now the group will have a collection of stories about what gives life to the organization, a shared dream of the future, and a shared idea of what needs to happen to help the organization move towards its dream future.

Provocative Propositions (future statements)

The final process is to develop a series of statements about what is going to happen. These are usual written as if the situation already obtained, so for instance the expression of us at our best might be 'we give excellent customer service in every interaction', rather than 'we aim to give excellent customer service'. These statements have become known as Provocative Propositions, which reflect the radical and visionary nature of the statements. The group should also be encouraged to make explicit links to the statements about what needed to happen which emerged and were mapped during the previous exercise. We would advocate undertaking the writing of these statements in small groups and each one being posted up next to the exercise statements to which they relate. The outcome of this phase is a series of statements that express how the organization will be, and some initial ideas about how that might impact on the current organizational set-up.

DESTINY

The destiny phase is concerned with planning, and forming action groups to take forward the actions identified during the discovery, dream and design phases. This involves a celebration of both the learning identified so far and the start of a process to move forward. The development of detailed actions and the formation of groups are to help ensure the continuation of the process of real change begun in these four days.

This can be done with task groups over a period of weeks or months. However, to illustrate the process we describe our experience of working in the destiny phase during the four-day systems-wide event. We suggest a four-step process, which we have summarized in Table 4.8.

Table 4.8 AI Summit: destiny

Day	Phase	Activities
4	Destiny	• From design to destiny – small group discussions on the outcomes from high-level design.
		• Action plan generation – small group activity to generate specific actions to deliver outcomes.
		• Inspired actions – large groups activity with individuals declaring intentions to act and appeals for cooperation team.
		• Task groups form – the declared outcomes and cooperation team become a task group with responsibility for task and plan their next steps.
		• Review – closing of session with celebration.

From design to destiny

The first exercise of the day we suggest is a small group discussion around the themes which emerged from day 3. Our intention here is to help the group reconnect to the previous day and to start the process of planning. The discussions could be in groups of four around a question 'What design themes (Provocative Propositions) excited you most from yesterday?'

Action plan generation

We may continue this small group focus into the next activity, but with two smaller groups coming together into groups of eight. This aims to generate specific actions that will help move the organization towards its desired future. At this stage groups could be self-organizing around the major design themes, and asked to work on the question: 'What specific actions or changes to processes will bring the ideas to life?' As with most goal-setting, the best contributions need to offer an organizational stretch, without creating an organizational strain.

Inspired actions

To change the feel and pace of the event we like to return to a large-group activity to report back the outcomes from each theme group. As the process moves from feedback from one themed group to another, we encourage individuals to declare their intentions to act to bring about the new processes and actions. These individuals then in turn appeal for assistance.

Task groups

As this process moves forward, task groups for each of the specific actions are being formed. These new groups then meet for an initial discussion. This discussion should review the themes and Provocative Proposition alongside the actions and processes planned. The groups' aim at this stage is to break the task down into a series of actions and form an initial plan about how the task will be actioned and by when.

Review

As the event moves to its final session, the objective is to review the event and to achieve closure for everyone. We think the closure of the workshop needs to acknowledge the progress made and the efforts and energies committed by those involved in the process. It also needs to act as a point of encouragement with a continued commitment to action using Appreciative Inquiry as a way of moving forward. Days away discussing the future can be fun, so it can be good to acknowledge this.

SUMMARY

In this chapter we have briefly described the 4D model of Appreciative Inquiry and offered a practical step-by-step approach which could be used as a design for an Appreciative Inquiry event over one or more days. We have offered this as a starting point, and would always argue that Appreciative Inquiry needs to be tailored to the needs and time available, so a one-day meeting or a three-month process would be equally appropriate in the right context and right situation.

We hope that this chapter has clearly highlighted the importance of conversational processes to Appreciative Inquiry as a practice. While each phase has a specified outcome, the process of engagement by all is as important as the final result. Within the Appreciative Inquiry approach it is recognized that change happens as people meet and talk together, not just after. So although the event concludes with the production of an action plan, that is not to say that nothing has happened until this point. The new relationships people have formed during their experience of the event, and the different conversations they have had, are of themselves an important change in their experience of the organization. The stories they have told that hadn't been told before, the dreams they have created of the future, and the ideas they have developed of how things can be and what needs to be done have all acted to change their experience of the world and so have effectively changed the world. The energy generated by the event is supported by the action plans; it is a not a product of it.

In the next section we will be examining more closely the aspects of conversation that impact on the ability of an organization to identify its life-giving properties and to use these to grow towards a positive future.

Part 2

Advanced ideas and practice

In this section we separate out some of the specific elements of organizational conversational process to allow us to examine their influence and effect more closely. Understanding the elements that make up the whole is key to any skill development. For example, musicians need to learn scales, to read music, to keep time and so on to be able, in time, to play fluently combining these many skills.

For conversational practitioners some of the key skills are using questions, hosting conversations and working with organizational stories. We explore these skills in some depth in Chapters 5, 6 and 7 respectively, to help you develop your practice. We then move on to extending your range of conversation-based processes by introducing four more, namely: World Café, Open Space, Future Search and the Circle. Finally, in Chapter 9, we examine what it means in a broad and general sense to be a conversational practitioner; we look at the particular sensibility and focus we bring to all our organizational interactions.

5

The power of the question

INTRODUCTION

In this chapter we are going to explore in more detail one of the key skills of an effective conversational process practitioner, the ability to ask powerful and impactful questions. To be able to do this skilfully in a variety of situations we need to understand the nature of questions, and to have some idea of the likely impact of different questions in different situations. This chapter will present some ideas concerning how questions can be distinguished by intent and effect, to help you to shape your questions with skilful thought, tailored to the situation in hand.

NOT LOCKS AND KEYS

The effect of a question (that is, the account produced in response to it) is influenced by factors such as who is asking and in what context. Sometimes people seem to forget this and think that to get a particular answer they have to find the 'right' question, as if questions and answers were a series of keys and locks! To help illuminate the fallacy of this way of thinking, here are some possible answers to the seemingly factually straightforward question 'What is your name?'

'Why, who wants to know?'
'I'm David's sister, Sandra'
'To you, I'm Teacher'
'Granger, Sandra Granger'
'Forgotten again!'
'Ms Granger'
'Bit late to be asking now!'
'Call me Sandy'
'Granger'
'Boss will do!'
'My friends call me Sadie'
'You don't need to know that, what you need to know is...'
'Mrs Granger'
'Well I was christened Simon, but most people call me Sandra these days'
'Sandra Granger'
'The name on the passport is Sandra Blossom'
'My maiden name was Hammond'
'Mummy'
'You remember me, surely?'
'I'm your niece, Sandra, Debbie's daughter'

Which of these answers (or one of many others) is given is a product of, among other things, who asks, in what context to what perceived end. The amount of information contained in the combined question and answer about the relationship between the people involved is huge. A question is no longer to be perceived as a blunt tool that performs the same task pretty much regardless of who is wielding it, or where, or to what end: that is, to produce a pre-determined 'right' answer to the question, like a key fits one lock. Rather, questioning is a resource that, like pigment or clay in skilled hands, can work in an infinite variety of ways to produce an infinite variety of effects, yet is never entirely predictable in its outcome.

Having looked at some of the broad contextual factors relevant to the inquiry process, let's move on to look more specifically at the shape of questions and the effect that can have.

LOOKING AT QUESTIONS

1. Question shape

Questions have different shapes that influence their effect. Almost anyone who has ever received any management development training knows the difference between open and closed questions. Open and closed questions differ in the amount of information they invite in response. So 'Did you have a good time last night?" invites a yes or no answer. 'What did you do last night?' invites a more expansive answer since yes or no as an answer won't really fit the question. In this way open questions invite more information. All questions contain a certain amount of assumed information. The greater the assumed information in the question, the less fresh information is invited in the answer. It is this property of questions that allows us to use them for different purposes, ranging from exploring something new to clarifying our understanding, for example, 'What have you been up to recently?' works to help us generate new information, while 'I believe you went to Tunisia last year, is that right?' works to confirm our existing information. And there are a range of questions in between (Figure 5.1).

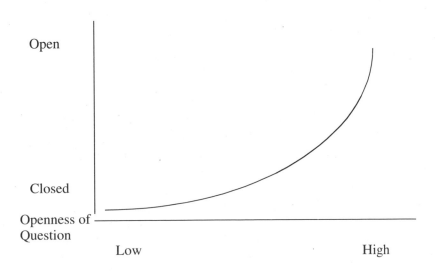

Figure 5.1 Effect of question shape on information generation

Sometimes, after a basic introduction to the property of openness and closedness in questions, people are left with the idea that open equals good and closed equals bad. This dualistic classification discounts the idea that the usefulness of your question shape depends upon your purpose. Closed questions that carry a lot of information can be crucial to developing shared understanding, developing relationships and assisting us in going on meaningfully together. The ability to achieve moments of shared accounting is as important as the ability to create different accounts, and the usefulness of closed questions in doing this should not be overlooked.

2. Beginning the question

Questions have other shape properties, for instance how they start. Apocryphally, all journalists are taught as part of basic training that there are six fundamental questions in any situation they are investigating to which they must seek an answer; these are how, what, who, when, where and why. Obtaining answers to these questions, it is asserted, will allow them to create a full and compelling news story. This is interesting to us as we are also interested in being able to create full and compelling stories. Being able to call forth accounts or stories of organizational life is a skill central to all the practices and methodologies presented in this book. We examine the whole idea of stories in organizational life in more depth in Chapter 7. Within Appreciative Inquiry specifically, the process acts to produce rich descriptions of past events (the discovery stage), future possibilities (the dreaming stage), transition (the design stage) and intent (the destiny stage). These accounts can be characterized as stories of organizational life.

When asking questions we need to be constantly mindful that the way we shape the question affects the probability of different types of response, and so directly affects the development of the relationship and the potential for future communication. It is within these factors that the potential for organizational change lies. As skilled practitioners we need to move from asking questions 'instinctively', that is, just as they occur to us in the form they occur, to asking questions thoughtfully. To apply thought is to be mindful of the possible impact of question shape and content on what happens next. We move now to considering different forms of 'thoughtful' questions.

3. Appreciative questions

A major category of thoughtful questions we are likely to use within Appreciative Inquiry is going to be appreciative questions. Of course we can also use them in other conversational processes. Appreciative questions are those that seek to elicit answers about what gives life to the system – about the good, the real and the beautiful in organizational life. They also ask about the aesthetics and wisdom of the organization. The basic premise underpinning the living-human-system approach is that if a system exists, then something is working, something is giving, preserving, nurturing and encouraging the life of the system. So the potential exists for evolving into other states and forms. By focusing on what is giving life, we can create greater potential for healthy and adaptive growth and for the evolution of the system.

To be able to inquire appreciatively into an aspect of organizational life we have first to generate our appreciative inquiry topic, as discussed in Chapter 4. Once that has been agreed, we then move to the discovery stage of the process. Here we want to elicit accounts of positive experiences. Paradoxically our 'inquiry' may at this stage have the form of an instruction. This directive mode encourages people to engage with the task. This distinction is important at this stage. To ask directly 'Can you think of a time when...?' is inadvertently to suggest an evaluative process 'Can I?', to which the answer might be 'No'. Whereas the direct instruction 'Think of...' contains in it the assumption that such a time, state or event exists and so encourages search activity instead, and invariably such an account can be generated. Here, then, are some examples of what an opening to a discovery appreciative interview might look like, with the particular Appreciative Inquiry topic in italics:

> Think of a time when you really felt part of a team working here, a particular episode or incident. (*team-working*)
> Think a time you've worked with someone from another discipline and it worked really well, when you knew that your working together really made a difference to the quality of care and service a client received. (*multidisciplinary working*)

However, appreciative interviews can be formed to suit a variety of situations with almost no content focus:

> Describe an episode when you felt absolutely at your best working here.

Think of a time when you were using all your resources, were fully engaged, were at your best in this organization.

Appreciative questions can be used in any conversational processes. The common theme is that they focus attention on what is working, or what is positive in a particular experience or possible future. They make reference to positive emotional states or positive anticipations of future states. Typically, appreciative questions incorporate pinnacle adjectives, 'the most' or 'the best' for instance, and include life-giving words. Life-giving words are those that describe strong positive emotions, such as 'passionate', 'excited', 'joyful', 'courageous' and so on. People are sometimes nervous of using such language in organizations because it is outside the normal restrained organizational lexicon. Be bold, everyone has emotions, everyone is alive, everyone can respond to these words.

What is most attractive to you about the dream you have created?
What are you most looking forward to about starting to move towards the future?
At this point, what do you feel most passionately about, have the most energy to do something about?
Out of all the things we've identified that we could do that would move us towards a better future, which is the one you are most excited about?

4. Questions to elicit rich descriptions

Rich descriptions work best when the person telling the story gets to tell it from inside the experience, rather than as an outside observer. This is a very important distinction as the body reacts differently to the two relating perspectives. When someone is telling the experience from inside, parts of the brain are activated which set off a neuronal pattern of firing that is similar to the original experience and so the original emotions, state of arousal, and muscle tone are re-created and re-experienced in the body: the telling is an 'embodied' experience. When we tell the same story but from the outside of the experience, as an observer watching the episode on a screen, we are much less likely to experience that embodiment and re-creation of the emotions of the original experience.

Some people are more easily able to relive past experiences than others. One very effective way to assist people in this is to get them to describe what was happening at the time, and how they felt, in as much detail as possible, drawing on all five senses. Example descriptor questions might be:

Who else was present?
Who else was aware something extraordinary was happening?
How did you know they knew?
Then what happened?
Where did this take place, describe the room to me?
What sticks most vividly in your mind about that episode?
Which feelings were you most aware of at that point?
When did you first become aware that something special was happening?

All of these questions ask the respondent to attend to their memory of that episode and to expand their recall of it. You'll notice that all of these questions have an appreciative focus on the good and positive in the situation.

5. Oracle questions

Some people are more able to tell a good story, in rich detail, than others. The experience of interviewers frequently is that once they have asked for the story to be articulated, they never have to ask another question as it all comes flooding out. However, some people are less able to tell their story with fluency and may speak with brevity or dry up, and then the interviewer needs to work harder to get a story told. One way you can encourage the development and extension of the story is to use oracle questioning. To act as an oracle means to find your next question by picking up a phrase mentioned by the storyteller, echoing it, and inquiring further into it. As a technique it allows them to go further into their story while reducing the risk of you introducing your content. They might say '... and I realized everyone was listening then...' You might then say 'Tell me more about what it was like when everyone was listening' or 'What was the feeling like in the room when everyone was listening?' To do this effectively you need to use their exact phraseology and not be tempted to paraphrase or 'improve' their articulation. In an appreciative context you are listening particularly for words and phrases that sound as if they express or describe an aspect of the experience that can be affirmed and appreciated. In another situation you might be particularly listening for aspects of this story that you haven't previously heard in other accounts of this episode.

Oracle questioning is a useful technique in many interviewing or conversational situations. By shifting the focus from the central narrative to parts of the experience at the margin of recall and awareness, and bringing them to centre stage, it works to increase the richness of the story or to create different variations of the story. It can be particularly useful if you feel you are getting a 'rehearsed' story where nothing new is actually being said. By redirecting attention to a minor detail of the recital, you stand a chance of getting the person to articulate something they hadn't before, and so to move from a rehearsed to a generative account.

6. Circular and linear questioning

Linear questions focus on establishing simple cause and effect relationships. We are more likely to be familiar with this form of questioning than with circular questioning. Circular questions are focused on revealing recursive patterns of behaviour and interaction. Both have their place in our conversational process. Let's examine the difference in more detail. In 1987 Tomm, a systemic family therapist, put forward a model to help us understand the relationship between question form (circular or linear) and question intent (orientation or influence). He then documented the likely effects, for both the interviewer and the family (or organization), of questions asked from the four 'questioning spaces' his model created.

As you can see in the model in Figure 5.2, the questioning space is located across two axes: linear–circular, orienting–influencing. The linear–circular axis reflects the questioner's perspective on change and the achievement of change. So some questioners might assume a straightforward linear pattern of cause and effect, while others might assume a more circular, systemic pattern of cause and effect. The conversational process approach generally assumes a more systemic pattern of cause and effect. The orienting–influencing axis reflects the questioner's intent, either to orient themselves to the system or to have an influence on the system. Again the conversational approach recognizes these as two concurrent aspects of engagement, being aware that are both happening at the same time. However, at any particular point our intention can be more towards one than the other. Let's first consider the difference in a linear or circular question approach when initially orienting ourselves towards the organization.

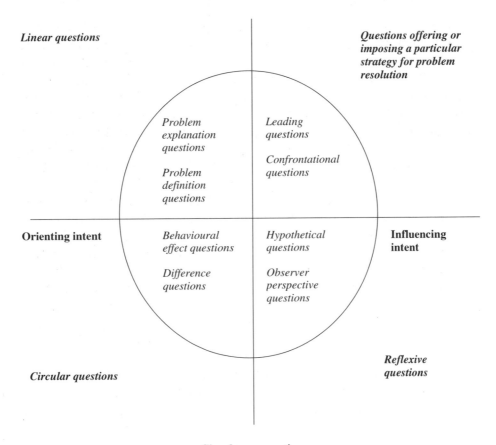

Figure 5.2 Linear and circular questions

Source: from Tomm (1987)

Orienting towards the organization

Tomm suggests that in the early stages of our intervention with an organization we may be more concerned to orient ourselves towards the organization. This means we are interested in asking questions the answers to which we hope will allow us to gain an understanding of the organization. These orienting questions can be of a linear or circular nature, and the asking of each is likely (but by no means guaranteed) to have particular and different effects. These effects have important implications for the possibility of achieving organizational change.

7. Linear questions

Linear questions are based on a simple cause and effect model of organizational actions. In trying to establish the linear sequence of events that led to the current situation, they might ask such questions as, 'What is the problem? Who caused it? Why did they do that?' or they might focus on defining the problem, 'What exactly is the issue here?' Many people habitually think in terms of simple cause and effect and so have often already considered these questions. When asked these types of questions they readily give their, possibly much repeated, answer. In this way these forms of question have a tendency to call forth existing stories about the issue.

People tell their stories about the world in the hope that doing so will change something. In other words, we create and give accounts of life for a purpose, usually to make sense of what is happening and/or to change what is happening. In difficult or stuck situations this account may well include stories of fault and blame. In an organizational context, encouraging people to articulate and repeat these accounts or explanations contains two possible dangers. The first is that, purely by the act of being heard, they experience their account as being endorsed or validated and so it becomes even more entrenched in their mind as 'the truth'. The second is that it is the nature of such explanatory stories of what went wrong or who is to blame, to invite judgement. The innocent inquirer may inadvertently find themselves being strongly invited to form a judgement as to the rights and wrongs of individual people's behaviour. Such an invitation can be hard to resist, especially in the face of powerful and persuasive stories of accountability, blame and exoneration.

8. Circular questions

However, it is possible to use circular questions at this orienting stage. Circular questions are focused on revealing the patterns of behaviour in the organization; they are used to call forth the patterns of connection within the system. There are many forms of circular question, some of which we will look at in a moment. The main point is that with effective circular questioning the system isn't directly confronted and so doesn't feel the need to defend individual actions and beliefs against our judgement; rather, as we gently inquire into the system using effective circular questions, 'the warp will pass through the weft, until the design will be clearly seen in the fabric, without the necessity of posing the most feared and defended against question' (Cecchin, 1987). For us, this analogy brilliantly illuminates how the hidden stories and beliefs that underpin the patterns of behaviour slowly come to everyone's awareness, and are changed in the telling.

Circular questions about relationship

Circular questions explore relationship. For example, a question might ask one person to comment on another person, in their presence, as in 'What do you think Mike believes to be the most valuable asset you bring to the organization?' A number of things happen here. First, Mike is likely to interested in this interaction, even though he is not taking part; secondly, he might learn something about how someone else understands him; and thirdly, the person to whom the question is addressed may be articulating a story that she hasn't considered, let alone told before. This is likely to shift their relationship in some slight or profound way; that is, something will change.

Circular questions across time

Circular questions also explore relationships across time, so you might ask something like 'When was the last time this problem didn't exist? What was different then to now?' and of course questions about the future. These are particularly relevant to Appreciative Inquiry with its emphasis on dreaming and the future. Penn (1985) notes that future questions 'rehearse change'. By focusing on possible futures, the system increases its view of its own evolving potential. Exploring possibilities for the future leads to the creation of new maps of how the system can be, of possible relationships within the system. Dreams about the future offer a source of learning to the system. Future questions, she suggests, illuminate the present conditions of the organization as, not immutable, but as context bound; and that since concepts of the future and change are married, all future questions suggest that change is possible. Future questions cut into ideas of pre-determination; they address questions of how you would like to be, as opposed to how you are because of the past.

Future questions

The basic Appreciative Inquiry future question is 'How would life be if more of these good things were happening more of the time?' However, future questions can be used in a more focused way, often by using 'if', as in 'If in two years' time your team was working brilliantly together, what stories do you think you would be telling about the difficulties you are experiencing now?' You can also use 'just imagine', as in 'Just imagine that this project is a fantastic success. What will people be saying about this team?' You can also ask the miracle question, 'Suppose a miracle were to happen overnight and things became much improved. What would be the first little thing that you would notice was different?', and pursuing the circular vein you might ask 'Who else would notice? And how would you know they had noticed?' These questions imply patterns not facts and ask how if the pattern were different, things would be different. In this way they are based on a living-human-system understanding of the organization rather than the more traditional organization-as-machine. The moment a question offers alternatives to the current belief system, it creates opportunities for new stories and so the potential for change.

Circular orienting questions are more likely to have a liberating effect upon the organization than linear questions. With linear orienting questioning, existing accounts are reinforced, it is unlikely anyone's beliefs will change and the sense of being trapped in an impenetrable mess continues. With circular orienting questioning, as the patterns of interaction and relationship are brought into the light and into awareness, different meanings of being together are created. And the interviewer, no longer required to take sides or make judgement, can instead focus on being curious, listening, forging connections around, across and through the system, exploring gently the weft and the warp and accepting the unfolding story.

9. Influencing questions – linear

As the change process proceeds, the interviewer is likely to be concerned to move to a more influencing orientation; he or she wants to influence the system to change. When this intent is expressed from a linear perspective it tends to express itself as a desire to impose particular strategies or solutions upon the organization, usually by asking leading, loaded or confrontational questions, eg 'Why don't you...?' or 'What would happen if you were to...?', as the consultant attempts to get their own sense-making and so their own solutions adopted by the organization. This has a constraining effect on the system; its inventiveness is constrained to considering the options inherent in the question. At the same time this mode of intervention has an oppositional effect on the consultant as they try to oppose the logic of the organization and impose an alternative. Frequently these attempts at influencing a system don't work, and sadly it is not uncommon to then hear the consultants, in their frustration, blaming their stubborn clients, who either reject outright, or more often politely accept and then ignore, their considered advice. It doesn't necessarily leave clients speaking well of consultants either.

10. Influencing questions – circular

By attempting to have influence through asking circular questions the interviewer is more likely to have a generative effect upon the organization. The questions are reflexive, they encourage the organizational members to articulate the patterns of interaction in which they are bound up and by so doing to extend their understanding of cause and effect from a predominantly linear perspective (He makes me...) to a more interactive, circular or systemic understanding (When I..., then he..., then I). Reflexive questions explore the connections in the system and people's understanding of them. So you might ask 'What do think Mike might need to hear to be able to believe that you welcome feedback?' Or 'If you were to tell Beth how excited you are about the future, what might she feel able to do?' or 'If you could offer one piece of advice to Mike about how to make it more likely that these good futures will happen, what might it be?' Reflexive questions allow the system to talk to itself about itself in new ways and so become more aware of its capacity to behave differently and to be different, to co-evolve to new forms of organizing. Such questions, and the responses and sense making they provoke, serve to open space for the system to see new possibilities and to evolve more freely of its own accord. In this way change is evolutionary, growing from inside the system, rather than imposed from outside the system.

SUMMARY

In this chapter we have considered the power of the question to shape what happens during organizational conversation. Tomm offers a useful reminder that question and answer, as we suggested earlier, is not a linear case of cause and effect: 'Differentiation of questions does not depend on their syntaxic structure or their semantic content. It depends on the (consultant's) intentions and assumptions and the ongoing context and sequence of interventions.' In other words, there are no guarantees. He also notes that 'What actually happens when we ask a particular question depends on the uniqueness of the organization and structure at each moment. The actual effects of a question are always unpredictable' (Tomm, 1987). Awareness of the essential unpredictability of the effect of any particular question on the ongoing systemic interaction has a strangely liberating effect upon the inquirer, leading them to become more creative. If one question 'doesn't work' in terms of eliciting a positive story, or opening space for the system to evolve into, the interviewer searches for a better one, a more effective one, a more useful one to try to open other spaces to release the natural healing capacity of the client system. This stands in contrast to the search for the 'right question' that will unlock the truth. Instead, awareness grows that questions asked aren't right or wrong; they are more or less useful when measured against our intent of enhancing the system's capacity for positive change.

6

The power of conversation

INTRODUCTION

At the heart of all conversational processes like Appreciative Inquiry is a meaningful encounter between people in powerful conversation. This chapter explores the nature of conversation, reflects on the power of conversation, considers its role in organizational and personal change and offers practical insights into how a conversational practitioner can support powerful conversations.

WHAT IS CONVERSATION?

Theodore Zeldin (1998) begins to capture the essence of conversation when he writes:

> Conversation is not just about conveying information or sharing emotions, nor just a way of putting ideas into people's heads... conversation is a meeting of minds with different memories and habits. When minds meet they don't just exchange facts: they transform them, reshape them, draw different implications from them, engage in new trains of thought. Conversation doesn't just reshuffle the cards: it creates new cards (1998: 14).

As we reflect on our own experience of relationships in the workplace and in our private lives, we can observe that the vast majority of encounters we have had with others focus on sharing factual information. The e-mails advising us of new initiatives, colleagues and friends asking for opinions, and chat about what we did for our holidays all have a role in the workplace and in life generally. They provide guidance, offer feedback, create rules, help coordinate and create a social environment but are not in themselves conversation. They are important talking interactions but not conversation as we intend to define it.

It's not just talking

Zeldin helpfully view distinguishes between talking and conversation:

> 'It's good to talk' is the slogan of the twentieth century, which put its faith in self expression, sharing information and trying to be understood. But talking does not necessarily change one's own or other people's feelings or ideas. The twenty first century needs a new ambition, to develop not talk but conversation, which does change people. Real conversation catches fire. It involves more than sending and receiving information (1998: 1).

We and Zeldin see conversation as something special, and therefore by implication, something that is relatively rare.

It's not just dialogue

As well as distinguishing between talking and conversation, a distinction can be made between the concept of dialogue and conversation. In examining the meaning of the word conversation, Baker, Jensen and Kolb (2002) note that its earliest recorded usages relate to 'living together, commerce, intercourse, society, intimacy, sexual intercourse, to be united in heaven in conversation' (2002: 10). Nearly all of the definitions emphasize the communal, sensual and emotional aspects of conversation.

The word 'dialogue', on the other hand, has within its origin references to words like 'debate 'and 'discussion'. Thus they argue that 'the root of "dialogue"' is more related to 'opposing voices in search of truth', a definition that emphasizes conflict and a more rhetorical approach than 'conversation'. Dialogue tends to focus on communicating knowledge about ideas and exchanging views. When we are engaged in dialogue we are expected to show a high degree of rational thinking and the willingness to weigh up arguments to determine the truth. Expressing strong emotions in dialogue is viewed as a distraction from this core activity. In conversation on the other hand, emotion expressed or otherwise is a vital aspect of the experience.

Our understanding of the conversation experience does not preclude dialogue, but has an added dimension that creates a shared understanding supported by an emotional experience. In other words, conversation is by definition an emotional experience. It may involve dialogue, but, above all, it will move us as people to a different emotional place than that which we occupied before the conversation. What happens subsequently is our choice. We may choose to act differently, or we may not, but we will have experienced something different.

The experience of conversation

Conversation is a human experience between two or more people, which, by the expression of thoughts and feelings, results in the creation of new ideas, perspectives, understandings, and an increased potential for action. We know we are engaged in a conversation rather than dialogue or talk when we experience:

▌ a sense of being listened to, and of listening to others;

▌ an atmosphere of trust and openness;

▌ a liberty in expressing thoughts and feelings;

▌ a sense that what is happening has some importance and value;

▌ affirmation of our self-value and the value of others;

▌ an awareness of new perspectives and ideas;

▌ knowing that something is different as a result;

▌ the development of shared meanings and understandings;

▌ a sense of equality between participants.

The experience of conversation may also include:

▌ a profound, even life-changing, insight or 'aha' moment;

▌ a release of emotion;

▌ the sense of being taken to a better place;

▌ a close sense of unity between participants;

▌ a decision to make change happen;

▌ excitement;

▌ sense making at the deepest levels.

THE POWER OF CONVERSATION TO TRANSFORM

The power of conversation in the workplace – an example

One of the authors has a story of a powerful conversation set in the context of a hospital that resulted in significant improvements for patients.

Conversation with Dr John

The hospital in which I worked at the time was facing a significant challenge in coping with the high numbers of emergency patients coming through the Accident and Emergency Department. To help generate some new ideas to tackle this challenge I invited Dr John, a senior clinical leader, to attend with me a day conference about new approaches to emergency medical care. The quality of presentations was high, and over coffee during an interval I held a conversation with Dr John. We both reflected on what we had heard presented and openly shared our different perspectives. At one point during the conversation both of us felt very energized. We realized that while our own hospital's challenges had seemed overwhelming, as we talked it became clearer what we needed to do and that we were the people called to carry out the work. We both experienced profound insight and the consequence of the conversation for us was a renewed vision and a sense of the possibilities for the future of this vital service. The exact content of the conversation I can't recall, but I had a sense that this was an important moment that led, I believe, to a whole series of important changes for the health system in which we both worked.

On our return a day later I picked up an e-mail in which Dr John expressed his commitment to lead change and even give up his clinical activities for six months to give much needed time to the project. A few days after that I had a conversation with another senior doctor and together we developed a plan that built on the ideas promulgated at the conference. Within a week a series of conversations took place in which these ideas were refined and more widely shared. A few weeks later I had a meeting with the chief executive of the hospital. He shared with me his ideas for change, which exactly matched the content of conversations I had been involved in. Of course they were now his ideas! During the following two months the plans took shape and a new approach to caring for emergency patients was implemented.

While, undoubtedly, many other factors were at work influencing the situation, the role of conversation stood out for me as the most important aspect of this change process. What would have taken months of bureaucratic wrangling and power play was beginning to be accomplished within a couple of weeks through conversation.

Some of the lessons learned by both of us included:

▌ The opportunity to have a productive conversation can take you by surprise.

▌ Out of our normal place of work we sensed a greater openness to conversation with each other than had we been back at the hospital.

▌ Conversation developed because we both found a common passion – the improvement of patient care services.

▌ The power of conversation in securing significant changes in very short periods of time.

▌ The ability of conversation to both create and rapidly spread ideas and energy.

This experience resonates with others who have shared our excitement about the power of conversation:

> I believe we can change the world if we start listening to one another again. Simple, honest, human conversation. Not mediation, negotiation, problem solving, debate or public meetings. Simple, truthful conversation where we each have a chance to speak, we each feel heard and we each listen well' (Wheatley 2002: 3).

So, for some people like Margaret Wheatley and us, the potential power of conversation extends far beyond the scope of this book and into the realms of changing the world. Having paid attention to conversational experiences, often within the context of an Appreciative Inquiry process, we are no longer tempted to view her words with hardened scepticism, but sense a profound truth that deserves our full attention. The notion of changing the world resonates deeply with the optimism of a conversational practitioner. In practice, however, we need to maintain an optimism that is tempered by a recognition that such aspirations are only realized in our daily lives one small step at a time.

THE FEAR OF CONVERSATION

This reality prompts a question: If conversation is such a powerful agent of change, why is it not given far more formal acknowledgement in our organizational cultures? The answer lies in the fear that many in traditional executive positions of responsibility have of such a powerful process. It is an understandable fear given the way conversation can prompt emotional responses and unplanned action. This is a cause of anxiety for those with formal power who are tasked to exercise careful control of resources and people. They aim to reduce unpredictability in organizational life, while conversation has the potential to create more not less unpredictability. So it is that many people at work rarely experience conversations in the context of meetings where they might be most expected. Instead, meetings are places where agendas are strictly adhered to and little, if any, time is given over to free-flowing conversation. The priority is given to maintaining executive control and exchanging information, not 'wasting time' having a conversation. Any benefits conversation might offer in terms of more creativity and better staff engagement are set to one side. Rarely is the discouragement of conversation a deliberate strategy by senior managers. It is something that becomes an unspoken aspect of organizational culture, particularly where the culture places a premium on control and positional power.

UNDERSTANDING THE FEARS AND AMBIVALENCE TOWARDS CONVERSATION

Apart from the fear of loss of executive control, there are a number of other reasons why people in organizations may resist engaging in conversation:

▌ The fear of expressed emotion. Conversation involves us being present as ourselves and so it conflicts with the 'professional', some-what emotionally detached, persona we often bring to our work environments. Emotion is an integral aspect of conversation. This can be difficult for each of us to handle in an organizational context where rationality is often the most valued of all attributes. We have become trained in our cultures to 'manage' feelings in a work environment by either ignoring or sublimating them. A conversation has the potential to bring feelings to the surface in a way we fear might cause hurt or unintended consequences. This fear can be compounded by a sense that conversations appear to have no boundaries, and without a safe 'container' or conversational process we can feel too exposed. It therefore feels psychologically safer to stay within our professional persona.

▌ The fear of being perceived as different from our colleagues. Organizational cultures help create a sense of belonging and uniformity of approach. Where conversation is not generally valued, as we begin to use it, it can make us appear different and can result in pressure on us to return to more accepted organizational behaviours. Conversation is rarely seen as 'proper' work and in using it we run the risk of being labelled as an unproductive colleague.

▌ The need to manage anxiety. From Kleinian psychoanalytic perspectives 'it is possible to understand the structure, process, culture and even the environment of an organization in terms of the unconscious defence mechanisms developed by its members to cope with individual and collective anxiety' (Morgan, 1997: 228). The rules and regulations, the management boards, the language and rituals, the job titles and work routines all offer a sense of security. If you accept this notion, then it is possible that conversation, because of its apparent lack of integration into formal organizational structures and its uncertain outcomes, can potentially be perceived as threatening these mechanisms. Conversation can take people to places beyond the boundaries of feelings, thoughts and actions usually accepted within an organization and so can be perceived as something that will destroy defence mechanisms and increase uncertainty. In the authors' experience this sense of anxiety can lead to a very prompt rejection of any proposal to enhance conversation. Where conversational approaches to change, such as Appreciative Inquiry or Open Space, are considered, organizational leaders are often keen to establish how boundaries around conversations will be proscribed and managed. For some organizations the fear is too strong and there is a sense that what will follow free-ranging conversation will be so destructive to the organization that it will threaten its very existence.

SOME ISSUES FOR THE CONVERSATIONAL PRACTITIONER TO CONSIDER

The challenge for conversation hosts is to recognize that these fears are likely to manifest themselves as conversation is offered as a process to support change. If we experience a hesitant or even a very negative response to the proposal that conversation be encouraged, it will help to offer understanding of why this should be the case and then work with the organization to create a structure for conversations. This structure can both support the emergence of the benefits and manage the perceived risks for leaders and participants.

In summary, we think the aspects of organizational cultures to which the conversational practitioner needs to give particular attention include:

I The need to be aware of any personal ambivalence about participating in conversation and the reasons for this.

I Potential high levels of anxiety amongst people who fear the expression of emotion in conversation.

I Organizational cultures that place a premium on 'professional detachment' are less likely to want to embrace an approach that seeks to engage staff as people.

I Concern on the part of leaders that conversation is a waste of time. This may lead to a conversational approach to organizational development, such as Appreciative Inquiry, being viewed as unacceptable.

I Gender and power dimensions in the use of conversation.

I Defence mechanisms that people use in order to protect their own sense of psychological safety.

THE AMBIVALENCE OF ORGANIZATIONS TOWARDS CONVERSATION

We have suggested that while on the one hand people can see something of the power of conversation to change thinking and actions, on the other hand, in a formal organizational setting, there can be many anxieties that serve to discourage conversation. In spite of this we know that conversations happen all the time as part of the 'shadow' or informal aspect of organizational life. They take place out of the spotlight and away from formal meetings where they cannot be controlled. It's in the hallways, by the water cooler and outside during a 'cigarette break' that the informal aspect of organizational life is developed. It's in these places that people's thoughts and emotions are expressed to one another and where conversation is most likely to happen. Here you will often find people at their most engaged and full of ideas.

What we think is beginning to counter ambivalent feelings towards conversation is the recognition by a small but growing number of senior executives of the benefit of attempting to harness the power of conversation through the use of processes like Appreciative Inquiry. Having been schooled in the scientific model of management, their expectation used to be that once a decision had been made by the organization, then that's what would happen. But their experience, in this rapidly changing and complex business environment, is that time and time again the formal organizational structures seem ineffective in precisely carrying out their intentions. As a result they are starting to look to conversational processes as a means of using the power that resides in the informal culture and deliberately building it into the core of the formal organization.

A conversational practitioner addresses these challenges by offering an approach that gives structure and introduces a degree of risk reduction to conversational activity. The uncertainty about conversation as a transformational process remains very powerful even when a 'container' for the conversations like the World Café is offered. As you encounter such ambivalence it helps to retain a sense of purpose, and to have a range of skills and behaviours that build confidence in you by the organization.

HOW CAN A CONVERSATIONAL PRACTITIONER SUPPORT POWERFUL CONVERSATIONS WITHIN ORGANIZATIONS?

The conversational practitioner as a resource

With knowledge of the philosophy, and experience of applying conversational processes in organizational contexts, the practitioner is a valuable resource available to the organizations with which they work. We have already explored in this book the skill of surfacing the powerful questions, and of contracting effectively to use conversational processes. Alongside these skills is the passion to serve as hosts and model conversationalists.

The conversational practitioner as a host of conversations

The traditional role of the facilitator in organizational development and learning activities is well known. The work they do is primarily to design and coordinate processes that help organizations achieve their development objectives. It is often interpreted as a very upfront role with a focus on encouraging people to engage with the learning process. Encouraging conversation and holding conversational 'space' requires some of the skills of the facilitator and also the mindset and heart of a host. At the heart of being a good host is the ability to let go of personal control of a process and to hold onto the principles of self-organization, participation, ownership and non-linear solutions.

Hosting is a pattern and a practice which values people as people and helps them express their humanity in the context of meaningful human relationships. This is both different from and complementary to more traditional ways of working, which are primarily based on rational planning mechanisms and which often aim at establishing control in order to manage outcomes. In working with conversation you will soon appreciate that what it calls for from you is not just a set of change 'tools' but also a new way of being and relating to others. This new way of 'being' is not a woolly change in aspects of your personality but is focused on your skills and presence as a host of conversations.

For most of us to work this way, change is needed since we have become so used to controlling processes and engagement with people that to let go of this way of working and being takes practice, new skills and a new mindset.

This book has already explored one of the key attributes, which is the ability to help surface powerful questions. In preparing to use conversational processes the host is, from the earliest moment, alert to the questions that are beginning to be voiced and sensitive to questions which may not even be voiced or acknowledged but are nevertheless present. Much of the early work of the host is to hold conversational spaces where questions can come to the surface.

The conversational practitioner as a conversationalist

Given the centrality of conversation in conversational processes the practitioner needs a deep understanding of the skills, behaviours and emotional presence that prompt powerful conversations. We suggest that the following abilities and attitudes can be developed in each of us to support our practice as conversationalists.

Listening to others

It is very difficult to overstate the critical importance of the role of listening in any conversation. As we listen carefully and actively our minds and our hearts begin to open and we begin to construct our own reality through what we hear moment by moment (Ellinor and Gerard, 1998). In our experience, listening is a challenging discipline that asks of us to be quiet and open with ourselves. As we do so we can begin to hear and be affected by what others are saying. It is possible to read plenty of books about listening 'techniques' and still miss the point. One of the challenges for us is to develop our authenticity as a listener. This means we listen, not because we have to but because we are genuinely curious and care about the speaker and what they are seeking to communicate (Stone *et al*, 1999).

To participate in a conversation effectively, it's also vital that we are present, attentive, curious and caring. We have to confess that is not our daily experience. What passes for conversation seems often to be about 'waiting to talk' rather than wanting to listen. The other person almost becomes part of a theatre audience. As the actor centre stage we want to speak our lines and wait for the applause. To shift from being focused on ourselves to concentrate fully on another person is perhaps the biggest challenge we all face in the conversational process. As we shift attention so we have the possibility to create a life-enhancing and life-giving experience. If you have experienced another person paying you full attention because they care for you, then it's a memorable moment.

The other side of the coin is that not being heard saps away at our sense of 'being here'. We are not sure if we have worth and are uncertain about our place in the world. The implications for our practice as a conversational host are considerable. Through our work supporting conversation we can potentially help individuals find greater fulfilment and a sense of personal worth.

Listening to yourself

Stone *et al* (1999) helpfully observe that in listening to another we are also at the same time engaged in listening to our own internal voice. The danger is always that our internal voice can block off what we need to hear. In deep conversation this is almost inevitable at times as the words of the other person spark in you a whole series of thoughts and emotions. The discipline is to hold these in your mind and heart whilst you continue to open yourself to receive what the other person is communicating. It is helpful to consciously spend time listening to the internal voice and use it as a way to stimulate curiosity about what is going on for the other person. It is also realistic to recognize that sometimes your internal voice is just too noisy and that you need to speak and not just listen.

Listening for shared meaning

As we host conversations amongst groups of people, so we need to be aware of the emergence of shared meaning. We can listen superficially and miss the streams of meaning that become present as conversations interconnect. Instead, what we perceive is just a lot of chatter. To counter this we can develop an ear that is attuned to the interrelationships between the perceptions and insights that are occurring in the room. As we do so, the 'whole' becomes apparent and will become so not just to ourselves but to others as well. This happens as we voice what we have heard. Practically, if you listen to groups' conversation and behaviour over time, you will also begin to get a picture of the world view or thinking that sits beneath the surface and drives the groups' strategies and results. A role of the host is to take opportunities to feed back and test out your observations of emergent themes and issues to a group. Reflecting in this way usually assists the group in coming to a shared conclusion about a subject. Also, by speaking it out amongst the group, new insights occur and people have 'aha' moments where they understand the significance of something they have heard in the conversation.

There is a judgement to be made here about the value of your own insights as host. After all, you will have your own perspectives and bias that will influence what you notice. One way around this is to ask others in the room for their own sense of emerging themes. Another approach is to employ a graphic artist who can 'cartoon' the group's conversation across a wall, enabling the themes and key words or expressions to become highly visible. This approach is particularly powerful when working with large groups who are tackling complex problems and issues. The unfolding cartoon acts as a mirror back to the group and helps map the development of a series of conversations.

It is worth remembering that listening for shared meaning is also an incredibly important part of one-to-one conversations. In listening fully to one another we give a sense of value to the other person and deep insights become the norm rather the exception. Being listened to in this way even conveys a sense of existence and identity to both participants. Conversation is truly life giving (Ellinor and Gerard, 1998).

Offering others help to listen effectively

Margaret Wheatley (2002) offers us a helpful observation when she stresses the importance of listening and, more particularly, the need for us to recognize that we need each other's help to become better listeners. She talks of acknowledging the difficulties we face in listening effectively. No matter how good our intentions may be, there will be many distractions in our lives and our personalities that make listening a struggle. In holding a conversation space like an Appreciative Inquiry process the host needs an awareness of the challenges facing people as they listen deeply to one another and to offer them words of encouragement to help one another.

THE INNER LIFE OF THE CONVERSATIONAL PRACTITIONER

Developing our listening skills will contribute to our effectiveness in hosting conversations, but to become master practitioners we need to learn how to become truly authentic in each conversational space. Such authenticity can help draw out authenticity in others and helps build a community of hosts such that, in the end, we each host one another. Space does not permit a detailed exploration of all the facets of personal authenticity, but the following are some of the key aspects that warrant our attention.

Maintaining personal centredness

Margaret Wheatley once observed that the best thing a leader could offer to people in a time of turmoil was a sense of having found a degree of inner peace. She argued that, from a position of personal peace, you are able to move effectively as a leader through the situations being faced by the organization. A sense of peace, of centeredness and spirituality, supports the host in creating a safe space around him or her where people are likely to feel more at ease and open to the possibility of conversation.

Developing personal values

In true conversation our values become obvious quite quickly. If we really don't believe in the value of human conversation in creating change then that will become clear. We are not going so far as to say that conversation will be completely ineffective but that most is to be gained by all concerned if the host 'walks the talk' and is consistent, as far as possible, in their life and practice. The challenge for a host is to clarify the values from which they operate with regard to other people.

Remaining self-aware

Given the emotional challenges conversation can present, a good degree of self-awareness, we think, gives the conversational practitioner greater freedom to choose particular conversational approaches which suit the circumstances. We also believe that self-awareness is critical in being able to hear and act upon feedback in a way that supports the personal learning of practitioner.

Holding intention

To work with conversation requires a degree of intentionality. It is necessary to maintain a purposefulness and seriousness about the way you convene conversations or participate in them. That's not to say you have to become humourless and dry, but rather that you should be always alert to the possibilities of a conversation developing. We should ensure that, as best as we are able, we remain present and an active, positive, participant.

Being authentic

In meeting people who regularly host conversations, we have been struck by the authenticity they demonstrate in the way they relate to people. Conversation is not, for them, another tool they adopt during work time but rather part of a way of life to which they have committed themselves. Authenticity involves a decision to live in a particular way with a particular set of values. Conversation then becomes not a form of game playing but rather an attempt to be honest and real with others. It means taking down the mask we often hold in front of us. But it goes beyond that. It asks us to be open to the possibility that we ourselves might be changed (Scott, 2002).

For the conversational practitioner to practise conversation, they themselves need to be open to the possibility of change for themselves, not just for others. This moves way beyond conventional approaches to consultancy where the consultant offers a set of skills and insights to an organization and then moves on largely unchanged to another organization. Authentic practice involves the challenge of personal change.

WHAT WILL WE AS CONVERSATIONAL PRACTITIONERS BRING TO OUR WORK WITH ORGANIZATIONS?

Separating the 'doing' of a conversational process from the 'being', a host of conversations feels a little artificial. The two belong together in our view. When we are present and in relationship with people in an organizational context we have already begun our work, perhaps at a subconscious level, but it is work none the less.

First and foremost, the conversational practitioner will act as a catalyst for conversation. While the practitioner may have skills and insights into a variety of organizational processes, their main focus will be to understand how conversational change processes can be of benefit to the client. The client needs to be made aware that it is not always possible to be definite about the outcomes or what other issues may emerge through the process. Working with conversation is about creativity and developing new understandings, some shared and some not. Yes, there may be optimism at the start of a process of conversation, but there may also be pain and struggle as the process unfolds.

Second, the practitioner will bring their skills as a conversational host. To do this requires a constant awareness of what being a host involves. We deliberately set aside as much of our own agenda as we can and offer ourselves in the service of others. Through displaying the characteristics of a good host combined with modelling excellent conversational skills, we co-create a conversational environment that opens up entirely new possibilities and depth of relating. This can be unsettling, and part of what we bring is a sense of relative comfort at working in the midst of discomfort.

Third, we bring our knowledge of conversation as a change process, both in its principles and its practice. These inform the conversations we have with the client about the processes they and we will engage in.

Fourth, and perhaps most importantly, we bring with us an approach that supports the creation of new meaning and depth of understanding. Specifically, the notion that, as the conversations we host take place, reality is constructed between us as individuals. This 'reality' may be a completely different one from that which existed before the conversation took place. Change, in its broadest sense, may have taken place simply because shared understandings of the situation have changed through the conversation.

The power of conversation cannot be underestimated.

SUMMARY

We have explored in depth the nature of conversation and contrasted it with dialogue and other types of interaction. We recognized that the potential power of conversation to transform situations can sometimes provoke fear and ambivalence in people and organizations. To work with these feelings and to be effective in supporting conversations in organizational contexts we considered the role of the conversational practitioner as a host of conversations rather than as a traditional Organization Development (OD) facilitator. We concluded this chapter by describing the skills and personal attributes of a conversational host and some of the challenges the role can present.

7

Extending practice: working with story in organizations

INTRODUCTION

So far we have introduced the key theory and practice of conversation-based processes, using Appreciative Inquiry in particular to illuminate the points we have made. We hope this has inspired you to experiment with this different approach in your work. If it has then you may have noticed that the whole atmosphere and tenor of the work is different. This chapter offers complementary ways to create this type of experience, to increase your flexibility in your response to organizational challenges. This chapter will first of all further examine the place of story and conversation in organizational life. Then, drawing on that understanding, we will present two techniques that work with story and conversation in different ways: reflecting teams and domains of inquiry. Lastly we will consider some story-based sense-making tools, useful in highly complex or fragmented situations where it is hard to make sense of what is going on. To make clear the connection between what the chapter has to offer and what has gone before, we perhaps need first to spend some time identifying the common ground.

THE COMMON GROUND WITH THE CONVERSATION-BASED APPROACH TO ORGANIZATIONAL CHANGE

All the ideas and ways of working presented in this chapter and indeed this book are based on a systemic understanding of the relationships between people. To have a systemic understanding of relationships and organizations is to recognize the interaction between people as being of the greatest interest when observing organizational life. These interactions are, correspondingly, seen as the potential site for influence or intervention. This stands in strong contrast to most ways of looking at, and working in, organizations, which place a strong focus on the individual person. Such perspectives see the individual, and change in the individual, as offering the greatest potential for organizational development. We can see this in the emphasis on measuring people (psychometrics) and on the deficit model of personal development (identifying 'the skills gap'). Working from a more systemic perspective we are more interested in such organizational features as: relationships between people; the beliefs held that inform those relationships; patterns of communication within the organization; the meanings created by these recursive patterns; and the potential and constraint such meanings create for various possible further actions. Translating this back into Appreciative Inquiry terms, we can see that our discovery, dreaming, design and destiny activities impact on precisely these things. These activities exert influence through the impact they have on patterns of behaviour in the organization, and on the beliefs held about the organization. Changes in these things allow new ways of being together to emerge. We do all this by facilitating the creation of new stories about the organization, through conversation.

USING STORY

The idea of organizational stories being a source of organizational change is relatively new in organizational development and we want to spend some time here considering what we mean when we talk about organizational stories. The idea of organizational stories is built on, or out from, the common organizational activity of giving account. Within organizations we are always giving accounts of what has happened, should happen, or will happen. It is important to note that 'an account' isn't the same as what actually happened, it is a 'story' about what happened. Even when we are giving the most truthful account we can, the account is the translation of lived experience into words, and inevitably something is lost and gained in the process. We can never really tell it exactly as it was; what we can do is tell it exactly as it was to us. In this sense our story about what happened is as accurate an account as we are capable of giving, yet at the same time it is essentially a fiction, a representation of experience put into words. However, the important thing is that this lack of an exact correspondence between what happens to us (our lived experience) and how we can relate it (the story we tell) be viewed as a resource rather than a problem. The lack of a possibility of the one true story allows for an infinite number of possible stories. There is always more than one story that can be told about what has happened, is happening, or is going to happen. Here lies organizational resource for change.

Deciding what to believe

How, you might ask, from this wealth of possible stories, do we decide which ones to believe? We usually choose to believe the stories that make most sense to us, that is, fit best with our understanding of how things are. When these two facets of life (stories told about our experience and our lived experience) don't fit well together, we experience difficulties in making sense of what is happening. For example, discrepancies can arise between stories other people create about our life and how we are experiencing it. If the story I'm being told about what's happening to me holds little in common with my current interpretations of my lived experience, then I am likely to find myself in a dilemma. Do I believe your version of events or mine? We see this frequently in organizations where the managerial story about challenge and the future (for instance, 'We are forging ahead to new challenges, equipped to meet them and raring to go') fails to resonate with the front line's current experience expressed as 'We're worked off our feet, we don't know what is expected of us and we don't know what the future holds for us'. In response to this lack of cohesion in accounts, the story the frontline staff might generate to make sense might be 'Management have lost touch with the real world' or 'That's just management talking, it means nothing'. Meanwhile the managers will also be struggling to make sense of the gulf between how they understand the world and how other people are behaving. To bridge that gap the managerial story about their staff might be 'They are such Luddites' or 'They are only concerned with their own jobs'. In this way we can see that the stories we tell make sense of and define our worlds, express our worlds, and connect or disconnect our worlds.

Stories and their relationship to 'the truth'

For most of us the more the 'story' resonates with our lived experience, the more likely it is to seem like the truth and so to be given the special status of 'the truth'. Truth is unquestionable; it is impossible to argue with the truth. To stake a claim to the truth is to attempt to establish an unassailable position for a particular version of events. From a systemic perspective, what is presented as 'the truth' in any given system is only one possible account of life, from an infinite number of possible accounts. Not all accounts or stories are equally valid though, and we measure their validity by reference to the author, the audience, our shared experiences, other stories we hold dear, their relationship to our lived experience, and its relationship to the stories we tell about ourselves. Working with an awareness of this, we need to be able to access, and hold on to, the conviction that there is always another possible story.

Story and its relationship to Appreciative Inquiry

To help you with this, let's relate this back to the practice of Appreciative Inquiry. One way of viewing the discovery phase is to say that it generates new stories in the system. When we have people telling often previously untold stories of when things went right, we are seeing the system tell different stories about itself. That in itself, as you will have noticed, changes things. You may also have noticed that people frequently struggle with the 'both/and' nature of what we are creating with them. We are saying 'What you were saying about the problems, and what you are saying about the good things, are equally true.' Many people find it hard to give up the notion of a single truth, and wrestle with the dualistic choice of 'we are either a problem system or an appreciative system, we can't be both'. Ideally we can move the single organizational story of 'this is how it is' to a story about possibilities: 'It can be this way and many other ways.' We do this by working with the stories present in the system to open up new possibilities of ways of being.

Once we start to appreciate organizational stories as a powerful source of change in an organization, we begin to see a rich and complex pattern of possible organizational resource. Barnett Pearce's taxonomy of organizational stories allows us to develop a more sophisticated understanding of this resource (Figure 7.1).

From this we can see that when we work with stories, we have a rich source of stories to call upon. Of particular interest, often, are the

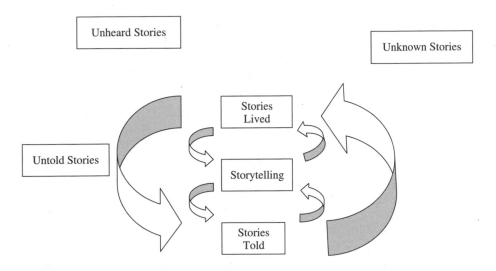

Figure 7.1 Organizational stories

unknown, unheard and untold stories in the organization. We can work with each of these to create more organizational stories, that is, to create more organizational resource. Each of them requires a slightly different approach. For instance, to move the unknown story to the known story, we have to create a context where this new story, which creates knowledge for the organization, becomes told. To generate the untold story, we have to create a context for its telling. And to allow the unheard story to be heard, we have to attend to speakers and audiences. To help this make some sense, let us tell you a little story about some work one of us did a while ago where shifting the story pattern was key to the system resolving its issues and moving on.

One of us was invited to join with a system that was in the process of forming: two previously separate organizations were coming together as one. Neither of these two voluntary organizations had particularly wanted to join the other. They were driven to this action by a shared dependence on a particular funding body which had made it clear that it would no longer to fund two separate, small organizations, but would continue to fund a slightly larger single organization. They needed to amalgamate. One organization was notably bigger than the other.

When we arrived at the 'new' organization we noticed that there were a number of different stories about the current experience being told within the system. For instance, the predominant, public stories present in the formal meetings set up to facilitate the merger were of the great difference between the two organizations. The gulf seemed insurmountable. There were also different stories about the nature of the coming together: was it a genuine merger or really a takeover? The formal story was that it was a merger, but to some people it felt more like a takeover. These stories in turn were fuelling strong individual stories of having to stay in the new set-up to protect what had gone before. At the same time, many people did not want to be part of this 'no longer us' new organization. The negotiating ground for many of these contested versions of events was the discussion around 'the formal contracts' involved in coming together. A heavily contested contract-based legal process, which no one was looking forward to, seemed the sole way forward.

What struck us particularly was the tremendous emphasis being put in these conversations on the difference, and so uniqueness, of the two organizations. They had different histories, different values, different ways of working and different cultures. Being in the formal meetings you would have been led to believe that these two organizations were strangers being coerced into an unwanted, unequal, arranged marriage. What struck us as interesting was that, in contexts other than the formal meetings, there existed stories of connection. The organizations shared some of the same clients, and some of the people involved had worked for both organizations or had sat on each other's Boards of Trustees. At the point that we joined the system these stories weren't being brought into the formal meetings. There were two separate conversational arenas – we can call them the public and the private arenas – where different stories were being told about reality. We could say that in one arena stories of difference were being privileged almost to the exclusion of all others, while in the other there was more opportunity for other stories to be told.

One of the more impactful sessions we had working with this group was when we focused, in a session that was part of the formal process, on identifying what was common or shared. By offering a process where people could share some of the things we had been hearing in the private conversational space we were able to bring 'unheard' stories into the formal merger process. The system's sense of itself as two very separate and distinct systems, locked in a conflict unto the death, began to shift more to one of a larger system of people, concerned about similar things, with similar values and career paths, that crisscrossed over each others like tracks in a forest. The shifting of the pattern of stories allowed various different things to happen. For example, it made it possible for key people who wanted to move out of the emerging system to do so with a clear conscience, knowing that 'the system' held some of the things that were dear to them. And although discussions as to the contractual nature of the new organization continued, they were no longer the main action around which all the unresolved concerns and questions were being played out. It became possible to start to build a joint future without betraying the past. Bringing different stories to life in different contexts changes things.

WORKING WITH STORY

1. Reflecting teams

Within organizations stories can be simple or complex, single or multiple, loud or muted. Sometimes when faced with a single, simple, strong, organizational (or individual) story it can be difficult to create openings for alternative stories to emerge. We have illustrated in Table 7.1 some different types of questions that can be used to help story development and exploration.

However, we want to move on to consider how we can use people's physical positions to help them hear differently and so create different stories about what they hear. One way this can be done is by placing people in different positions relative to the story. By establishing reflecting teams we can free people from the constraint of an ordinary conversation or discussion, so allowing them to listen differently. Why might we want to do this?

Why use reflecting teams?

The beauty of a reflecting team is that it places people in a position where they are free to listen, and then comment on what they have heard without having to engage with the other people directly. This positioning frees them from the normal conversational obligations of, for instance: responding to everything that is said; being obliged to defend themselves against any perceived criticism or attack; thinking about what they are going to say next; turn-taking; managing their facial expressions; and seeking clarification. Freed from such resource-engaging preoccupations, people have much greater resource for listening, and, as the title of the process suggests, reflecting. A typical reflecting team set-up might look like Figure 7.2.

Table 7.1 Questions to help story development and exploration

Categories of Questioning or Question	Examples or Explanation
Contextualizing questioning	So how come this is so energizing for you? Where does that passion come from?
Appreciative questioning	Tell me about a recent experience when you found yourselves in agreement about something.
Questions to connect meaning and action	If you see that there can only be one winner here, how does that make you act?
Questions to widen the context	If we asked your other colleagues about this, what would they say?
Hypothetical questions	If you believed you could do this, what would you do next? If we weren't talking about this, what would we be talking about?
Questions that embed a suggestion	If you decided that the most helpful thing you could do would be not to do what they have asked, what might you do instead that would be helpful?
Tracking questions	So when X did that what did Y do and when Y did that what did Z do?
Ranking questions	Among your colleagues, who would be the most likely and least likely to think that you could do this?
Episodic questioning	Give me an example of an interaction with your manager where you didn't get frustrated.
Questions to connect thinking and feeling	So when you think that way what do you feel? What would you need to feel to think that they were on your side?
Questions to encourage difference	How would your description of what is happening differ from what we have just heard?
Dyadic questions	How do you think they made sense of what you are doing?
Triadic questions	If I were to ask John to describe Janet's attitude to Dimple, what might he say?
Temporal questions	How far back do we need to go to get to when this wasn't a problem?
Historical questions	When did you first begin to notice that things were changing?
Position questions	If you were leader of this organization, what is the first thing you would do to resolve this?
Questions to explore untold accounts	What story would you like someone to tell about this?
Reflexive questions	What could I usefully ask you at this point?
Questions to explore contradictions	How do you make sense of this...?
Questions about emotion	If the emotion could speak so that it could be heard, what would be the signs that it had been heard?

Informed by Oliver and Brittain (1999)

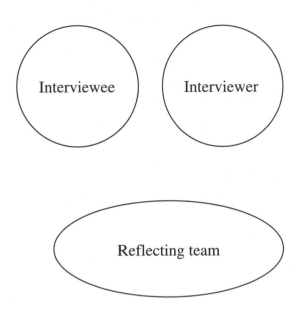

Figure 7.2 Categories of questioning

This illustrates a set-up focused on an interview of an individual (perhaps the group leader), while Figure 7.3 illustrates a group arrangement (perhaps when you are working with two groups at the boundary of their relationship, such as a board of directors and the senior management team). Sometimes a group with one shared identity is divided, for the purposes of the exercise, into two groups. We are going to use the arrangement of two separate groups that need to work better together to illuminate our explanations of working with the reflecting team process.

How to use the reflecting team process

(a) Setting up the reflecting team
The basic process for utilizing a reflecting team is as follows. The two groups can be designated a talking group and a reflecting team. A conversation takes place between the interviewer and the talking group. While this is going on, the reflecting team are asked to minimize eye-contact with the talking team and to just listen to what is being said. Depending on the particular purpose of the intervention, further

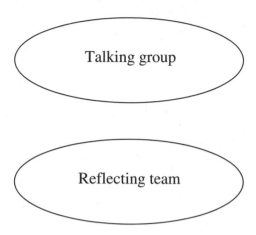

Figure 7.3 Reflecting teams

direction can be given to the reflecting team about what particularly to listen out for. This further direction might focus on content. So you might ask them to listen out for such things as: differences in accounts being given; stories of success, talents, skills or abilities; back-stories not being told; unquestioned assumptions; maybe even what they hear as unsaid.

Alternatively, you might want the reflecting team to focus more on their reactions, and so guide them to notice when they felt curiosity and what about, any 'aha' moments they experienced, when they were 'struck' by something said, when they felt bored, or when they realized they were hearing something new. Of course, you can also give no particular direction and just see what the reflecting team pick up. Different reflecting teams will hear different things depending on many factors, including their relationship with the talking team. They will certainly hear things differently from you, and also hear different things. In this way, bearing in mind that what we are listening for influences what we hear, we can work to identify and amplify particular aspects of the situation that interest us.

(b) working with the reflecting team
At some point you will want to halt the discussion and work with the reflecting team. There are various ways you can do this:

▌ You can interview the reflecting team.

▍ The reflecting team can just 'have a discussion' about what they have heard.

▍ You can set a purpose for their discussion. 'Given what you have heard, please identify three things you would like me to inquire into further.'

▍ You can ask them to work in one of the specific domains of experience (explained later in this chapter).

▍ You can ask them to speak directly to the talking group.

One other way to work with the reflecting team is to switch their roles so that the talking group becomes the reflecting team, while the reflecting team becomes the talking group. In this way the two groups swap roles. You would then conduct a conversation with the new talking group. People are inevitably interested to hear what other people have to say about what they have heard. We are curious to know what sense people make of us. It can be a revelation to hear what people have heard or their reaction to what they have heard. Iterations of this process allow subtleties and nuances of conversation to be heard and developed, creating new and different stories and new and different conversation.

Reflecting teams can offer the benefits listed in Figure 7.4.

It is useful to remind reflecting teams when they shift to becoming talking groups and are asked to reflect on what they have heard that, even though they are not speaking directly to, they are still speaking in the presence of, the people they have just been listening to. This means that they need to be mindful of them as one of the audiences as they speak.

(c) What next?

Working with the reflecting team process offers great scope for creativity and responsiveness to what is emerging in the conversation. From this initial starting point outlined above, there are various directions in which you might move, some of which we outline here.

After the new talking group have spoken, reverse the roles again to return to the original set-up and continue the interview or group discussion. The opening questions will be influenced by what has just gone before, so you might like to ask your talking group 'Out of what we have just heard, what most caught your interest?' If for some reason the reflecting conversation didn't connect for the talking group, then you can ask them 'What would you have liked the team to have asked?' or 'What were you disappointed they didn't comment on?' or 'What

Reflecting teams can offer:

Metaphors
Stories
Direct suggestions
Hypotheses
Possible connotations
Alternative descriptions
Unique outcomes
Sparkling moments
Personal reminiscences and feelings
Other questions to be asked
Restatement of words heard
Theoretical explanations
Pragmatic suggestions
Observations on voices they could hear behind the story told
Possible audiences for the story as told, and other possible audiences they became aware of
Emotional connections, where they heard passion, sadness, hope
Stories not being told
Stories that couldn't be told
Stories that inform action
Stories that contain moral imperatives
Stories of obligation
Curiosity

Figure 7.4 Reflecting teams can offer

does this lack of connection at this point suggest to you (tell you) about what we are talking about?'

Alternatively, you might ask the people who have been listening to reflect on the reflecting team's reflections.

You might suggest that the reflecting team becomes an interviewing team, allowing you to move to a different position as one of them steps into the interviewing space. The team can then become a consulting team. This means that they act as a resource to the interviewer, coming forward with questions or suggestions about where to take the interview/conversation if the interviewer gets stuck. Or the interviewer can use them as a reflecting team, asking them to comment amongst themselves on what they have just heard until he or she feels able to recommence the conversation.

With larger groups you can use cascading reflecting teams, where a series of teams get to reflect on the reflections of the previous group. Or you can have a set of parallel small reflecting teams and release the talking team to go around and 'listen in' at different groups to what is being said. You could then invite some feedback from each of the reflecting teams and the original talking team before moving on.

Endless flexibility

As we hope you can see, there are many different way to work with this process, limited only by our imagination, logistics, acoustics and time. It might be pertinent at this point to remind ourselves of the point of the exercise! Essentially, by placing people in these different positions to each other, and by encouraging quality listening and reflection, you are greatly affecting the normal pattern of interaction amongst the group: you are changing something. You are also bringing more of the story landscape into view as unknown, untold, and unheard stories join the stories told and the telling. This acts to increase tremendously the resource available to the group in its sense making and storytelling. In this way you are building the group's capacity to create a better future.

2. Domains of experience

Another way of working with stories in organizations is to use the model of the domains of experience in conversation (Maturana and Varela, 1987; Lang, Little and Cronen, 1990; Oliver and Brittan, 2001). See Figure 7.5.

First let's understand the model

In essence this theory suggests that conversational content and intent can be classified into three different domains: the domain of aesthetics, the domain of explanation and the domain of production. Generally speaking, we manage to conduct our lives and conversations without giving particular attention to these different possible domains. However, when life and so conversation becomes complex, complicated, busy, noisy and heated, it can be instructive and useful to work to separate out these domains so that we can better see and hear what we are saying in each. Having separated out these elements of the conversational experience to enable us to consider each in a more focused way, we can then reintegrate them in a way that allows us to connect better with each other and to make better sense together going forward (Figure 7.6).

Figure 7.5 The domains of experience

When working with domains can be useful:

When the system is experiencing rigidity
When there is disconnection in the system
Confusion
Too much certainty, a dualistic story, either/or
Too many voices are being drowned out
Experiencing difficulty in having a creative conversation
Conventional discourses not working
Dilemmas, especially moral
Systems trapped in a paradox – such as strange loops of belief
Stuck systems
When there is confusion about what conversation we are in
When there is too much disconnected complexity
To talk about context
To expand the terrain of discussion

Figure 7.6 When working with domains can be useful

How does it work?

These three domains give us a way of classifying utterances in conversation. With this simple classification system it becomes possible to hear, in a conversation among a group, that different participants are focused on different aspects of experience, and that they don't necessarily realize this. It may become apparent, for instance, that while some are keen to work out what happened (are focusing on the domain of explanation), others feel the priority is to decide what to do (want to be in the domain of production), while yet others seemingly want to digress to discuss how the whole thing feels (feel a need to be in the domain of aesthetics). We sometimes describe the experience of being in a group like this as being 'at cross purposes' with each other. It can be experienced as being in conflict and the quality of listening and connection can rapidly deteriorate. This concept of different domains, all equally important to the experience of living, gives us a way to reorganize such a multi-layered conversation so that we all stand a better chance of hearing the contributions being offered in each domain and connecting them. In essence it slows conversation down and separates out some elements.

Working with the domains of experience

There are different ways you can work with this understanding of the complexity of conversation. For instance, you can ask the group to have three sequential conversations based on the three domains. You can structure the three conversations in any order; however, it is often helpful to end with the domain of production, where the contributions are informed by the experience of the previous two conversations. In each conversation participants are encouraged, for the duration of the conversation, to behave 'as if' the world were one of aesthetics, or explanation, or production. This helps people to temporarily let go of their concerns that belong in the other domains and to participate fully in the one they are in.

Another way to work with domains with a group is to split them into three groups and give each one a domain in which to conduct their conversation; they converse sequentially. The other groups listen. The groups can then come back as one large group to discuss what they have heard and learnt and to see where they are. Alternatively, they could re-form into small groups containing members from all the previous conversations and hold discussions. You have probably already spotted that you could use this to structure reflecting team discussions!

Below, each of the domains is discussed in more detail to help you set up a domain-specific discussion.

The domain of explanation

Working in this domain is to work with story and hypotheses, the central focus being: how can we explain what is happening? This is a divergent conversation where we are looking for multiple, creative explanations. While exploring these concerns we will move around the system, considering how we could explain things from different points of view. We work with the fragments of stories and accounts that we have been offered to see if we can connect them into a useful, higher-context story. We are explorers across the landscape of the system, playing with different ways of accounting for and making sense of what we experience, creating many maps with no need to decide on a definitive one. We will use metaphors to help us see things and explain things. Working in this domain we refrain from giving advice or drawing conclusions. We are explorers.

In this domain we are working very clearly with narrative and story. All positions are partial, meaning that we owe no particular allegiance to any idea we come upon and so are free to move to another position, or 'take', on the situation at will. Multiple descriptions of the world are to be encouraged. This is a both/and conversation. Legitimate activities in this domain include story making, enquiring, questioning, reflecting, making connections and diversifying. We are looking for variety, and we are being curious, that is, privileging the voice of others rather than our own concerns. Not so much 'How do we make sense of this?', rather 'In what ways can we make sense of what we experience?' Answers will involve the elaboration of many different stories and perspectives as we attempt to understand the coherence of the action or behaviour of any person in the system. In essence this is the question of Why? To which there are many possible answers.

The domain of aesthetics

Working in this domain we are interested in considerations of fit, of elegance, beauty and form. Here we are working with a consciousness of sensitivity and sensibility. We aspire to develop a situated sensibility to the conversation, that is, to be conscious of context, connection and the reflexive nature of human interaction. Reflexivity and moral responsibilities are considered. There is an ethical dimension to our conversation; we connect our conversation to our values. We might well consider purpose here. We are looking for patterns. We are seeking the elegance of coherence, both/and rather than either/or.

Here we might make judgements: which is the most elegant explanation, which offers the greater sense of purpose? How could we create a story from what we know that highlights people acting with a sense of values? What ethical reactions do we have to what is going on? There is no requirement that at any point views converge; however, we may wish to focus on coherence amongst our contributions, work to ensure an elegant fit between what has been said and what we want to say. In this domain we can make judgements about whether to privilege a modernist (certainty) view of things or a postmodernist (uncertainty) view of the situation. In this domain we might consider the relationship between theory and practice, or identify some theoretical frames that could be used to contextualize action. We are focused on doing what we are doing elegantly and gracefully. Our emphasis here is fit, learning and ethics. In essence this is the question of How.

The domain of production

This is the domain of action. Here we decide what to do. Here we act 'as if' we had certainty about the situation and so can make decisions. In this domain we are concerned with facts, with rights and wrongs. Here truth is possible; we are in a world of order and certainty. It is a more modernist and convergent conversational frame than the other two. Legitimate activities here include instruction, stating of opinion, rhetorical argument, fixing of problems. We might use deductive logic and make reference to discipline, contract or legalities. Most of us are used to working and talking in this domain. Many workplaces unconsciously consider it the only legitimate domain in which to be functioning at work. Many workplaces produce ugly, ill-fitting plans for change, uninformed by a consideration of explanation or aesthetics.

We hope that this section has given you some ideas and processes to incorporate into your conversational practice, extending the possibilities of working with story and connection in organizations. We want now to offer you some ways of creating temporary stories, that is, ways of making temporary sense of what you are experiencing with a particular system. These temporary stories can create a 'holding' story around which a fragmented system can momentarily coalesce. They can also be useful in helping you to act purposefully as a host in your conversations.

SENSE MAKING: CREATING TEMPORARY MOMENTS OF CLARITY IN AN UNCLEAR WORLD

In contrast to the processes outlined above (reflecting teams and domains of experience) that work with the flow of the existing system complexity, the idea we are going to introduce below, that of organizational strange loops and paradox, works to introduce temporary, and partial, moments of clarity or stillness. The greatest danger here, of course, is that we mistake these temporary, and partial, moments of clarity that we can create for the permanent fixed story and believe that we have struck gold, having finally established 'the truth of the matter'. To help guard against this we need to bear in mind the uncertain nature of any hypothesis we may form both about what is happening and what is needed.

3. Strange loops and paradox

Working with organizations it behoves us to be aware that, as Morgan (1997) notes, 'organizations are complex and paradoxical phenomena that can be understood in many different ways'. One of the ways this paradoxical nature shows itself is in the ability of organizations to contain two mutually exclusive stories that serve to keep the system in an oscillating process of living first one story and then the other. It hardly needs to be added that this paradox is not part of the present story told or in the telling. In other words, the existence of these two mutually exclusive stories that are informing people's actions is not part of the organization's awareness of itself. The stories, and the awareness of the stories, are likely to exist as disconnected fragments. We are often alerted to the presence of a central paradox by a sense of puzzlement; something seems disproportionate or out of kilter given the story being told. An example may help.

Some years ago one of the authors was asked to work with an organization to help them appoint a CEO. This was a new position within this small voluntary organization. The organization was currently a cooperative, so clearly this would be a significant change. Even so, we quickly became puzzled by the contrast between the expressed need for assistance with making this appointment and the considerable experience that existed in the organization of creating roles and appointing to post. The organization knew how to recruit and select staff, so why did it feel it needed assistance with this particular appointment?

The next thing that emerged was that the decision to appoint a chief executive for the organization kept having to be remade. In other words, they kept making the decision yet not enacting it. Further exploration discovered a lot of different stories about the status of this decision, from 'very much still under discussion' to 'definitely decided'. We started to form a hypothesis that the act of appointing a chief executive was highly meaningful and highly problematic, yet deemed vitally necessary for this organization. While the story about the essential need to appoint a chief executive (which was connected to the demands of the wider funder/client system and need not detain us here) was not apparently contested, there was clearly a deep ambivalence about doing so that was holding the organization in an unproductive state of flux.

One way of looking at this was to view the organization as oscillating between two possible states of being, we have a leader, we don't have a leader, and not being happy with either. Working in the domain of explanation, we connected this with a key organizational story of being a cooperative, which was a strong story of identity, to come up with the representation shown in Figure 7.7.

With strange loops of belief, what happens is that each story plays into the other. In this instance, if we start on the left-hand side, the story is 'We don't have a leader (state), we are a cooperative (identity), we

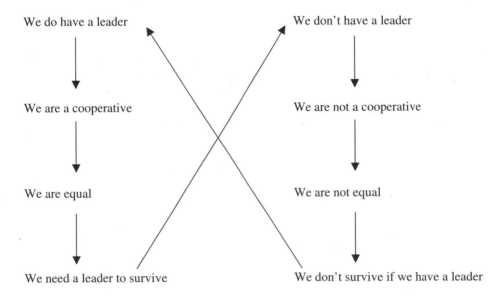

Figure 7.7 An example of a strange loop

are equal (values), we need a leader to survive (survival)'. However, 'If we have a leader (state), we are not a cooperative (lose identity), we are not equal (betray values), we don't survive (death)'. At this point the system would switch over to the life-affirming story of 'we don't have a leader'. This belief map is not 'how it actually was'; it's a story of paradox that connects the stories we were hearing and the action we were observing. It doesn't matter if it was 'the truth' or not, it was just a hypothesis.

What it did, though, was give us a sense of what we might want to inquire into to allow this set of stories to shift. From here we chose to inquire into the stories around 'being equal'. The inquiry gave life to stories of equality that didn't mean all being the same and did allow for the development of specialist skills. From here a story emerged that the role of chief executive could be 'another specialism within our existing equality'. Interestingly, the emergence of this story also meant that it was now possible for people from inside the organization to consider taking on the role, which previously was, if not unthinkable, certainly unsayable!

SUMMARY

In this chapter we have talked some more about the nature and function of story in living systems. We have suggested both some ways of using story and of working to increase the complexity of the story landscape. We have highlighted the importance of connecting different organizational stories, through conversation, to increase cohesion, coordinated action and the possibilities of system growth. In addition we have outlined a technique for introducing temporary moments of clarity to allow for reflections and the formation of hypotheses to inform the choice amongst the infinite possibilities of what to do next to help grow the system possibilities and resource. In the next chapter we will look at developing your conversational practice with an understanding of Open Space and World Café.

8

Developing your conversational practice

INTRODUCTION

In this chapter we want to help you extend your conversational practice by introducing four further conversation-based approaches to organizational change. We will first examine some of the common themes these approaches share, then we will introduce World Café, Open Space, Future Search and The Circle in more detail. Throughout this exploration we will be considering how these approaches complement the approach which we have already introduced, Appreciative Inquiry.

In our experience there is much to be gained from learning about these different approaches and potentially using them in conjunction with Appreciative Inquiry. At the heart of each is a conviction that conversation between people has the potential to transform individuals and the wider world. They also share with Appreciative Inquiry a deep sense of our ability as humans to draw upon the positive aspects of our lives to co-create a better future.

It's interesting to see how these various conversational processes have emerged during the past couple of decades alongside Appreciative Inquiry, in response to people's need for a different way of relating in organizations. For example, the developers of The Circle explicitly drew their inspiration from ancient village council practices, while others like Harrison Owen (1997) created Open Space in response to an expressed need for people to connect more effectively when attending conferences. The World Café came about through experimentation with different ways of engaging in conversation and sharing ideas, while Future Search focused on how to bring a whole system into a room to plan the future together.

It is common to find the creators of these processes acknowledging one another in their writings and collaborating in new projects. We are all benefiting from the new insights and approaches that are emerging as these pioneers engage in powerful conversations with one another. All of them are keen to make their learning available across the globe and to stimulate further work on and development of these processes. Where available we have included web addresses for the relevant websites so that you can gain a deeper understanding of these processes than it is possible to convey in this chapter.

COMMON THEMES

Later on in this section we will provide some outlines of each of the processes. First it's helpful to consider some of the features they have in common.

1. A belief in the transformational effects of conversation

First, and this maybe an obvious comment, they all are founded on the belief that meaningful, heartfelt conversation between people transforms lives, organizations and systems. The processes they have formulated are all intended to foster conversations which otherwise might not happen. They are deeply rooted in social constructionist philosophy and as such are based on the assumption that the 'doing' of change is so intimately bound up with the conversations people have about questions which matter that it is impossible to see the join. The one is so inextricably linked with the other that 'change' and 'conversation' are almost interchangeable as words and concepts.

Each of these processes is designed, therefore, not to be a prelude for change but rather to be a space where change of mind and heart actually occurs. The practical outworking of this change emerges naturally and within the flow of ongoing conversation. In effect conversation is becoming, in this paradigm, an overarching metaphor for change and development.

This then begins to explain why such attention is given in each of the approaches to the search for, and the formulation of, powerful questions. They each argue that conversations take place as people engage with questions that mean something to them. The role of the host in these conversational processes is therefore to encourage and support the search for questions. There are many ways that are suggested within each approach but the key is for the host not to get in the way of questions emerging or to impose their own. Practically, of course, this is hard. Time constraints and sometimes the demands of the client can put a great deal of pressure on the host to come up with the key magic question. It is best to resist this and explore with as many people as possible involved in the process a range of possible questions.

2. An understanding of the role of the host

Second, you will note from the use of the word host that your role in these processes is seen as quite different from the traditional facilitator's role. Within these processes it is not generally envisaged that the host will act as a 'manager' but rather that people will take responsibility for themselves and for one another. In Open Space, for example, this is taken to the limit where, after briefly introducing the process, the host steps back to silently 'hold the space'. The assumption is that people who are present have the wisdom needed to grapple with the questions they are facing. They are attending because they are interested in the questions and so will take ownership of both the process and the content. It is true that each of the processes offers a different role for the host. While in Open Space the host occupies a largely silent role, World Café suggests that the host actively facilitates a whole-room conversation at the end of two or more rounds of table conversations. This difference notwithstanding, the focus is on the participants as the source of wisdom and change.

3. Conversation engages the heart

Third is the expectation that people will engage at a heart level as much as with their heads. This means that feelings are welcome and that the processes are designed with 'rules' that seek to make the space safe enough for people to engage with one another at this level. True conversation, after all, prompts feeling and as we allow that to happen so we find ourselves open to new ways of being and doing. A key concept related to this is the notion of authenticity. The idea is that we bring our whole selves into the conversation rather than just our professional identity. Ideally the space created by these processes should be safe enough for us to remove, or at least part remove, one of our many masks to reveal a little more of ourselves and to open ourselves up to seeing and hearing others in a fresh way. At the same time, each of the approaches we are considering does not simply ask us to do so with no purpose. Each conversational space is established with a theme or question that draws our attention and interest. Becoming authentically present is focused around grappling with the depths of the questions with which we are faced, not simply as a gratuitous exercise in self-revelation.

4. The importance of the connections between people

Fourth, each process is underpinned by the assumption that connection between people is more likely to bring about a better world rather than solely relying on a small group of leaders to guide us and make decisions. There is a sense in each process that we have an essential equality between us. Our organizational roles, knowledge base and life experience may be different, but as we all sense ourselves to be equally valued and empowered to contribute, real shared commitment to change occurs.

5. A commitment to the power of inquiry

Finally, at the heart of each process we see an explicit commitment to the notion of inquiry. Conversational spaces are created specifically to inquire into the questions that really matter. The belief is that we become what we inquire into. Our energies focus around the inquiry, making real lasting change much more likely. Here we can see the most obvious link between Appreciative Inquiry and these processes. With a shared focus on inquiry through conversation it becomes much more straightforward to integrate these processes together in a way that allows the spirit and principles of Appreciative Inquiry to be applied in a very wide range of contexts with many types of questions and people. Appreciative Inquiry encourages participants and hosts to be creative and courageous in the way they engage in inquiry. Making use of the following approaches facilitates such creativity.

THE WORLD CAFÉ

By re-creating a café atmosphere, around small tables or in small-group clusters, anywhere between 12 and 1,500 people or more can feel relaxed and encouraged to have a series of 20- to 30-minute conversations around a question that matters. Volunteer table hosts remain at the tables to connect conversations whilst participants move twice or three times to new tables, bringing insights from their previous round. Generally, after two or more rounds of Café conversation, the overall Café host facilitates a whole-group conversation that surfaces underlying themes and key insights. The process can then be repeated with a new question.

There are seven integrated design principles that underpin this approach:

1. Set the context. Begin by clarifying the purpose and broad parameters within which the conversations will take place. This context should be set out on invitations to the Café and repeated at the start of the event.

2   Create hospitable space. Using music and room decoration, people arrive into a space that is different from that which they normally experience. The intention is to create a café type of environment that encourages relaxation and a sense of being at ease.

3. Explore questions that matter. Focus collective attention on powerful questions that build engagement and a sense of inquiry.

4. Encourage everyone's contribution. Invite full participation through careful listening to each member and speaking with intention.

5. Cross-pollinate and connect diverse perspectives. Through intentionally creating diversity by inviting many perspectives into the Café dialogues, build the density of connections among people while retaining a common focus on core questions.

6. Listen together for patterns, insights and deeper questions. Focus attention on common themes without losing individual contributions.

7. Harvest and share collective discoveries. Make collective knowledge and insight visible and actionable.

A Café is most appropriate when:

▌ You want to encourage the sharing of knowledge and an in-depth exploration of key challenges and opportunities.

▌ People need encouragement to engage in meaningful conversation with one another for the first time.

▌ It is important to build mutual ownership of outcomes.

A Café is not so appropriate when:

▌ A solution to a challenge has already been pre-determined.

▌ There is a very limited amount of time available (less than two hours).

▌ You want to make detailed implementation plans.

▌ People have already taken highly polarized positions around the questions you are proposing. In this case, Cafés can be used, but require hosts who are also highly skilled in complementary conflict resolution approaches.

How well does World Café fit with an Appreciative Inquiry approach?

The short answer is very well indeed! The spirit of inquiry is very strong within the World Café process and it works best when questions are framed appreciatively. Appreciative interviews are best carried out prior to a Café and can help shape the questions for the event. If you intend to undertake detailed action planning as part of the final destiny element of an Appreciative Inquiry process, then it is worth considering a priority setting and implementation format which enables task groups to concentrate on their work rather than a Café conversation which, by its very nature, encourages movement between groups, and the generation of multiple ideas and possibilities for action. Other than these caveats a Café approach offers a very flexible process that will accommodate almost any content arena and embraces both the Appreciative Inquiry philosophy and process.
http://www.theworldcafe.com

OPEN SPACE

Open Space begins with self-selected participants meeting in a circle. They are invited to consider a pre-determined theme. The process then moves on to working with a community bulletin board, and then a marketplace that helps participants structure their own agendas and meetings. A series of self-managed conversations lasting usually about one and a half hours then follows and the event concludes with participants back in a circle, with each given an opportunity to make a closing comment. An Open Space event can last half a day or as long as three days, depending on the issues being considered.

As its name implies, Open Space has a very loose structure and relies on people taking their own responsibility for hosting conversations on subjects that matter to them. The interventions by the host are very minimal. The host's prime role is to 'hold the space', thereby allowing others to enjoy the freedom to converse that this method encourages.

Open Space operates with four principles:

1. Whoever comes are the right people.

2. Whatever happens is the only thing that could have happened.

3. Whenever it starts is the right time.

4. When it's over, it's over.

And the Law of Two Feet: If during the course of the gathering someone finds themselves in a situation where they are neither learning nor contributing, they must use their two feet and go to some more productive place.

During Open Space events, conversation hosts are encouraged to take notes and these are then used to write up a report of proceedings.

An Open Space event is most appropriate when:

▎ A diverse group of people must deal with complex and potentially conflicting material in innovative and productive ways.

▎ People want to give time and energy to real-life issues which are of passionate concern to those involved.

▎ You have short timescales and want to create a very engaging and empowering environment.

An Open Space is not so appropriate when:

▌ A decision has already been made and people have limited opportunity to influence outcomes.

▌ Leaders want a strong degree of control over the agenda that people discuss.

▌ There is lack of clarity about the theme of the event.

▌ A suitable physical space with many breakout areas cannot be identified.

▌ There is a need to present a significant volume of material to an audience.

How well does an Open Space event fit with an Appreciative Inquiry approach?

One of the keys to a successful Open Space event is the choice of a theme or question that powerfully resonates with people. Using an appreciative theme is an ideal approach and Open Space offers a very helpful process to support an Appreciative Inquiry process after the Appreciative Interviews have been conducted. Since Open Space relies on people's energies it is a good way of sensing what will or will not secure people's commitment to take action.

Underpinning Open Space is a desire to support individual and organizational learning through encouraging powerful conversations and so its philosophy really fits well with Appreciative Inquiry. It is a matter of judgement where best to use the process if you are following the 4Ds cycle. In our experience it is particularly suited to the final destiny stage where you want to support people's enthusiasm for implementing those elements of design that they feel particularly passionate about.

http://www.openspaceworld.org

FUTURE SEARCH

A Future Search conference typically involves 25–100+ people focused on joint action towards a desired future for a community, organization or issue. Its structure is designed around the need to achieve five key tasks:

1. Review the past.

2. Explore the present.

3. Create ideal future scenarios.

4. Identify common ground.

5. Make action plans.

To achieve these, the creators of Future Search, Marvin Weisbord and Sandra Janoff (2000), have specified a number of what they describe as 'conditions for success':

▌ The whole system in the room.

▌ Global context, local action.

▌ Common ground and future focus, not problems and conflicts.

▌ Self-managed small groups.

▌ Full attendance.

▌ Healthy meeting conditions.

▌ Three-day event.

▌ Public responsibility for follow-up.

During a Future Search event a wide range of processes will be used to surface knowledge and support learning. These include small-group work, brainstorming, mapping and dialogue sessions that bear a strong resemblance to Open Space in design. The focus is very much on the future and looking for an ideal outcome. The emphasis is to support people in finding common ground and building on that foundation. Participants are encouraged to self-manage processes during the conference.

A Future Search conference is most appropriate when:

▌ Stakeholders want to create and act upon a shared vision for their organization or community.

▌ The 'whole system recognizes the need for change sufficiently to engage in a major commitment of time and resources.

▌ People are willing to self-manage their own learning.

▌ As diverse as possible a group of participants attend.

A Future Search conference is not so appropriate when:

▌ The 'criteria for success' outlined above cannot be met.

▌ There is weak leadership around the system and an unwillingness to engage.

▌ There is unlikely to be sufficient variety amongst participants.

▌ There is perceived to be no scope or freedom for people to take action they determine as important.

How well does Future Search fit with an Appreciative Inquiry approach?

There are some striking similarities between the two. First, the emphasis both place on appreciating the present and valuing what was good in the past. Second, the emphasis on shared learning and exploration around a theme or question that elicits deep interest and encourages conversation. Third, the focus on using the knowledge and understanding people have created together as a basis for planning the future. The Future Search conference and Appreciative Inquiry 4Ds offer processes which complement one another, while the Appreciative Inquiry philosophy provides a strong set of underpinning values and beliefs about how change happens through conversational processes. http://www.futuresearch.net

THE CIRCLE

In past centuries, village communities across the world gathered in council when they needed to access corporate wisdom. Usually there was a small amount of ritual and some basic courtesies that governed how the village council functioned. But everyone had a voice and everyone was listened to. In the past decade Christina Baldwin (1998) and her colleagues at PeerSpirit have rediscovered the power of circle conversations and developed a series of agreements, principles and practices which make it a highly accessible and valuable process creating safe spaces for people to engage in conversation.

A circle can be large or small and last for as long as is needed. At the centre of the circle are objects contributed by participants to signify their presence in the circle.

Those who have called the circle together have also, in advance, crafted a helpful question that will draw out the wisdom of those present on a subject that matters to the group. The use of a talking stick passed around the circle ensures that everyone has the space they need to contribute their wisdom and to be listened to.

A circle can convene several times in one day or over months or years.

Meeting in this way enables people to reconnect with their core purpose in life and work. The conversations can be literally life transforming. When used by teams these conversations change not just the individual but enhance shared commitment and direction. As wisdom is surfaced so new ways of doing things become obvious. It builds the confidence of the team to take on new and difficult challenges.

A circle is most appropriate when:

| People want to engage deeply with one another.

| Powerful questions need to be considered by a group who have a common interest.

| Participants are open to the spiritual aspects of meeting in circle.

A circle is not so appropriate when:

| The organizational context and culture is highly resistant to deep conversation.

| People want to engage intellectually with an issue but not emotionally or spiritually.

| Potential participants find the ritual too disturbing.

How well does Circle fit with an Appreciative Inquiry approach?

Circle offers a process that can be well used within the 4D's process. Its philosophy and particularly its spirituality fit neatly with Appreciative Inquiry. The conversational disciplines that the Circle encourages are consistent with Appreciative Inquiry practice and process. Its use of appreciative, optimistic questions as its focus and its encouragement of open-mindedness and learning also strongly complement Appreciative Inquiry. The emphasis of the Circle is upon creating a strong and safe

container for people to be honest in conversation. In an Appreciative Inquiry context this is very effective and helpful.
http://www.peerspirit.com

A REAL-LIFE EXAMPLE OF USING CONVERSATIONAL PROCESSES TO ACHIEVE ORGANIZATIONAL REBIRTH

Carolyn Baldwin is Assistant Headmaster at All Saints' Academy in Winter Haven, Florida, United States. The story that follows is her personal tale of how she used most of these conversational processes within an Appreciative Inquiry process between 2001 and 2006. What stands out is her personification of being an appreciative inquirer within her school, combined with her willingness to consider whichever framework seemed most appropriate at the time. We think the results speak for themselves!

APPRECIATIVE REBIRTH IN AN EDUCATIONAL SETTING

A little background...

All Saints' Academy was born of the vision and commitment of members of the parish at a local Episcopal church in 1966 and enjoyed much comfortable success as a parish elementary school. In the mid-1990s the energy of the vision keepers shifted to the design and building of a college preparatory grade 6–12 school and the attention to the lower school languished and division developed among the parish leaders and the board leaders of the new upper school. At a very low point, the lower school was asked to move from the physical location at the church which it had occupied since 1966 and the continued existence of the lower school as an entity was seriously questioned. With the support of a few loyal friends the decision was made to keep the lower school and relocate it, all within a six-week period of time. The school relocated and opened on time, but suffered an additional setback when the Head of the Lower School was not rehired and that decision was made public in October, although the Head did not leave until June. The school community was in great division about this decision for most of the school year. The school was in need of an appreciative approach when I entered the scene as Head of the Lower School in July 2001.

Setting the stage, preparing the ground...

1 July 2001 marks the beginning of an appreciative adventure into the dream stage and rebirth of the vibrancy of the lower school division at All Saints' Academy. As I walked around the school facility on my first day of work in July 2001, I took note of many things in the environment that could be worked on right away to give the school community, teachers, parent, and students the message that they were appreciated and cared for. It was a very unfriendly and unappreciative place for most staff and I suspect many others. During that summer the partitions came down, walls were painted, furniture was rearranged, and new plantings were brought in. I did everything I could within my budget constraints to make it clear in the environment that a new day was dawning. I wasn't quite clear what that difference was to be because I knew that difference had to emerge from all of us.

Beginning the dream...

I have been a student of appreciative approaches in leading for more than 15 years. I have seen and experienced the effectiveness of World Café' the Art of Hosting, Circle, Open Space and Appreciative Inquiry as methods of encouraging learning conversations. For our first meeting together as a community I chose a Circle methodology for our meeting to invoke the presence of shared leadership. During that first faculty meeting, held in Circle, we also spent time in pairs in an appreciative interview with questions about what our experience of the positive core of the lower school had been and what of that positive core we wished to carry forward with us into the future as we created our future together. Since this was our first meeting together as a community, the Circle 'check in' took two hours, as we approached the method seriously and were sure that each and every voice was heard. The appreciative interviews that helped us discover our positive core took the afternoon. The final activity for the day, our first day together, was to capture words that represented our positive core, about 20 words, and then post them around the building everywhere, so that as we began our year together we could be reminded of our positive core and what we were taking with us into our future. This first of many days to come ended with a feeling of great energy and positive direction. The methodology was very different from anything that the community had experienced previously, but was not threatening because it was positive. Energy was created because everyone had a part.

Discovering who we are and what we wanted to design...

From the data in the appreciative interviews (the positive core) we began to talk as a faculty about what new programmatic and instructional methodology might be suggested for us to grow. Here are the results:

▎ We discovered that string music was once a strength area and we re-established a string music programme very successfully as a regular part of our instructional programme for all students.

▎ We discovered that we are committed to global learning and dropped our language instruction from kindergarten to beginning at age 3 for Spanish and started a Mandarin Chinese language instruction programme at kindergarten. Our students will be trilingual by grade 5, which is very unusual in the United States and is very much valued by our parents.

▎ We have begun to offer multi-aged enrichment programmes and classes for high-ability students with global partnerships in China, Pakistan, Canada and Mexico.

▎ We celebrated our academic excellence and honoured that this core was very powerful and still strong.

▎ We recommitted ourselves to the school community and to each other as colleagues and a learning community.

These are just a few of the actual curricular and other changes that came directly as a result of the insight gained from the appreciative interviews conducted by the faculty with one another and actually grew from the positive core that the faculty uncovered in our organization that we wanted to carry forward and develop in more visible ways. These have developed over a period of five years through many faculty conversations. In this work together we have used Circle, Open Space and World Café and all the methodology has always been used with a positive and appreciative frame of mind and with an attitude of co-creation.

The structural design of any organization is forged by the board and work needed to be done in an appreciative way here as well. The board needed to be able to see that the lower school was a vital part of the healthy structure of the overall school and was of great benefit to the newly established college preparatory upper school. After numerous strategic appreciative conversations with board members regarding the value of the lower school in the organizational picture, an external consultant was effective in helping us with the 'bigger picture' design.

As a result, a design was made to make to school one 'whole', not two parts.

Finding our destiny...

We are in year number 6 of our appreciative way of living at All Saints' Academy and much has happened as a result of our choice to live in the positive. Life has returned to the lower school. So much life and so many children want to attend that a new design had to be made. On 1 July 2001 there were 147 children enrolled at the lower school. Today there are 405 children enrolled at the lower school, with waiting pools of families established. The board's design for a 'whole' school, not two parts, has been implemented with the unification of the school into a 'whole' on one campus and a new 42,000 square foot state-of-the-art lower school facility that is our new school home. Our community tells us that we are the preferred independent college preparatory school in our region in our enrolment and fundraising success. For me the most rewarding place to see our destiny is in our classrooms each day, where children are excited and engaged. Teachers have genuine relationships with students and there is a joyful presence about the building. Parents are in evidence everywhere and every day. There is a community spirit that lives and breathes. Our positive core is posted and palpable. We are practising each day, living our dream. This is our destiny...

BRINGING THEM ALL TOGETHER

There is no reason, as Carolyn's approach demonstrates, why all of these conversational frameworks may not be used during an Appreciative Inquiry process. Some may have more merit at different Appreciative Inquiry stages than others, but potentially all have a valuable contribution to make. The ability to judge which process to offer and when develops as you practise Appreciative Inquiry and engage with the people with whom you are working. Some may suit some groups of people and cultures more than others.

The confidence and ability of the practitioner is also an issue. Courses, training conferences and retreats focusing on one or more of these processes are increasingly being offered across the world. They tend to offer the benefit of learning from experts, practising the processes and engaging in powerful conversations with like-minded people. To find out more have a look at the websites in this chapter.

Needless to say, the more you practise hosting conversations the more likely you are to be able to offer, with confidence, a range of different formats.

SUMMARY

In this chapter we have introduced further creative conversations for change. We have identified common themes and introduced four specific approaches, namely: World Café, Open Space, Future Search and The Circle. We have also presented a long-term case study of the effect of this way of thinking and acting in a community over time. In the next chapter we will be looking in more detail at some of the general practice skills that facilitate being able to work in an appreciative way through the medium of conversation and conversational processes such as we have been looking at here.

9

Becoming an appreciative conversational practitioner

INTRODUCTION

A key skill underpinning all these conversational approaches is that of being appreciative, and of being able to work in an appreciative manner across a range of conversations and processes. This chapter will introduce some skills to help you bring an appreciative consciousness to all aspects of your work, and indeed life. We will first remind ourselves of our general purpose, then explore the spirit of appreciative inquiry, and finally, identify some key appreciative skills. In examining the spirit of Appreciative Inquiry we will be considering the importance to this approach, and indeed all the conversational approaches outlined in the previous chapter, of appreciation, curiosity, generosity, playfulness and irreverence.

In terms of skills we will be examining the development of an appreciative eye and ear, the skill of noting and naming the positive, and the development of the art of judgement. The nurturing and development of these spirits and skills contribute to changing our own life experience as well as changing the experience of the organization. It is by working at this deeper level with Appreciative Inquiry, and other conversational approaches, that we move beyond being mere organizational technicians with an additional technical skill to being people who truly see things differently and can offer organizations a genuinely alternative understanding of themselves. This difference shows in various ways, one being that we bring a different sense of purpose regarding our role with an organization.

PURPOSE

Wherever we are situated in an organization, and whatever our job title, is important to have a sense of our purpose and intention in our work. It is clarity of purpose that helps ensure our activities are informed and guided, rather than being random or formulaic. From an appreciative perspective we can define our overarching purpose to be that of 'enabling individuals to respond creatively to a changing situation' (Harman, 1999). This succinct definition encapsulates the common thread that pulls together all the conversational approaches explored in this book. We can perhaps understand this definition even better by seeing it in contrast to the more prevalent understanding of the purpose of those in charge during times of change. This more common understanding can be characterized as being 'the direction of resources (including human resources) to accomplish a predetermined task' (Harman, 1999). Understanding our purpose to be helping individuals to respond creatively to a changing situation is key to understanding our interest in increasing the organizational resource of stories that is a feature of a conversation-based approach. To increase the range of stories an organization has about itself is to increase its knowledge of itself and its ability to respond creatively to changing situations. The effectiveness of the conversational process lies partly in its ability to increase the story resource of an organization. To help generate a wide range of helpful stories, we need to bring a particular spirit of inquiry to our work.

WORKING SPIRIT-FULLY

Working spirit-fully is about being fully aware of the spirit in which we approach and engage organizations. We suggest here that such ideas as appreciative, curious, generous, playful and irreverent help to express the essence of this spirit.

The appreciative spirit of inquiry

What does it mean to work within a spirit of appreciation? In general terms it means maintaining awareness, perhaps in the face of contrary appearances, that good things that can be appreciated are happening in the organization, or have happened in the organization at some time. Being appreciative means being aware that the current picture isn't the whole picture. In practical terms it means seeking, by inquiry, to construct stories of good intent for all players in the organizational drama. To work within a spirit of Appreciative Inquiry is to be constantly asking yourself: 'Where is the good here?' 'What can I find to appreciate, to affirm, here?' An example would be to reveal, through inquiry, the positive intent in a particular action currently viewed by the organization as 'bad'. To illuminate this idea further, here is an example of just that.

Some short time ago, one of us was working with a public sector organization that wanted to achieve transformational change. A central plank of this change programme was a new IT system. As is often the way with such things, this centralized IT system was going to replace all the locally grown ways of doing things. In the specific example that concerns us it was going to take the process of booking rooms at the municipal village halls away from a small dispersed dedicated team who took bookings over the phone, and give it to a centralized 'customer service' team for whom it would only be one of their many duties.

Senior management were getting very frustrated at the reaction of some of the original staff to this proposed change. These staff didn't seem to regard the streamlining and computerization of their service as unbounded good news. The project managers' story about of what was going on was to see this 'obstructive behaviour' as a product of these people's self-interest, dinosaur tendencies and general obstruction to the future of the Council. Given the central and important position of the project team, this account was rapidly becoming the dominant organizational account about what was going on. This in turn led to the voice of the booking staff, who were suggesting that there might be problems for customers with the proposed new system, being ignored on the familiar grounds of 'Well, they would say that wouldn't they? They just don't like change.'

As outsiders coming into contact with the system, it would have been easy for us to accept the dominant story about what was going on. For a start it fits with the prevalent and popular 'resistance to organizational change' account of people's behaviour during change.

It also, from the senior managers' point of view, fitted the facts. Being appreciative conversational process-based consultants with a systemic understanding of organizations, we were interested to see what other stories or accounts of what was going on we could generate. We were looking to create accounts that were appreciative, rather than condemnatory, of these people's actions.

Appreciative Inquiry interviews revealed that this small specialist team knew their client group very well. They knew their needs and took pains to make sure they were met. 'For instance', a staff member we interviewed said, 'the old folk don't want to be in the next room to the brass band practice or when the crèche is open and all the young children are running about, they get worried. We know what people want, we know the layout of all the halls, so we make sure it doesn't happen. Also, most of our clients don't use computers, some aren't that happy on the phone and prefer to pop in to see us to sort things out.' They were worried that, with the best will in the world, the centralized call centre staff would not be able to provide this level of service. So, from their point of view the managerial story of 'this change is necessary to improve customer service' didn't make sense. And an appeal to them to accept the changes in the interests of 'increasing customer service' was meaningless and ineffective.

In other words, through Appreciative Inquiry we were able to generate an account of how their 'resistance' to the change was an attempt to protect good customer service, not to obstruct it. Having heard this story it was possible to take a more appreciative stance towards their behaviour of objecting to the proposed changes. We could now say that they were working to protect something that was precious to both them and the Council, that is, good customer service. With this point of connection, we could move forward.

A curious spirit of inquiry

To be curious and to remain curious is an important aspect of inquiry. Organizations or groups often want to settle into one fixed account of what is going on, or of what happened, or of who is to blame, or of what the right thing is to do. When they can't agree on one fixed story they experience themselves as being in conflict. And they experience that as problematic because they can't resolve the conflict and so they can't take action. Our role isn't to answer these questions for them. We aren't there to decide who is right and who is wrong. Our role is to wonder what purpose this or that account serves for the organization:

to wonder what might happen if they talked less about one thing and more about another; for instance, if they talked less about the problem and more about the dream.

In more general terms we are curious about the patterns of interaction before us. Having said that, we are often particularly interested in the exceptions to the general pattern. This places us in an interesting relationship with 'scientific inquiry'. Scientific inquiry is based on discovering general principles, the reliable principles that allow for predictability of events and control of the environment. Science is interested in establishing the central tendencies, and there is a convention when doing scientific statistical analysis that the researcher may ignore pieces of data that don't fit (known as 'outriders') so that they can identify a central tendency. Interestingly, Seligman makes reference to the strain this convention can cause, and the important data it can hide, when talking about the development of his interest in positive psychology (Seligman, 2003). Let us tell you the story.

Seligman was originally known for his work on learned helplessness (Maier and Seligman, 1976). Conducting behavioural experiments on dogs, Maier and Seligman established that repeated experience of being unable to escape an unpleasant event (in this case these poor dogs received electric shocks through the floor of their cage) led first to a lack of even attempting to escape and then to an inability to take the opportunity to escape when it became available (ie once there was an escape route, like an open door, out of the cage). This research attracted great excitement as it was seen to offer a possible understanding of the development of depression and hopelessness in people. It suggested that, when consistently battered by bad things they couldn't avoid (childhood abuse, bereavements, redundancy), some people learnt to be helpless and became effectively 'beyond help', being unable to do the minimum necessary to start making things better for themselves. It offered a behavioural explanation for this inexplicable behaviour: the phenomenon of learned helplessness.

What was not so highly publicized at the time was that a number of the dogs thus experimented on didn't display this pattern of behaviour at all. Instead they never gave up trying to escape or protesting at the treatment they were receiving. Rather they persisted in jumping up at the walls, or barking. Seligman refers to his unease throughout his research at 'the(se) embarrassing findings I keep hoping would go away' (Seligman, 2003: 23). The embarrassing findings being that one in three of the dogs did not learn to display the 'typical' pattern of learned helplessness. It is interesting also that one in eight didn't have to be taught, as we might say, to give up hope, rather they apparently had none to start with. Turning his attention to these findings led him to ask 'What is it about some (dogs and) people that imparts buffering strength, making them invulnerable to helplessness?' (Seligman, 2003: 23). By turning his attention to the outrider data, by being curious about the lack of fit of some of the data, Seligman started on his journey of discovering resourcefulness in situations of helplessness. This in turn led him to the development of the field of positive psychology.

This account is an excellent example of how being curious about the exceptions can generate resourcefulness for the 'central' part of the issue. What he went on to learn about the nature and development of optimism and hope has helped both adults and children become better able to avoid the miseries of pessimism and 'learned helplessness' (Seligman, 1996).

A generous spirit of inquiry

Being generous to others is a state easy to aspire to, not always so easy to achieve. In our context, taking a generous stance or working with a generous spirit implies many things. At a most basic level it can mean being generous with our resources, for instance our time, our attention, our skill and knowledge, our interest. It can mean being generous to others and their needs, giving them time to tell their story, not getting impatient with their apparent inability to get straight to the point. It can mean being prepared to look for the best, being generous in our attributions of motive to others. It can mean focusing on what someone can do rather than what they can't. It can also entail more complex forms of generosity, involving, for instance, being prepared to give up strongly held beliefs (stories) in order to help move things along.

A playful and irreverent spirit of inquiry

To work playfully within a spirit of irreverence is to say that nothing is beyond question; that nothing we encounter is beyond our curious reach; that nothing is beyond appreciation; and that nothing, we might say, is sacred. Oliver (1996) suggests that irreverence is 'a disrespect towards any idea which constrains (therapeutic) movement or creativity'. This means all rules of politeness, good practice, normal procedure or convention could conceivably be broken in service of the greater purpose of 'enabling individuals to respond creatively to a changing situation'. This is a tremendously liberating stance for those who would act to change things; however, it is not without responsibility. If we are no longer acting in reference to rules of politeness or an existing 'code of practice', then what other moral code are we acting with reference to, or in the context of?

We will explore this important question more in the second part of this chapter, where we make reference to the art of making judgements. For now we want to note that this idea of irreverence and playfulness allows us to break rules in the service of a higher context. These rules might be of the nature of 'the client is always right' or 'start where the client is at' or 'don't interrupt', or might be rules that relate to the particular organization or conversation we find ourselves part of. We can include in this those rules of the 'don't mention the elephant in the room' nature that exist in all contexts. We have liberty and licence to ask the un-askable, to say the unsayable, hear the unmentionable, and to enjoy the unenjoyable. Below we illuminate this idea with a non-work-based example of the benefits of a playful spirit, which had particular resonance for one of us at a certain time in our life.

Many years ago one of us read an article by a journalist about a day out with two or three families and their assorted young children. The day had taken some planning and some effort to organize. The hoped-for lovely hot sunny day punting on the river with relaxed children delighted by being so close to nature had somehow in reality become a wet, cold, rainy day on the river with wet, miserable, whining children and punts that were hard to steer in the cross-wind. Everyone was soaked, the children were hungry and the adults were tired. It was raining. At some point one of the adults said to the others 'Are we having fun yet?' The inversion of the idea of fun in this question is playful and transforming. At the time everyone burst out laughing and it made the author realize that, strange though it might seem, actually she was: this is about as good as it got under these conditions. It was good to be out with friends and there was more of the day to look forward to.

One of us liked this story so much, it resonated so strongly with our experience of the perils of planning 'nice days out' with children, that we have adopted it as a fail-safe mood changer in grim times when everything appears to conspire against us achieving that's day vision of family fun; and when we are in danger of turning in on ourselves to establish who is to blame for this dream failure! To ask 'Are we having fun yet?' serves to remind us that the responsibility for 'having fun' lies with us here and now, to remind us that the situation isn't, in the overall scheme of things, that serious if we can make reference to fun in the context of it. It changes things.

The idea of playfulness and irreverence is strongly present in the dreaming phase of Appreciative Inquiry. People new to Appreciative Inquiry often express the most concern about this part of the process. This may be partly because of a culture difference between the United States, where Appreciative Inquiry originated, and other parts of the world. The idea of dreams, and the significance of dreams, forms a strong thread of American cultural life. The American Dream is part of the cultural lexicon, and Martin Luther King is famous for his Dream. Native Americans weave dream-catchers. Other parts of the world don't always have such a strong cultural place for dreams. However, there may be some other aspect of culture that is helpful; for instance, Britain has a long and honourable history of 'fools', of humour, and of playful irreverence that we can call on to help us both understand and be effective with groups during the dreaming phase of Appreciative Inquiry.

When we take people to the dreaming place we are inviting them to play, to act 'as if' the future were uncertain. We want to take them to a place where established truths could be inverted. To dream gives us licence to step out of known constraints for a while, and calls on our long history of finding ways of doing that. For example, the monarchs of Europe used to employ Fools in their courts. The role of the Fool, in part, was to say things that perhaps no one else might dare to say in the presence of the king or queen. They would do so in rhyme, song or perhaps as a riddle or a story. Drawing on traditions such as this can be helpful when we are seeking to engender the spirit of playfulness, and an appreciation of irreverence, in our work with organizations.

APPRECIATIVE PRACTICE SKILLS

We want to move on to consider some of the specific skills relevant to developing consistent and fluent appreciative practice. We have already made reference to the skills of facilitating the 4D process (Chapter 4), of hosting conversation (Chapter 6) and forming questions (Chapter 5), and of working with story (Chapter 7). We want now to consider some more advanced and generalized skills that help us act appreciatively. The more we develop these general skills in ways of looking, hearing, speaking and acting, the more we are able to work from an appreciative perspective in all sorts of contexts without necessarily needing the structure of the 4D model or a World Café, the security of a clear label for what we are doing, or indeed express permission from others to practise in this particular way.

Freed from any supposed pre-conditions for practice we become able to act appreciatively in a variety of situations. Every conversation becomes an opportunity to work appreciatively; every encounter is an invitation to show appreciation. In the same way, every invitation to join with a group or organization is an invitation to bring our appreciative and conversational skills into play. To have well-developed appreciative skills is to be able to travel freely across the organizational terrain, engaging with many existing forms of organizational thinking and action in a conversational manner, and from an appreciative perspective. We want now to consider in more depth three of the specific skills that contribute to this more general ability.

1. Appreciative eyes and ears

People sometimes wonder whether everyone is capable of conducting an appreciative interview. Our experience of working with many groups of people is that, given appropriate guidance and context, everyone can be a 'good enough' appreciative listener and interviewer to cultivate appreciative stories. However, while it is helpful to recognize that everyone has sufficient basic skill, we can also recognize that as appreciative practitioners who are always listening for the good, the beautiful and the real in organizational life, we are likely to become more skilled at hearing it. We are always listening for 'What gives life here?', not just when we are conducting discovery interviews. This means that, even when confronted by unremitting tales of misery and woe, we are still listening for the good, the beautiful and the life-giving. We are listening for what isn't being said as well as what is. For instance, we might be listening for the life-giving stories about the organization that aren't currently present in the conversation.

With appreciative ears and eyes we are always listening and looking for signs of life, of engagement, of interest. Often such signs are only detectable in small differences of presentation. So we will be paying attention to small shifts in tone of voice, facial patterns, and use of language. We are listening or looking for sufficient difference to allow us to offer an observation or question. We are listening particularly for signs of passion, whether currently expressed positively, 'I love my job', or negatively, 'I hate my job'. Both give us something to work with. The first we might pursue with a straightforward 'Tell me more', while in response to the second we might ask a different question, such as 'What would need to be different for you to be about to say something different about your job?' As appreciative practitioners we are working to develop the ability to hear the differences, construct how to bring them into the conversation and then to grow, amplify and fan the differences. We work in this way to increase our participants' ability to respond creatively to a changing situation. This stands in contrast to the mode of listening in a conversation solely for the facts and data it contains.

2. The skill of naming the positive

Very closely related to the development of appreciative eyes and ears is the ability to name the positive aspects of the situation or the positive attributes of others. This doesn't come easy to many of us. First, we are skilled from years of training in spotting the flaws in the situation (and indeed each other!). We are good at spotting, and commenting on, what is missing, what is wrong, what is faulty. Many of us rise academically, and up the career ladder at work, on our ability to offer just such critiques. From this start, working to develop appreciative ears and eyes that see and hear what is present, what is right and what is working can initially be difficult. To find a way to bring such discoveries into focus and to name them can be a further challenge. Interestingly, a common reaction to the experience of doing discovery interviews for the first time is a sense of discomfort at having been asked to 'blow your own trumpet'. This can be seen as an expression of our general lack of skill, and lack of ease, at talking in an appreciative way about things or to people. It is an expression of our discomfort at naming and speaking about good things; especially good things about ourselves. Given this, it is useful to understand why the ability to appreciate and name the good things you see in others (or yourself) is important.

One way of understanding the self is to see it as being made up of abilities that we identify as being us. This understanding of who we are has an effect on our understanding of what it is possible for us to do. So as new abilities are named, and owned by us, our sense of our potential grows. The naming of abilities for individuals, groups or organizations is thus an appreciative, and an affirming, act. On the whole we are very bad at spotting and naming our own abilities. It is also, in the main, culturally prohibited to do so. Given this general context, the naming of abilities is a useful exercise that can be carried out with individuals, groups or organizations. Being able to name the abilities displayed by one's self and others in different situations has an impact on our understanding of ourselves. Here is an example showing how the naming of abilities can work to boost confidence, enable individuals to grow, and enhance their ability to act creatively in changing circumstances.

Many years ago one of us was involved in a project to help get mothers who had been out of the workforce for some time back to work. The group were a motley crew. Many of them were single parents, and had been living on benefits for a long while. It would have been easy looking at this uncertain, poor, very unconfident, rather depressed group of women to assume that their whole lives had been stories of failure. As part of the process of helping them to prepare CVs we needed to get a sense of their skills. We arranged for them to appreciatively interview each other about their life histories, and in particular their educational and work experiences. We instructed our interviewers to listen for the skills and abilities they heard exhibited in the stories told.

Some fantastic stories came to light. One woman had been a musical prodigy, a concert pianist in her late teens/early twenties. Another, once seeking a job at age 16, had travelled the length of Oxford Street asking in every store until she secured something. Neither of these women regarded themselves as having done anything exceptional or as having much to offer an employer! Our admiration as a group of these accomplishments was clear on our faces. Knowing the story to be true to their life experience, and seeing and hearing our appreciation of the skills clearly present in such behaviour, allowed them to start to incorporate stories about themselves as resourceful, talented, dedicated, and tenacious into their sense of selves. In this way people grow, and their ideas of possible futures expand when their abilities are named.

To be meaningful, our comments that work to name the positive need to connect with current organizational or personal stories in some way; they can't just be a 'feel good' exercise. We have all had experience of the fatuous 'appreciative' or 'positive' comment such as 'marvellous, marvellous' offered to us, that appears to be context-free, knowledge-free, connection-free. Positive comments offered in this a-contextual way don't connect with us, and so hold no value and little meaning. In contrast, when, as appreciative conversational practitioners, we work to name or articulate the positive we are working to pick up on a possible, but as yet unarticulated, story inherent in what is going on. We are naming and bringing into the light a hidden or unrecognized positive element of the story, one that has something to offer the situation. In this way our positive comment, or naming of abilities, is connected to the person's lived experience, and so has a greater chance of being experienced as affirming and life-enhancing.

3. Making judgements about what to do next

In our everyday interactions we are constantly making judgements about what to do or say next. However, if we were aware of this all the time life could become unmanageable. Instead, in many interactions, we can call on a 'default' mode where we are barely aware that we have choice in the matter at all. These are ritualized exchanges, based on a shared known routine, for instance 'Good morning, how are you?' 'I'm fine thanks, and you?' 'Good.' 'Good.' 'OK then, see you later.' 'Yep OK, bye.' 'Bye.' Such an exchange allows us to pass each other in the corridor, acknowledge each other's presence and move on the next part of our lives in an accepted way. Similar routines exist around many social activities: buying things in shops, ordering dinner in a restaurant. All parties know pretty much how the exchange should go and it keeps life moving along. Organizations have many of their own ritualized exchanges for similar reasons. They evolve over time and allow organizational life to keep going without everything having to be created anew all the time. While these organizational conversational and behavioural routines are working, all is well. However, as circumstances change, they can become a hindrance rather than a help to the organization.

Much of our work is about changing the normal routine of the organization by introducing difference. For example: we put different people together; we ask different questions; we pay attention to different things; we privilege different voices and accounts; we introduce different ways of thinking; we comment differently on different things; and we bring different organizational stories into the light. As we work to do this we are constantly making judgements about what to say or do next. Working appreciatively, we need to be doing this with reference to an understanding of purposeful action as 'a moral endeavour through which moment by moment judgments are made with reference to visions of the good and the bad' (Hawes, 1993). To act with reference to these visions of the good and the bad means we are acting with integrity, mindful of the great or the good we are hoping to achieve, not just the exigencies of the moment (Oliver, 1996). We are acting responsibly, mindful of the impact of our choices. We are making situated judgements about what to do, about what is most likely to move us all towards 'good'.

Ah, but who defines the good? In a moment we will consider the need to have our own answer to that question. First we want to consider the challenge of working in an organizational context that contains stories of the 'good' and the 'bad'. Often these stories are un-coordinated across the organization. Sometimes they belong with an earlier understanding of the organization and have somehow become detached from specific context and developed instead an unquestioned status of 'goodness'. Organizational stories tell us, and the organizational members, what a good outcome will look like, what it wants to achieve. Yet sometimes the stories of values, and the definition of good, may be contributing to the current difficulties.

For instance, one of us once worked with a group of shopfloor engineers in a manufacturing environment who were convinced that a key component of 'good' in their context was keeping the machines running. Downtime was 'bad' whatever the reason. This deeply embedded belief system was running up against a newer belief system, emerging in response to a changing client environment, that frequent machine tool changes were 'good' as they increased organizational responsiveness to client demand. At the same time, machine overruns were seen as 'bad' as they added to stock unnecessarily. So on the one hand there were people with a deeply ingrained need to keep the machines running, and another group with an emerging desire to keep stopping the machines to change things. The organization was struggling with the conflict caused by these different behaviours as there was a lack of an organizational space where these unaligned stories of good and bad could come together. Instead the 'lack of fit' was expressed by mutual blaming, lack of comprehension of the action of others, and a sense of the righteousness of one's own world view.

So in this instance an older story of 'the good and the bad' was clashing with a newer story. The challenge, as ever, was to connect the existing stories and move the organization to a newly evolved story that encompassed everyone. What was needed was a story of the good and the bad that would allow people in the organization to coordinate their actions without running constantly into conflict. In this instance, by creating organizational spaces where these stories could come together, and all participants could be recognized as endeavouring to 'do good', we were able to help the organization move forward.

So we can see that although organizations are full of stories of the good and the bad, we can't always rely on them to guide our 'moral endeavour'. If we can't call on the system to define the good and the bad for us, what do we call on? We need to have a wider context to refer to. For some of us that may be our professional code of ethics, for others it may be a religious faith, and for others a more generalized personal belief system about the rights and obligations of people in relation to each other. An awareness of this is our counterweight to the persuasiveness of the internal logic of the system, and to the frequently perceived immorality of a postmodern perspective where it is sometimes asserted that everything is relative. We need to know our own set of values, and to be able to be explicit about the beliefs that inform our moment-to-moment actions. In this way we can be ethical practitioners even as we disavow the illusion of control and predictability in the impact of our actions. To become better at making these moment-to-moment judgements skilfully is to develop an 'ability to judge the fitting action to take within multiple possibilities and uncertainties' (Oliver and Brittain, 1999).

SUMMARY

In this chapter we have considered what we can call on to help us become flexible and skilled appreciative conversational practitioners whether from the position of leader, manager or consultant. We have identified our overarching purpose, the important aspects of the spirit of inquiry, and some key practical skills. We have also carefully located our practice in an ethical and moral space.

In the next chapter we will consider the challenge of getting started in these ways of working, answering some frequently asked questions and giving guidance on practice. The rest of this last section will then be devoted to case studies that illuminate how different people have put these ideas into practice.

Part 3

Using conversational approaches in the organization

In this last section we will be looking at case study examples of using a conversational approach to assist organizations to respond creatively to changing situations. We open with a section on introducing Appreciative Inquiry into your work and your workplace. We have chosen to focus on Appreciative Inquiry for this chapter as, at present, this is the more widely known of the different approaches we have introduced in this book, and so is the one that we get asked most questions about. Many of the points made are equally applicable to the other conversational approaches we have discussed.

We then present four different case studies. First, David Gilmour and Anne Radford present their experiences of working with Appreciative

Inquiry in the UK with BP. Caryn Vanstone and Bruno Dalbiez then present their work across the European Union and in Finland with Nokia. The third case-study chapter draws on work within the American Association for Quality and is written by Arian Ward, Paul Borawski and Juanita Brown, using World Café. The final chapter in the case studies is again from America, working with Orbseal Technology Center, and is by Jacqueline Stavros and Joe Sprangel.

We were conscious in commissioning the case study chapters that case studies often are simply a story of success written by the 'consultants'. Our experience as managers and consultants tells us that the world is often more complicated. We asked our case study writers to include the ups and downs, and a lessons learnt section. We also asked them to work collaboratively in writing their chapters to bring together different perspectives and voices.

We hope that these case studies will prove a useful illumination for you of how some of the ideas presented in this book can be put into practice.

10

How to introduce Appreciative Inquiry and related approaches to your organization

---

INTRODUCTION

This chapter is designed to help you start working with Appreciative Inquiry. To do this we are going to look at some of the common concerns and queries people have when setting up and running their first Appreciative Inquiry event. We will start by considering the commissioning and contracting process, and will suggest some ways to work with these. After this we will examine in more detail the challenges posed to new practitioners by each of the stages of the 4D model, and will suggest some tips and guidance for practice.

1. Change happens in the here and now, as well as later.
2. Everyone involved can influence what is happening.
3. It fosters good feelings.
4. It's highly participative.
5. The mode of delivery can be flexed to accommodate different requirements.
6. It draws on lots of the resource, and resourcefulness, of the organization.
7. It works with what is known, not what isn't.
8. It increases what is known.
9. Everyone can participate, it requires no specialist skills or knowledge.
10. It honours everyone.
11. It is oriented towards building different futures together rather than apportioning blame for past problems.
12. It fosters optimism and hope rather than recrimination and despair.
13. It works to help the system change rather than changing the system.

Figure 10.1 Some of the benefits of an Appreciative Inquiry approach

GUIDANCE IN GETTING STARTED: COMMISSIONING CONVERSATIONS

When initially introducing the idea of Appreciative Inquiry to an organization the first challenge is often to get enough connection with the organization to build rapport and trust. These are necessary prerequisites to being able to encourage the client to invest time, money, energy and resources in something that may seem unfamiliar and rather different to what they had been expecting you to propose. To help you with this initial challenge we have developed some tips as outlined below. The commissioning conversation is the part of the consulting process where ideas are explored about what the issue is and what can be done. From an Appreciative Inquiry perspective these early conversations are an important part of the whole process: how we commission and contract for the work is an important part of working appreciatively. In writing this guidance we are aware that readers will have differing organizational or consultancy experience. The ten points we make are summarized in Figure 10.2, so that you can selectively read sections that sound as if they may have something to offer you.

1. Feel your way into the conversation

As mentioned above, an important function of early conversations with an organization is to establish some sense of connection, to build

1. Feel your way into the conversation.
2. Work to find points of connection.
3. Offer what is needed to maintain connection and interest.
4. Offer what is needed to allow your audience to see what you are offering.
5. If necessary, break your proposal up into stages.
6. Offer to accommodate what they already want to do.
7. Demonstrate by example.
8. Be coherent to the client, coordinate yourself with them.
9. Acknowledge client fears and concerns.
10. Go in undercover.

Figure 10.2   Ten tips for commissioning conversations

rapport and trust. In these early encounters, it is important to be alert to body language and tone of voice cues so that you can feel your way into the developing conversation, and can gauge how what you are saying is being received. You want to be able to connect sufficiently with the organization to be able to offer something different across that bridge of connection. If your starting point and your language are too disconnected from the existing organizational conversation, then what you are trying to say may be dismissed out of hand. First you must build the bridge. Listen for the language they are using to describe themselves, their issues and their desires for the future, and work to incorporate the way they think and talk about themselves into the way you present your ideas. In this way, you can start to feel your way into, and join with, the ongoing organizational conversation rather than expecting them to join you in yours.

2. Work to find points of connection

To help bridge the difference between what you are saying and what they are used to hearing in this context, listen for their invitations to connect your ideas to what they already know. For instance, someone might say 'So it's a bit like positive thinking?' It can be helpful to hear comments like this as an invitation to inquire into their understanding. By asking about how they understand positive thinking you create an opportunity to listen out for the features offered in their explanation that you can build on to form a connection between their current understanding of the possibilities in the world and those that you are offering. The fact that the two methodologies present in the conversation may have many points of difference is irrelevant at this point. For the moment you are focusing on the similarities in order to be able to forge bridges of connection across the areas of unfamiliarity or difference. These similarities will allow you and your commissioner to make sense with each other, and to continue the conversation together.

3. Offer what is needed to maintain connection and interest

In these commissioning conversations there is a need to strike an appropriate balance between the familiar and unfamiliar if you are to maintain both connection and interest. By listening to their reactions to what you are proposing you can get a sense of whether they are closer to being overwhelmed by unfamiliarity or under-whelmed by over-familiarity. In either of these situations, often what is needed to bring the conversation back to a more productive place is a little of what is missing. By this we mean that if they are suggesting that what you are proposing doesn't sound so different from other things they have done, tried or heard about, then you may want to emphasise the specific features of Appreciative Inquiry that are different. If they are more concerned that it all sounds a bit faddish or new age, that is, too different, then you might want to reconnect with the core business concern, prioritize the points of similarity or familiarity and choose words that resonate better with the words your companion is using.

4. Offer what is needed to allow your audience to see what you are offering

Sometimes people just can't hear what you are saying or see what you are offering unless it is presented in a particular format. Many are the times during a discussion of possibilities that we have felt that we have made at least one if not many proposals for how we might proceed. However, at the end of the conversation, our commissioner might say something like, 'Well, that's all very interesting, but what will you actually do?' This suggests to us that they haven't heard what they need to, to be able to visualize what could actually happen. Often, sequencing possible activities works to achieve some point of clarity, as in 'Well, I think first we'll need to decide on our affirmative topic, and then organize some more conversations with people.' For some people this will be sufficient for them to form a picture of what is actually going to happen. Other people may need to hear some familiar 'action' language, such as 'Well, I think first we'll have a meeting then we can undertake some individual interviews ...' before they can gain a sense of what might happen. Sometimes it helps to offer a written proposal, or to demonstrate a rough possible sequence on the flipchart, as some people can't hear until they can see.

5. If necessary, break your proposal up into stages

One of the challenges of the traditional consulting process is the delivery of a proposal, either just verbally, or more often, in a written form. Delivery of either of these means making a rather definite statement about the sequence of activities. For ourselves we like to keep things flexible, as in 'Well, depending on what comes up in the first round of discovery interviews, we could consider expanding our group of interviewees, or perhaps we'll be able to move straight into a dreaming event.' Some people like this, but of course some people hear it as indecision, lack of precision, or vagueness. They need to hear something more decided and concrete than possibilities to be convinced that something positive will happen. One way to get around the difficulty of presenting a process from beginning to end when you have a number of ideas about what might be appropriate after the first interviews (depending on what they create) is to present the proposal as a series of stages or phases. In this way, you can offer the commissioner great clarity in the early stages, and increasing opaqueness further down the line.

For instance, stage/phase one can be very clearly defined and costed; stage two might perhaps offer two possible ways forward in outline; and stage three could be labelled 'to be negotiated'. Remember that it is the nature of consultancy that contracting has to be regularly revisited as things change. At this stage you need only to offer your commissioner as much clarity or detail as they need to be able to get a sense of what you are offering and to be able to proceed within the constraints of their organizational requirements.

It might be worth noting that at the opposite end of the scale are the people who need no structure and who say 'That all sounds really interesting, let's arrange a time for you to come in next week and talk to some people.' For your own sanity and profitability you may need to offer a little more structure, particularly to help clarify the point of crossover from 'negotiating to get work' to 'actually doing work', ie when they start to pay you. A little more clarity about what you propose to do and with whom can also help to ensure that the organization gets the best from its investment in your time, eg that the appropriate people are available for you to meet when you are next in.

6. Offer to accommodate what they already want to do

It is not uncommon for a client to have an answer in mind when they ask you to come in and help with some particular challenge. They may well already have a structure for proceeding, and indeed may have started to put their plans into action. While it can be difficult sometimes to see why they are asking for your assistance when they seem to have it all sorted, it isn't necessarily a problem as most activities can be undertaken from an Appreciative Inquiry perspective. For instance, they may already be planning to undertake a staff survey. 'Excellent', you say, before enquiring whether it is possible to modify some of the questions, or include a couple of extra questions, so that people get a chance to talk about what excites them or about recent successes. If the survey process is already too far advanced to be modified, then you might suggest looking at the results from a 'good news and strengths' perspective as well as the planned 'gap analysis and areas of weakness' perspective. Similarly, perhaps they want to use the Myers–Briggs Type Indicator (MBTI) before they do any team-based work. Again this isn't necessarily a problem, as MBTI could be used as a launch pad for some appreciative discovery by inquiring into episodes where 'I have worked really well with someone whose style is very different to mine', for example.

7. Demonstrate by example

One of the most effective ways of introducing an appreciative approach is to conduct all your early conversations and negotiations in an appreciative manner. In other words, to treat Appreciative Inquiry not as a tool like any other that you pull out when you 'start the work', but as an a priori set of assumptions about the world. This is no more or less than consultants who employ an organization-as-machine perspective do when they conduct initial interviews focused on data gathering, or on 'ascertaining the facts'. Working from an appreciative stance, you will recognize that from the first moment that your questions are interactions, which will repay careful thought. So rather than saying 'Tell me about the problem?' (to elicit data), you might be asking 'How would things be different if the problem didn't exist? (to start creating alternative possibilities to the current situation), or 'Who most considers this to be a problem?' (to start to understand the relational patterns in the organization), or 'Who is most concerned that this problem gets sorted, and who least?' (to create awareness of differences).

In a similar vein, rather than asking 'How big is this problem?' you might be asking 'If people weren't spending so much time talking about this problem, what else might they be talking about?' Throughout the conversation you can demonstrate your appreciative stance by asking general appreciative questions such as, 'I appreciate things are hard at the moment; given this, what are you most proud about regarding your team at the moment?' or 'Tell me about this organization when its working at its best.' You might ask 'Who is affected by this issue?', for instance, but you will also be asking questions intended to have a transforming effect on existing perceptions and ways of talking about the issue, the organization and the people. You will inquire into and amplify things that sound like they might be a resource to the organization: energy, engagement, passion, to begin to discover what gives life to the organization. And you will be careful to respond neutrally to the aspects of the situation that seem unhelpful, such as accounts of blame, and stories of 'personality issues or clashes'.

If you conduct your initial commissioning and contracting interviews in this way, your interviewee will have a different experience from their usual 'briefing the consultant' meeting. They will also experience new thoughts, insights or perceptions as you ask them questions they hadn't considered. In this way you are already encouraging generative conversation, that is, the generation and articulation of new accounts of the world. By conducting your initial conversations like this, you give your interviewee a flavour of your way of working. They will experience change happening in the moment, and your ability to achieve change is available to them through direct experience rather than solely as a told tale.

8. Be coherent to the client, coordinate yourself with them

While you want your client or commissioner to experience you differently, you also need them to feel that they can connect with you, that you and they can form a working alliance. This means that you will need to present your ideas back in a language that connects to theirs. You need to be sensitive to what the client needs to see or hear to believe that you have understood their situation, appreciate their concerns, hopes and fears, and have something to offer. Like any client they need to feel heard and understood. At the end of the conversation it is usually helpful to offer a clear restatement of the issue or problem from the client's perspective and then to summarize the ideas for action that have emerged in the discussion. You can frame this account as clearly belonging to the client, 'So your perception is that this issue initially arose because... and your main concerns now are... and your hope for this intervention is that....' Having demonstrated that you have understood the essence of their situation, you can go on to articulate how your proposal for moving forward offers some different possibilities for what to do in the future.

9. Acknowledge client fears and concerns

Clients can be a little alarmed at the idea of asking people what they enjoy about work, or what is good about the organization. They can also be worried that using high-intensity emotional terms such as 'passion' will alienate their cynical older factory workers or their hard-bitten accountants or executives. They are sometimes dubious about the wisdom of giving those usually silent, perhaps those of lower status in the organization, a voice. They can be concerned about the effect of asking questions that might raise expectations, or encourage communication on topics outside the usual permitted range between different people.

It is only human to be ambivalent about things: your commissioners want change and they don't want change; they want to know what people think and they don't want to know. They want to empower others, and they want to maintain the existing privileges of power. Their fears and concerns are justified. If your intervention is effective then things will change in the social order and that upsets existing political, social and power relations. It is important to acknowledge the basis of these fears if expressed. They are taking a risk inviting you into their organization; it is not possible to predict the actual outcome.

Remember, however, that in the same way that you are not interested in their stories that scapegoat 'lazy workers' or 'power-crazed technicians', neither will you endorse workers' stories of 'don't care management' or 'empire-building managers'. In essence you aren't interested in stories of blame or individual inadequacy, because, given that these people are here and are going to continue to be part of the ongoing story, these explanations or accounts aren't useful to moving things forward. Offer reassurance that the process will be open and transparent and that everyone will have a voice. Make it clear again that the point of the exercise is to help people develop new, different and more helpful stories about what is going on that will allow them to do something different. Remind them that this process is about appreciation, positive emotions and growth, not criticism, blame and correction.

10. Go in undercover

Appreciative Inquiry is an approach more than a method. There are many different ways to practise it. Sometimes it is appropriate and helpful to clearly label what you are doing as Appreciative Inquiry; at other times the intervention could usefully have a more individual label, meaningful in the local context. For example, a number of projects have majored on the use of the power of imagination in the approach and have entitled their projects accordingly, such as Imagine Chicago and Imagine Scotland. A fanfare announcement of a project isn't always appropriate, particularly if there has been a recent succession of such things. We have frequently practised an Appreciative Inquiry approach under the more generic rubric of 'team building', for instance.

MOVING TO THE 4D CYCLE: COMMON BLOCKS AND HOW TO OVERCOME THEM

Once the project starts you will meet the people that you are going to take through the 4D process. This activity presents its own series of challenges. Below we have identified some of the key concerns new practitioners have about 'doing Appreciative Inquiry' and offer some ideas for overcoming these perceived difficulties. We have organized this into 'getting started' and then each of the 4D processes. We have presented it in a frequently asked questions format so that once again you can pick and choose amongst what is offered to suit your existing knowledge and experience. Just to remind you, the 4D cycle is shown in Figure 10.3.

Getting started

Q. How do I move the group from thinking about problems to engaging with appreciative interviews?
A. This is an important question as, when you first approach a group of people who have been experiencing difficulties with the aim of helping them move forward, they often have preconceptions of what is going to,

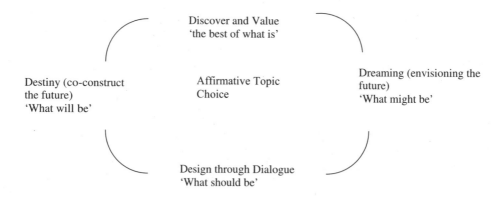

Figure 10.3 The 4D model

or should, happen at this point; and you will need to engage with those ideas. For instance, people are often expecting you to ask them such questions as what is wrong, what is the problem, and who is to blame; and they want to tell you. They also often want to tell you what should be done. If negative emotions are running high, they may fear that you are going to get them to confront each other in some way. When people are full of these fears and concerns, they may not be immediately ready to drop them all to engage in Discovery Interviews. Fortunately there are some things you can do move to a more productive place.

1. Let them tell the story they want to tell

With a smaller group, or with people known to feel strongly and negatively about the issues, we try to negotiate some initial individual interviews. These interviews are designed to be appreciative in their approach and the questions they ask; however, we also include a catch-all question at the end along the lines of 'Is there anything else you want to tell me, or you think I need to know to be able to help your team move forward?' This is the invitation to the interviewee to unburden themselves of any story that they feel it is imperative be told about the team and the team situation. Quite often the appreciative interview has done its work and the imperative has lessened and they hold their counsel. Other times people use the opportunity to state or indicate where they think the issue really lies. It is useful to know what sense people are currently making of the situation, who is being held accountable (scapegoat) and what emotions are around, without in any way endorsing these accounts. These individual pre-interviews allow people to tell their story to 'the outsider' in the least harmful way.

2. Do the 'before' work

Depending on your group and situation there are various things you may need to do before the group is ready and able to engage with discovery interviews. Introductions, accounting for your presence, setting the context and clarifying the desired outcomes, presenting a map for the day or the event, offering an explanation of the beliefs behind the approach; all of these may be appropriate for different groups and contexts and can be used to help prepare readiness.

Introductions

Whether you are working with a group who know each other well or who are strangers, an introduction process is important to starting the day. It gives you an opportunity to introduce yourself and account for your presence. It is an opportunity to tell a story about how you come to be acting as host or facilitator for the day. This is helpful to your audience who need to 'place you', or make sense of your presence, to be able to engage with you. It also gives you an opportunity to set an introduction task that sets a tone for the rest of the day. Depending on the group, some of our favourites are:

▌ Arrange yourselves in terms of length of service with this organization. This gives you a great way of working immediately with the history of the organization, by asking everyone from oldest to newest about the organization they joined. This process often reveals an ongoing story of change, which can make the current change seem less a strange and foreign event, and more part of an unfolding development. People can talk about what the organization was called when they joined it, what job title they revelled in, what the challenges of the day were.

▌ Find someone and tell them about a success you have had in the last week, at work or home. Then find someone else and tell them about a success, a different one. And then do that again with a third person and a third success. When people first hear this challenge they are often shocked. They can't for a moment believe they can manage three different successes. And yet they do. This is a great one for introducing a really positively emotional charged start to the day.

▌ Write down two things about yourself that other people here may not know that you are happy to have shared. You then gather the papers up, redistribute them, and ask people to find the person whose papers they have. Once everyone has found their person, the information is revealed. This process is great for starting to challenge people's conceptions of each other. This means it can be very valuable with groups that think they know (or more often you have been told know) each other very well.

▌ Talk in pairs and tell us about a time in your life which left you the most proud. Then invite the pairs to introduce their colleague and to tell the story based on what they heard. People find it easier to share proud moments in one-to-one conversations and these moments often create connections between the group, as well as creating a positive energy with which to enter the day.

Setting the context and clarifying desired outcomes for the day
It is important to set a context for the day or the event. Why are we here and what do we hope to achieve? Depending on the context we will emphasize different things. For example, if we are working in the context of a merger and acquisition we might talk about the need to look after fragile and precious things that can be lost in the hurly-burly of the change. In another context we might talk about the unintended consequences of changes on things like the opportunity for informal communication and the effect that can have on a group. In another situation we might reflect on the importance of quality conversation and how hard it can be to achieve that in the day-to-day pace and demands of organizational life. The pre-interviews will have given us some pointers here. Using the old standbys of hopes and fears and establishing ground-rules can also help with context setting. We often use the forming the ground-rules process to introduce ideas of 'working in the spirit of generosity and curiosity with each other'; of course, you could also use this process to mention 'appreciation'.

Offering an explanation of the beliefs behind the process
If people are concerned that the day sounds very good, but it's not addressing the problem, then we might make reference to 'every problem is the expression of a frustrated dream' or we might talk about this process being more like 'dis-solving the problem' rather than 're-solving the problem'. How much technical explanation it is necessary to give depends on the group, but beware of getting caught up in a 'Yes, but' conversation where you are engaged in an intellectual battle of persuasion. Usually this mental play only engages a few people while the rest wait for 'something to happen'. Better then to work with the social process to get enough agreement to 'give it a go' and then get started so that they can start to experience the difference.

Essentially you need by such methods to get the group to a point where they are able to bear being in the same room, and have some faith that it's 'going to be alright'. Sometimes we will ask the group 'OK, so are we ready to proceed?' or 'OK, is there anything else anyone needs to ask, say, clarify before we can go on/start the day?' It is important, of course, to pick up and check out the non-verbal cues offered at this point and call them. 'Daphne, you still look a little dubious.' Daphne might deny it, 'No, no I'm fine', or she might use the opportunity to express continuing doubt, 'To be honest I can't see that this is going to improve things.' It doesn't matter, we are not looking for consensus or 100 per cent commitment or wild enthusiasm, we are looking for sufficient agreement to move on without fear that anyone will refuse to play.

Q. Can I use this with: factory workers, accountants, less articulate people...?
A. Yes, and many other groups besides.
People are sometimes concerned that, being a process so clearly based on the use of words and language, there are some groups for whom it will be less applicable. Better perhaps to think about it being based on communication and relationship, aspects of life important to everyone. This process has been used successfully with groups of mixed nationality all using English as a foreign language, groups of engineers and shopfloor workers, and 'dry' accountants who 'intellectualize'. Have faith, the parts of human experience it connects to, that is a desire to be understood, to be heard, to feel good, to work with others, are greater than a lack of fluency in the English language. It will just be a different experience.
A. Use other media
You can also reduce the dependence of pure words by using Appreciative Inquiry with other media such as Lego, or Art or Drama.

The four stages

Discovery

Q. Will people be able to find a positive experience to talk about?
A. The short answer is yes they will, although initially they may doubt it or may find such an experience hard to recall. You can help by giving people time. Introduce the idea that this is what you are going to ask them to do and continue to talk for a while. You will notice that, once this has been floated as a request that is going to be made, people

immediately start to engage with the implied question and start to seek out something that fits. This is part of the beauty of Appreciative Inquiry: people hear the question and things start to change. They start to bring to mind episodes, events and stories that weren't present just a moment ago.

1. Work first with those who can

As you introduce the exercise, watch people's faces as they start to engage and you will see some people beginning to identify the episode they want to talk about. Use them to pair up with those who are expressing doubts that they ever had a good experience with these people, in this organization. You will find that one person's good experience will often trigger a memory for the other.

2. Make the pool of possible experience as wide as possible in the context

How wide a pool of experience you want them to call on depends on the context. When we're working with a team and one of the issues is the team dynamic, then we may want to restrict the range to 'with this team'. In a training context, with people from different organizations, it might be 'in a work context'. Whereas if we're coaching someone and we're trying to help them locate an experience that will act as a useful resource in their current context, then we might expand it to include any aspect of their life. It all depends on the context and the priorities and our in-the-moment hypothesis of what will be the most useful boundary for the exercise.

3. Use 'least bad' experience if you have too

If someone is insisting that they have never had a good experience, then we will ask them to identify the 'least bad'. If that leads to an assertion of generalized awfulness, you can push back with 'If you had to pick one experience that was marginally less awful than all the others, which would it be?' Either way you are working to get them to note and articulate differences in experience. It might be worth highlighting here that people who are seriously depressed have difficulty with these tasks of discrimination of experience. The process is robust enough to absorb the odd depressed person, although it may raise ethical issues regarding your concern for their mental well-being.

Q. Will people be able to interview each other well enough?
A. Yes, have faith, give guidance.
In our experience yes, we find most people manage well enough. We

give guidance on what we want to achieve and on useful and less useful questions (see Chapter 5). We emphasize that they are working to get the person to tell their story from inside the experience, not as an observer. It needs to be an embodied tale. We want the interviewee to re-experience the experience, good feelings and all. We also emphasize that, during this story telling, we do want to stay with the good aspects of it, and not to get drawn into the 'but of course it isn't always like that!' conversation. We are interested in a description of the particular event or episode, not the explanation of it.

Dreaming

Q. Do I have to use the word 'dreaming'?
People new to practising Appreciative Inquiry are often scared of the word 'dreaming'. It is unfamiliar and too closely related to day-dreaming, fantasizing and other ways of spending time that organizations tend to condemn.
A. No, you don't.
First, of course, if you are concerned about this, remember you don't have to announce 'we are now moving on to the dreaming stage of the process', if you feel the effect of doing so will be detrimental. However, we think in the main we actually do better to embrace the word and be upfront that this is about the creative use of imagination. We can point out that no one can predict the future; so all future predictions such as cash-flow forecasts and strategic plans are in that sense built on dreams. We can also point out that this isn't an exercise in pure fantasy, that we are building out from what we know is possible. This isn't 'blue sky thinking', disconnected from any current reality, this is using our imagination to think 'what would the world, life, this organization, be like if more of these good things were happening more of the time?' This is play-time. Remember, everyone dreams, everyone has played and still can (although it may not be a skill they utilize very often). It's just that they are not used to being asked to do it in a work context with other people and about particular things. The dreaming phase offers people the chance to escape from reality for a short while. And once they get going, most people really enjoy it and appreciate the opportunity to imagine 'how things could be'.

Q. What do I do if people dream impossible things?
Aspiring practitioners are also sometimes concerned that people will 'dream the impossible, things that can never happen'.
A. Nothing, that's fine.

They will, and that's fine. One of the purposes of dreaming is to generate a wide range of possibilities; it is not about forecasting reality. In a dream all things are possible. Believe us, people are very good at reasserting the demands and constraints of reality when asked or given permission to do so, it's the letting go of those even for a short while that is the challenge! So, if the dream of someone at your poverty-stricken charity organization includes the organization moving to glamorous offices in Jamaica, fine. If your hardworking executive's dream includes 20 extra people in his or her team, so be it. Encourage your participants to enjoy living in another world for a short while, they will return refreshed. Different ways of structuring the actual exercise are discussed in Chapter 4. Another aspect of the dreaming phase is that the dreams created are resources that help the organization move forward. We can sort out which resources to call on later.

Q. Does everyone need to dream the same thing?
People are sometimes concerned that different members of the group will have very different dreams.
A. No, this is a divergent process.
Again they will and that's fine. We are not seeking convergence here, we are creating possibility, resource, general direction and energy. Design and delivery are the phases where we focus on commonality of direction and purpose. Here we are interested in variety and expansion of possibility. Remember also that the context has been set by earlier, shared conversations, that they have a shared work environment, and that, depending on how you structure the exercise, they are 'dreaming' in the context of each others' dreams.

Design

The design phase is where ideas of future dreams of possibility and present perceived realities meet. Essentially this is the phase during which we select where to focus our energies and resources, out of the many possibilities. It is the phase in which we more actively make decisions about what to change, build or reorganize to move towards an engaging positive and possible future. It's where we start to construct a story about what we are going to do to make desirable aspects of our future more likely. There are various ways to do this, as outlined in Chapter 4. In essence though the questions is 'Out of all that we do, what do we want to keep, drop, add, or do differently, to move us towards a desirable future?'

Destiny

Q. How do I ensure things we have dreamt or discussed are carried forward?
The destiny phase really is what happens next. The energy created by
the first two phases, combined with the connections they are making
between how they are now and how they want to be, tend to fill people
with resolve. It's no longer that they know they ought to do something,
it's much more that they feel they want to. The concern here can be, as
after any event, how can I ensure that things happen, that people do
what they say they will do, that we use our resources wisely and don't
duplicate our efforts, waste time?
A. Work with the energy, go with it, help to coordinate what happens next.
There can be a tendency at this point to slip into more deterministic
ways of thinking, with a desire to produce a carefully documented and
controlled 'project plan' of what is going to happen. This approach
runs the risk of squeezing the life-blood out of the energy created by
the Appreciative Inquiry. Change processes that are based, as those
presented here are, on the organization as a living-human-system,
focusing on emotional life, relationships and communication, are by
their very nature messy and iterative, not neat and tidy. The base for the
motivation and energy is volunteerism. Too heavy-handed a demand to
relinquish control to a central person can reduce commitment, accountability and energy. The role of the consultant or manager, or group
leader, at this point is to encourage the development of coherence,
coordination, cohesion and conjoint action, not to centralize control.
This means they work to ensure that the energy, positive feelings, group
dynamic and aspirations for the future generated by the Appreciative
Inquiry process are continued. They do this by working to create clear
paths for people or groups to work together and stay connected, rather
than by working to get groups of people to fit tightly into a prescribed
plan. They work to create stories of what has happened and will
happen (coherence), help people work together (coordination), taking
simultaneous, in the context of what others are doing, action (conjoint
action) and ensure that it connects enough to hold together (cohesion).

SUMMARY

We hope that the ideas presented above about how to positively use
the opportunities presented by the very unfamiliarity of Appreciative
Inquiry will inspire you to have a go at introducing these ways of
working into your assignments and challenges. We also hope that our

tips about how to face the anxieties often induced at each stage of the process for those first starting down the unfamiliar road will give you some good places to start and serve to increase your pleasure in the experience and reduce your fear of the unknown.

11

Case study: Using Appreciative Inquiry at BP Castrol Marine

David Gilmour and Anne Radford

INTRODUCTION

In this chapter, the turnaround of the BP Castrol Marine business is seen alongside the increasingly difficult market situation of regular oil price increases and disruption of supply. There is a danger in seeing this case study set out in chronological order – it could give the impression that all the steps were planned ahead of time and implemented in a neat and systematic way. The reality is very different: armed with a set of principles that underpin the positive change approach, Appreciative Inquiry (AI), we used it to engage the UK Castrol Marine team and regional teams throughout the world during a two-year period to transform the business. As we used the approach at BP, our skills developed on when and how to engage customers and people in the business. This enabled us to gradually develop a culture of commitment and to mix this new approach to change, AI, with more traditional methodologies. The outcomes of taking an iterative and emergent approach have been seen both in terms of financial success as well as greater employee and customer satisfaction.

THE ORGANIZATION

Castrol Marine is a Performance Unit (PU) operating within the International Marine business unit within Refining and Marketing in BP plc. International Marine markets fuels and lubricants to shipping companies around the world and is a $5 billion+ turnover business with over 700 employees. Castrol Marine is a global marine lubricants marketing business selling and marketing in over 70 countries and has sales, marketing and technical teams resident in more than 40 countries.

THE ORGANIZATION CHALLENGE

Castrol Marine was acquired by BP plc in 2000. This integration was especially challenging as BP Marine itself was undergoing a significant business transformation through internal reorganization, development of joint ventures aimed at transforming the marine marketplace, as well as a significant systems implementation. The Castrol acquisition was judged to be a small but a valuable addition to its business. However, the size and scale of this integration were underestimated.

Despite the best endeavours of the management, the business lost momentum internally and in the marketplace, and its business performance declined rapidly. A major strategic review and implementation were initiated during 2003. The outcome was a significant reorientation of the business to define priority segments, position the brand clearly as well as provide internal functional support aligned with the segments.

David Gilmour was appointed PU leader, Castrol Marine in 2004 to implement this business strategy. His other main challenge was employee engagement and their motivation to deliver the business objectives. A new management team was also in place by 2004.

SELECTING THE APPROACH

Appreciative Inquiry was selected because it was thought that the principles and methodology would address the many different aspects of this business turnaround. This confidence was based on the approach having been used effectively in several situations in BP as well as in Castrol Marine. There were also many other examples of its use in international and global businesses.

The appeal was that people in the same location, across regions and throughout the business would work together to collectively discover best practices in their operations and generate a way forward. Because the process supports relational working, uses affirmative language and builds trust and commitment, strategic issues would be linked at the same time with operational issues. This would mean that decisions taken at the site level would be in keeping with the wider issues at the regional level and at a functional level in BP.

APPRECIATIVE LEADERSHIP

This approach also required the managing director (MD) to adjust his own leadership style by being more inclusive and guiding others so that they could develop their own leadership skills. In this way, people would gradually assume more accountability for their actions and work collaboratively with their local teams to make decisions.

The new approach was not universally accepted: some did not understand or like this leadership style or the level of involvement required. Those who had been in the business for many years welcomed the approach as a renewal of values long held in Castrol. Others recognized that they would be helping to lead the change rather than having it done to them. This together with further development work within the team provided a sound foundation for the work of the Projects, where speed, cooperation and flexibility were going to be needed.

MIX OF AI AND OTHER METHODOLOGIES

Appreciative Inquiry was used in conjunction with other methodologies such as project management, transition planning, performance management and strategic planning (Gilmour and Sutton-Cegarra, 2005). By applying dialogue as well as affirmative language, which come from social constructionism, people used the classical approaches and methodologies they knew well. This maintained the momentum of business improvement while developing the level of detail necessary for simultaneous implementation at the local site level. The combination worked especially well in the Design phase, the third of the four stages of the 4D AI cycle.

The only people who had formal training in Appreciative Inquiry were David Gilmour and Anne Radford. Everyone else learned about the approach as situations arose, such as managers preparing the design for their next meeting or preparing for a performance appraisal; and consultants designing a workshop. As people's interest increased, they delved into the field further through articles, books and websites (AI Commons, 2007). Recent interviews with thought leaders in the AI field have indicated that it is essential for the internal leader to have a solid grounding in AI (Whitney and Fry, 2006).

OBJECTIVES FOR THE CHANGE PROCESS

There was a need for change due to the lack of clarity in a number of key areas: customer segments, brand positioning, disappointing financial results, declining customer satisfaction and unclear strategic direction of the business for employees. The remit was to address each of these areas: deliver strategic clarity, and deliver an operational and organizational framework for clear customer segmentation, brand positioning, offer definition and offer execution, together with optimizing key business processes underpinning the business.

DESCRIPTION

While this case study focuses on the two-year change activities within Castrol Marine, all members of the International Marine Business unit (700+) were involved in major change during this time. This had a significant impact on the Marine Lubes business and the supporting functions, probably 500 in total. Many, if not all, roles were reviewed, reconnected into a segment-driven organization, and working relationships reframed. Over 100+ roles were eliminated and people were redeployed into other Group businesses. In addition to employees, customers were deeply engaged in redefining the offer, and moved between offers so that their needs were better met and the business met its brand promise.

The following timetable sets out the changes carried out in Castrol Marine from 2004 to 2006.

INTRODUCTION OF APPRECIATIVE LEADERSHIP: MANAGERS AND REGIONAL SALES TEAMS

2004

August 2004: In addition to making the decision to use AI throughout the business, David Gilmour decided to use the Appreciative Inquiry approach to modify the managing director's leadership style. The coaching sessions focused on using the principles of AI as well as the 4D cycle. In the discovery phase he looked for the best of his leadership experience in handling change. In the dream phase, the focus was on his image of himself as an appreciative leader, and in the design phase, he looked at ways to live his role as an appreciative leader. Each session was a 4D cycle. The following aspects formed a useful framework as he moved his leadership style to an increasingly relational one:

I Power and craft of the positive question.

I Framing and re-framing.

I Leadership from the future 'there to here'.

I Concept of internal dialogue: healthy = 2:1.

I Storytelling and hope.

I Wholeness… internal and external voices.

I Praise… circulating all the good you can.

An early decision coming from these sessions was to involve the managing director's direct reports (his management team) and the regional sales managers who became known as the Leadership Team and Extended Leadership Team, respectively, in developing a strategy for the business turnaround. One of the first events was a Sales Leadership Summit. This meeting was welcomed because the teams knew business performance was poor and they were concerned about the future.

November/December 2004: Two meetings took place focusing on leadership. In the first meeting, the Marine Leadership Team (the direct reports) identified examples of successful leadership in Castrol Marine, highlighted areas in the business which could be strengthened and would improve performance as well as highlighted their personal leadership skills which could help deliver the results required in the business.

In the second meeting, the Sales Leadership Summit with the Leadership Team and Extended Leadership Team, the two groups focused on the topic 'Irresistible Sales Leadership to Deliver Extraordinary Performance in Castrol'. The MD set the strategic context for the Summit. During the next two days, the two groups set out their high-level objectives in each of four key areas: safety, financial performance, working through people, and working with customers and the market. Regional teams prioritized the global possibilities and objectives, and designed their plan of action. Each person also identified the leadership skills they needed to use more to achieve the goals they had set.

During this period, the oil price and hence input costs rose dramatically, putting the financial position of the business even more at risk. Two significant price increases were put in place, aimed at mitigating these costs and raising margins to improve the business performance. This was a bold act of leadership for the new team in an industry where traditionally price lists were issued every three to five years. As the financial performance started to improve, it offered some encouragement that the business could indeed be improved. However, each price increase was a major challenge: contracts were complex which meant that each price increase put a huge burden on the internal processes in the organization. People, although encouraged by the market response, were getting tired.

THE EASY BUSINESS VISION

Six months into his role as leader of Castrol Marine, the MD reflected that the business needed to be easier for staff to work in and easier for customers to interact with. The employees were committed but tired, and customers were becoming disappointed with poor invoicing and poor delivery performance. He asked the question 'How can we make life easy for ourselves and our customers?' The answer to this question was crucial for the organization to be able to deliver the rapid and flexible response to changes in the business environment that rising oil prices were causing. This question generated the Easy Business project.

2005

Easy Business transformation

January 2005: A small group of senior leaders from a number of disciplines (marketing, customer service, supply, leadership and finance) came together to work on this project. Areas for the Easy Business transformation were identified as:

█ Customer Offer

█ Service Delivery

█ Customer Engagement and Relationship Management

█ Organization and Culture

█ Operational Excellence.

The group anticipated that Easy Business would deliver the following benefits:

█ Improve customer satisfaction by making it easier to do business.

█ Improve employee satisfaction by facilitating a better operational environment and improving the work–life balance.

█ Reduce the errors and time to invoice.

█ Reduce the levels of outstanding debt and deliver improvements in debtor days and cash flow.

█ Reduce support costs through a better operational environment.

█ More productive use of sales force time by reducing the amount of administration and problem solving required, resulting in more time spent with existing and prospective customers (AI Practitioner, 2005).

Project Engage: Discovering the core factors of Easy Business

January 2005: Project Engage was initiated to discover successful practices staff found easy to work with and customers found easy to interact with. The trends or patterns in these practices would indicate the core factors that needed to be preserved in the development of the Easy Business project, including a future 'Ideal Contract' between the customer and the organization.

A second project, Project Promise, was already in place. Its objective was to outline and clearly set out the customer promise. The team believed that by implementing Project Promise and Project Engage together, they would deliver Easy Business. Figure 11.1 shows the interaction between the two projects.

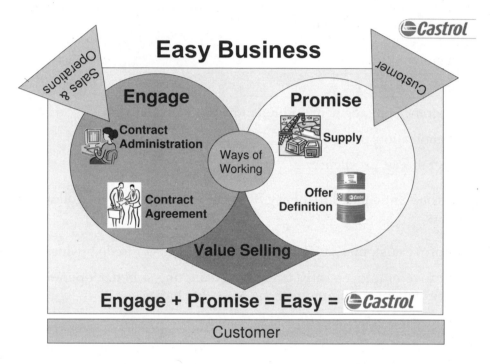

Figure 11.1   Interaction between Project Engage and Project Promise

February to April 2005: The first Project Engage workshop was piloted in early February in Madrid with a group of 20 staff from sales, marketing, trade, accounting and finance. Improvements were made and further workshops held in March and April in Athens, Singapore and the UK. These involved all regions and functions in the business. Over 100 people were engaged in the Discovery, Dream and Design phases, with learning and understanding being shared across continents. Bringing people together generated energy, joy and team spirit throughout the organization. Optimism started to reappear and people started to become more confident in themselves and their colleagues.

However, the business context started to get even worse – a fire at a key industry supplier put a major supply challenge to the industry as a whole. This challenge signalled the need to build even closer relationships with customers as well as the need to increase prices again to cover even higher costs. Emphasizing the value of marine lubricants to the shipping industry as a whole as a valued product and service replaced an earlier emphasis on marine lubricants as a commodity. Margin recovery started to be challenged, volume growth opportunities were not so clear – the business needed to reorientate itself to yet another round of price increases.

Easy Business: Designing and Developing to Ensure Success

April to mid-June 2005: Following completion of the four AI workshops, output was compared and contrasted and a clear design specification agreed by the project manager with marketing, customer service, trade accounting and finance. The different parts of the organization were again brought together in a 3-day workshop with the objectives:

I To understand the Easy Business implementation priorities.

I To gain an overview of the supporting tools and operating approach.

I To define the Easy Business detailed ways of working.

I To identify any risks to be managed during the implementation.

I To confirm the Easy Business implementation timing.

A key part of the transformation to Easy Business was redesigning the ways of working within the Castrol Marine business and the wider BP organization. Each area already had some rules and constraints defined as a result of the AI workshops. The groups discussed these and defined the processes required to implement them. This was a practical and pragmatic session that focused on what could be done, how it should be implemented, who would do it, how often and why. Processes were mapped using a 'swim-lanes' methodology depicting the tasks and flows of information between groups of people. Each activity was then broken down into steps and a new Operations Manual developed.

Again, owing to the inclusive approach adopted by the project, the team were able to move forward quickly, gaining agreement and commitment to the proposed implementation from both people in Castrol Marine and the supporting BP Marine organization.

Full implementation of Easy Business

May 2005: A significant number of employees were involved in the AI workshops and process design work.

June 2005: A senior leadership conference was held to align and engage senior managers from within Castrol Marine and the supporting BP Marine organization. They committed to deliver and implement Easy Business in the marketplace by the end of 2005. Each regional team also committed to develop a workshop for all staff in the region to work with the Easy Business concept and tools.

August to December 2005: On 14 August 2005, the first Easy Business contract was established with an important Taiwanese customer. This contract delivered simplicity in pricing and reduced customer set-up times considerably. A quote from the leader of one of the systems teams was, 'I love it!' She had just seen a glimpse of the future with her team's workload being considerably reduced and simplified.

However, yet another round of price increases was needed, which raised the question: Could EasyBiz be implemented and a price increase delivered successfully? The management leadership team responded with a commitment to a 100 per cent implementation of EasyBiz across some 500 customers across the globe and to deliver a 10 per cent price increase at the same time. By December 2005, over 90 per cent of the contracts had been changed, the price increase was implemented successfully and customers were carefully handled during the supply crisis with few lost deliveries. Handling these three major changes was considered a remarkable achievement since, even a few months earlier, implementing one of the changes would have been a significant challenge.

2006

Achieving outstanding financial performance

As the New Year approached, there was a clear recognition that although prices had been increased, the business was still making poor returns. A step change in profitability was needed, yet the cost of goods continued to rise as oil hit $60–70 per barrel. Two price increases were implemented successfully in the first half of the year. Profitability improved significantly and during the Q2 of 2006 the business success was being noticed in the wider BP group. At this point, the financial turnaround was complete – Castrol Marine had emerged as a top-quartile business delivering outstanding financial performance. At the same time, a new challenge started to emerge – how to sustain and deliver the transformation and turnaround.

Embedding the EasyBiz transformation

A deepening of the implementation of the EasyBiz transformation was made: invoice errors started to be tracked month by month; overdue accounts identified; and good practices were identified with the aim of improving the transactional effectiveness of the business.

However, other improvements were needed. The leadership decided it was necessary to address a perceived value gap by improving the ability of everyone in the business to articulate value to customers in the face of such dramatic price increases. This led to a commitment to develop skills in value selling and delivery.

To support this, the extended leadership team committed to improve its skills in recognizing, appreciating and coaching their staff. This training helped considerably to deliver the value proposition to customers through the regular day-to-day contact with customers. Embedding and sustaining the simplification would continue into 2007.

Global Strategic Inquiry to sustain growth

During mid-2006, Castrol Marine started a Global Strategic Inquiry to review progress to date, see where future opportunities lay and identify ways forward. It was also recognized that sustaining growth would require more leaders and, perhaps, a different type of leadership from those who initiated the turnaround.

For this Inquiry, people used an application of Appreciative Inquiry to strategic thinking, called the SOAR model (Strengths, Opportunities, Aspirations and Results) developed by Jackie Stavros and others (Stavros, Cooperrider and Kelley, 2003). Using the first part of the SOAR model, the Inquiry is looking for Strengths and Opportunities. This new way of doing strategy (for a business unit in BP) is generally being well received. There are those people who would prefer to manage the process themselves internally as well as those who would prefer to ignore the need for further change. It is a successful approach for those who:

▌ like the relational process used during the past two years; they enjoy contributing in this way – it feels like the natural way to do things and it doesn't feel 'corporate';

▌ are aware that strategy is not an end point;

▌ are aware that the way everyone looks at the business will determine what is done; people have seen the value of creative thinking to address problems that have been in the business for some time;

▌ see that implementation takes place at the same time as the strategy review; they have the experience of seeing how fast solutions can be implemented when people are fully committed;

▌ like to link classic approaches such as project management with new approaches such as Appreciative Inquiry;

▌ the stimulus of bringing in someone to lead the Inquiry who thinks differently and raises questions that move people from their comfort zone.

A senior BP Executive described the change:

> The Marine Lubricants business transformation has been accomplished over the past two years through a holistic and complete realignment of all elements of the business: strategy, structure, systems and processes, and capabilities.
>
> This is not the result of one or two big initiatives, but many fully connected and consistent actions. It is a story of discipline and execution: getting 700+ people to be clear on what to do and working together to do it. Significant cost reduction is an outcome of a clear strategy and simpler processes!
>
> A critical starting point was rigorous customer segmentation, leveraging the historical strengths of the Castrol Marine brand [such as]:

> ▌ Smaller companies, often owning a small number of ships.
>
> ▌ Greater reliance on trusted suppliers (limited or no dedicated lubricants procurement & technical staff).
>
> ▌ General cargo and specialist (eg ferry, fishing, offshore supply, etc).
>
> ▌ Itinerant tramper trade – requirement for supply at smaller, regional ports often with limited advanced notice.

OUTCOMES

The outcomes are best illustrated by the organization performance in Table 11.1, Figure 11.2 and Table 11.2.

Table 11.1   Market positions: 2004 and 2006

The business position in Q3 2004	The business in Q3 2006
The market	
• Cost of goods starting its dramatic rise through rising oil prices. • Fierce price competition as competitors seek market share gains, leading to price and volume decline for Castrol Marine.	• Record cost of goods (doubled over period) and scarce availability of key raw materials, leading to shortage in marine lubricants. • Between 5 and 6 price increases implemented with a net improvement in pricing (this contrasts with price decline for the previous decade). • Castrol Marine volumes are growing at above market growth.
The customer	
• Loyal customer base. • Customers dissatisfied with the basic offer – poor invoicing, poor delivery performance – and a lack of clarity around what was the basic offer. • Strong relationships between sales teams and customers' challenged by poor transactional processes.	• Loyal customer base, no significant losses in customer numbers and acquisitions rate beyond market growth. • Improving satisfaction with Castrol Marine with some improvements in delivery performance. • Development of a 'One Team' culture beyond the scope of the existing organization, enabling greater responsiveness and flexibility in meeting customer and internal needs. Bringing groups together – especially strong and appreciative links between accounting, customer service and sales.

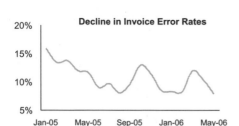

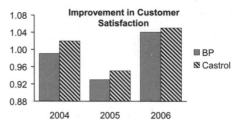

Figure 11.2   Business performance

Source: internal BP documents

Table 11.2   An overview of the transformational change in International Marine

---

The financial performance

- High fixed cash costs in relation to margin.
- Some improvements started to be seen due to price initiatives.

- Significant turnaround recognized at Group level.
- International Marine split into two material operations, reflecting the success of marine lubricants and fuels.
- Costs stabilized, overheads under control.
- Highest prices in a generation.

Internal processes

- Processes and relationships 'broken' owing to Merger and Acquisition with little rigour and discipline in application.
- Little investment in people capabilities owing to a focus on firefighting.
- Lack of common infrastructure and platform.
- High levels of internal complexity.
- Lack of understanding of customers and their needs.

- Well-defined contracting processes being implemented and embedded in organization supporting our customer offers.
- One Team approach being built.
- Clear segmentation and understanding of customer needs.
- Simple offer, internal processes well defined, easier to work.

Organizational climate

- Business challenged by management to improve.
- Business was given space to implement strategy.
- Fear of business failure and redundancies within the business.
- Transformation programme recently announced including staff reductions.
- Internal relationships between sales, supply, service and finance were fractured, resulting in a strong blame culture.

- Business is a reference for excellence in business marketing.
- Organization is currently being established as a separate business unit, away from the umbrella of International Marine due to scale.
- Staff reductions have taken place and people relocated to other parts of BP Group.
- Pride in performance, rising employee morale.
- Major investment in people capability (leadership and sales and marketing).
- Teams are empowered and execute agreed actions with discipline and rigour.

Information from a document 'Context for AI Dialogue: 30th June 2006' prepared by David Gilmour

REFLECTIONS AND LESSONS LEARNT

At the beginning of this chapter we indicated that there is a danger in seeing this case study set out in seemingly neat steps which might imply that they had been planned in advance and followed one after the other. The reality was very different. In this section, we highlight some of the learnings and observations which come from reviewing the phases, behaviours and activities of the past two years from a distance. While the need to deliver results is always present, the pressure to build momentum and commitment to a new way of working to deliver results was particularly acute during this two-year period. Being willing to work from a set of principles rather than a clear and pre-determined set of plans took courage from everyone involved. It was probably challenging, exciting, frightening and inspiring at times – sometimes all of them within a matter of minutes!

Changing one thing in a system changes everything else as well. In this case, the managing director believed he could only deliver the business results needed by using a process that would involve everyone. This, in turn, meant he needed to flex his leadership style. While he had been trained in the use of Appreciative Inquiry and has used it in several projects, the business turnaround was by far his largest application. While the big agenda was the business turnaround, the MD was in no doubt that he would be closely watched by his team to see whether this new leadership style was permanent, and if so, what its impact would be on them and their part of the business.

When the managers began to see and feel the benefits that started to come with this positive and inclusive way of working, the momentum and commitment built in the team. Even though it was a slow build, it meant that everyone was on board when it came to implementation and they delivered results quicker than in a traditional project. Our experience with traditional projects is that change management is one of the work streams, and usually late in the project. However, the success with this way of working shows that it needs to start at the moment of project conception.

Another key learning about this type of change is the importance of patience and belief in one's self. The time lag between the MD changing his behaviour and the team changing theirs required a significant amount of patience and a strong commitment and belief in the approach he was using. At times, it would have been very easy to give up or assume that a team would never change. Also, being watched for authenticity and consistency meant taking much more time than usual to explain what he was doing and why. In a recent Inquiry into the impact of the MD's change in leadership on his immediate team of managers, they were very aware that their own style of managing and leading had also changed significantly. They hadn't expected this and were not necessarily ready for it, but saw the positive impact on their own teams with a greater sense of people working together as a whole system.

While we seemed to be on a courageous path – by taking a strength-based approach and involving the managers to a much greater extent than before – in hindsight it would have been advantageous to have been even more courageous! In the Easy Business project, we engaged about 30 to 40 per cent of the population in its development. In its execution, we engaged about 90 to 100 per cent. The result was that we got 80 per cent success very rapidly. However, we had to work a lot harder with the remainder. This was due to a mixture of lack of motivation or understanding of what was required because of not having been involved in the earlier stages.

While there are many ways of turning round a business in BP, the preference tends to be to take a problem-solving approach. Therefore, there was an expectation in the group that the turnaround would be seen quickly and through financial results. There was little understanding in some areas about achieving financial success through deep-seated culture change or transformation. Acknowledging the difference in the culture of the BP group and the emerging culture of the Castrol Marine business required the MD and others to be translators between the two systems. More work could have been done to deepen peer relationships, and help them understand the different types of successes taking place in the business. When the financial results did start showing, they were far better than expected.

If more businesses within the group are to use these strength-based and inclusive approaches, senior management needs to be more aware of and have greater trust in the people who are doing the work at a local level. In the local experience and customer knowledge lie the success stories that show what to continue and what can be improved. The answers to perceived organizational problems always lie within the organization itself. These answers are characterized through peak experiences – when business feels 'the best'. Catching these experiences and learning how to share them and reproduce them is an uplifting and motivational experience (AI Practitioner, 2005). This also means that this kind of strategy work involves a degree of uncertainty and non-analytical processes such as stories rather than desk work.

Applying the principles of AI to traditional methodologies such as project management was crucial in making sure that each stage of the work was properly prepared. It enabled the MD, his team and their teams around the world to bring together both the inclusive and participative approach with the structure and rigour needed to successfully deliver a phase of the work. Project management technology was a familiar tool in the business and was adapted as managers and staff became more confident in using the new approach.

In the last point in this section, we refer to the external consultants and their willingness and interest in combining and applying AI to the methodologies they were known for and hired for. This enabled them to deliver the behavioural changes and business results within the overall framework of the AI principles. For Anne Radford, it meant providing AI instruction while designing various events or phases with the other external consultants. This was a very different way of training people in AI and required her to bring in just enough information for the current task. Her concern was to make sure that this gradually led to the consultants having as thorough an understanding of AI as if they had been on a more usual training programme.

In summary, projects that are deeply transformational and change perceptions of customers and employees need to have inclusiveness, inquiry and adaptability at the heart and from the start.

12

Case study: Revitalizing corporate values in Nokia

Caryn Vanstone and Bruno Dalbiez

INTRODUCTION

In this chapter, the authors aim to explore the story of an Appreciative Inquiry-based intervention, focusing on revitalizing the corporate values in Nokia.

THE ORGANIZATION

Nokia's long and diversified story started with the wood pulp mill established by Fredrik Idestam in 1865 (Nokia, 2007). The turn of the 20th century also saw the birth of two other companies, the Finnish Rubber Works and Suomen Punomotehdas Oy, a wire and cable manufacturer. Nokia Ab also started generating electricity during the early years, and the various businesses were merged during the early years of the 20th century. After the Second World War, the company started to export cables into the newly created USSR and by the 1960s it had started to work in consumer and industrial electronics. By the 1980s it had established itself as one of the leading firms in the emerging telecommunications market.

In 1989, the Company President, Simo Vuorilehto, started the transition from diversification to focus. Vuorilehto shifted from acquisition to selling, from international to domestic consolidation and within just a few months, 10 per cent of the company's revenues were gone. Whilst the financial communities were applauding Vuorilehto's divestment of failing units, internally people were increasingly unhappy working without the compelling vision of a growing, European Nokia championed by Vuorilehto's predecessor, Kairamo. By 1990 Finland's GDP was also in the red with the collapse of the lucrative Soviet trade. The company hit rock bottom – even rivals Ericsson were not interested when Nokia's leading shareholder tried to sell them his stock. A major change in direction and approach was required. It happened in the 1990s, under new CEO Jorma Ollila, who led and established Nokia as the global leader in mobile communications it is today, and championed the articulation of Nokia's values.

THE ORGANIZATION CHALLENGE

The largest increase in number of employees throughout Nokia's history took place between 1996 and 1999, when the company recruited over 20,000 new employees around the world. In 1998 Nokia was the world's largest supplier of mobile phones. By 2000, it had just under 60,000 employees in over 50 countries, and sales had increased to 31 billion euros. The Nokia Values created in the early 1990s had guided Nokia people through this period of extraordinary growth.

However, by 2000, the Group Executive Board (GEB) was feeling that it was time to revitalize them. They discussed the challenge – how to refresh and revitalize the Values, keep the incoming ideas and diversity alive and yet honour and continue the fundamentals that had supported Nokia's success over the last decade? Internal and external conversations led the Board to the conclusion that training everyone in the Values was not a good enough solution; a different approach was called for.

SELECTING THE APPROACH

Ashridge Consulting met with Nokia to explore alternatives. Ashridge suggested to Nokia that they think differently about the concepts of values, identity and meaning, drawing from Social Constructionist ideas, as articulated by Berger and Luckman (1966) and Gergen (1999). From this different mindset, values cannot be objectified or externalized (for people to organize themselves 'around'). They form in the interactions between people and gradually become institutionalized and routine within the prevailing cultural orthodoxy. They come to be recognizable, through repetition and storytelling, as being 'what is important around here'. Identity and shared values are therefore constructs formed, negotiated and continuously updated through ongoing, dynamic relational processes. This positions the Nokia Values as something that are both formed by, and forming, employees' sense making and behaviour at the same time.

Therefore, all knowledge, including the basic, taken-for-granted common sense of everyday reality into which we are constantly acting, is derived from and maintained by what goes on between us in the everyday experience. This knowledge includes the values and identity that people think of as 'the organization' and as 'who I am as an individual', which are merely externalized and internalized versions of the same ongoing conversation and storytelling in which people participate (Mead, 1934). 'In the end, we become the autobiographical narratives which we "tell about" our lives' (Bruner, 1987).

This challenged the notion of 'training in' the values at Nokia, as it asserts that values cannot be imposed from 'outside' the local interactions between people in their everyday workplaces. No amount of workshops, posters, mugs or mousemats, reward schemes, top-leader videos or websites would turn a set of ideals into something that people hold to be the lived reality of what is 'of value' in that organization. It would therefore be inappropriate to attempt to find a way of revitalizing a set of values centrally and 'enrolling' people in them. This, however, can be a difficult message for highly agentic and accountable company executives to take on board. Does this mean that one can do nothing formally to develop a common set of corporate values?

In our view, it is still possible to be proactive in developing shared values. Mead (1934) also proposed that meaning created and re-created through local interaction leads to what he described as 'significant symbols' – those things that have become understood in the same way by all parties in the interaction and which then guide patterns of behaviour.

In Nokia's case, the consultants' task was to create a structured process (to contain anxiety sufficiently to act) that would enable people to engage consciously in this conversation and storytelling in the workplace. This process should allow employees to connect up and explore the implicit and unofficial beliefs and values already present in their everyday experience, alongside the explicit and official espoused values. The assumption was that, from this interaction, new, shared 'significant symbols' would arise which would be understood to be the new emerging Corporate Values. The difference was that the directors would not be 'in control' of the values, but would be participants, alongside others, in co-creating and living them.

DESCRIPTION OF THE PROJECT EXPERIENCE

The Nokia GEB considered a proposal which would involve cross-sections of the entire organization in structured conversations focused on real, concrete stories of success and Nokia values in action. The proposal generated a positive response, and four members of the GEB volunteered to be part of a pilot workshop planned for November 2002. This would give them an experiential understanding of the approach before making any final decision about a large-scale summit.

Definition workshop

They convened a group of 20 employees drawn from a worldwide cross-section of businesses, functions, geographies and organizational levels. This group would experience the approach (based on the AI '5D Cycle' shown in Figure 12.1), and become the 'Core Team' who would co-own and sponsor the rest of the project. They felt that this first workshop should be facilitated by one of the established, worldwide 'gurus' of AI and Summits. So Dr Frank Barrett was brought in from the United States to work with Bruno Dalbiez (one of Nokia's internal consultants in Organization Development & Change) and the group of 20.

In November 2002, the group met for a two-day workshop. The objectives were to:

▌ Gain an understanding of the AI approach by experiencing it for themselves, and make the final decision whether to proceed.

▌ Turn what was a broadly described idea ('revitalizing the values') into some more precise topics of inquiry for the whole organization

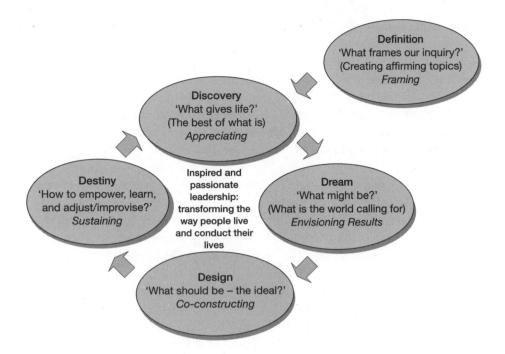

Figure 12.1 The AI process

to engage in. (On the 5D model, this was, for them, a Definition phase.)

▌ Plan the next steps and take ownership.

The workshop was not without ups and downs, which had to be worked through with skilful facilitative support. By the end of the workshop the group intellectually understood the relevance of the approach to their issue, and emotionally 'felt' the power of it on their own energy and behaviours. They agreed to go ahead with an inquiry process, leading to a large scale Values Summit based on the remaining 4Ds in the 5D model (Figure 12.1). This would be a three-and-a-half-day event for about 200 people in Helsinki.

The two-day workshop had successfully acted as a definition process, resulting in a clearer articulation of the topics they wanted to inquire into through the remaining 4Ds of the process.

The appreciative topics they created were:

▌ inspired and passionate leadership: transforming the way people live and conduct their lives;

| making a difference;

| exceeding our own and customers' expectations;

| pride in working for Nokia.

The AI interview protocol (set of appreciative storytelling questions prepared for use in the pre-Summit inquiry, and during the Summit itself) was created and agreed.

Pre-Summit inquiry

Through the winter months of 2002–03 a planning team worked together – both virtually using telephone conferencing, e-mail and internet technologies, and in face-to-face design meetings. This team was made up of representatives from the 20-person 'Core Team' from the November workshop, Bruno and an internal facilitation/support team, Caryn Vanstone from Ashridge Consulting and Dr Frank Barrett. The date of the Summit was set for April 2003 and the venue selected.

It is also fair to say that the Core Team and the Nokia GEB showed a good dose of 'sisu' (a Finnish term meaning a mix of long-term strong will, determination, courage, acting rationally in the face of adversity) in engaging and sticking with something that was very different from their normal ways of working. They did commit to a 3.5-day Summit experience, supported the team actively and made time to engage in the AI 1:1 interview process which preceded the Summit itself.

Every member of the 'Core Team' carried out AI Discovery interviews with between 1 and 15 Nokia employees each, worldwide, using the topic-based protocol. This was an important phase of the work. With hindsight though, it was too low profile in comparison to the investment in, and 'wow' of, the Summit experience. By going out into the everyday workplace, engaging people in conversations and storytelling processes (focusing appreciatively on stories of values in action, and value-based leadership) they were already starting to 'seed' the workplace with new patterns of discourse and meaning-making interactions. On later reflection, we came to realize that this IS the most important aspect of working with AI and Corporate Values/Culture, and we did not give it sufficient focus, time or resources in the Nokia project. In projects since, Ashridge Consulting have increasingly downplayed the event-based Summit approach, focusing more and more on a 'viral' method of inquiry at local level.

The Summit

The 200 participants in the Summit in April 2003 were personally invited by CEO Jorma Ollila, as a highly diverse representation of the organization around the world. The summit was facilitated by Caryn Vanstone and Dr Frank Barrett.

It followed the remaining 4Ds of the AI cycle, with 1:1 AI Discovery interviews, sense making and positive core articulation, before proceeding through Dream expressions and Design propositions. The final day was based on the principles of 'Open Space' (Owen, 1997), which allowed people to connect together in a self-organizing manner to identify and work on initiatives and experiments they felt passionate about.

The 'Core Team' and the facilitation team both remember moments of doubt, high tension and pressure, as well as extraordinary positive energy and joy during the Summit. During evening meetings with the Core Team and GEB, the consultants found themselves fielding questions and anxiety-laden demands – especially in the first couple of days which, to action-oriented executives, can seem slow and ponderous.

Of course, it is possible at any time for someone in a position of authority to believe that they have seen the 'right' pattern or themes, and to short-cut the group process by offering their answer. This is often what leaders are asked to do in organizations as it reduces the anxiety of emergent group process, makes them feel in control and suggests speed and 'moving on'. However, 'moving on' without the wider group having discovered their own answers will result in slower or no action later.

When, as an AI facilitator, you hold back leaders from a premature articulation of emerging themes and patterns (by holding to the process of discovery), they often feel frustrated and disempowered. The group can also feel at a loss for a while, and can turn to the facilitator to 'fill the gap'. Part of the skill of facilitating such events is the presence of mind to refuse such seductive invitations – from leaders and other group members alike – but instead to hold the whole group to the task of finding their values, identity and meaning for themselves.

'Removing the mantle of scientific authority and fostering democratic participation has been a chief aim of constructionist inquiry' (Gergen, 1999).

In addition, it was important that time allowed the 'norms' and embedded 'positive core' to be fully experienced, told and retold in different combinations in the room. This IS the process through which those 'significant symbols' (or organization Values that they wanted to foster) emerge in the group as a phenomenon within the relationships, behaviours and interactions between people in the room.

Post-Summit process

For several months after the Summit, Bruno and the Core Team continued to support the work, in an informal way. There was only an internal webpage to share news and progress and several face-to-face meetings of the leaders of specific initiatives. The assumption was that empowered and enthusiastic Summit participants would create their own conversations and energy locally.

OUTCOMES SO FAR

The ongoing change from a Summit takes two forms – the formal changes (projects, initiatives, etc) and the informal changes (personal, emergent, localized).

Formal outcomes

On the final day of the Summit, 18 action groups of volunteers formed around projects co-created in the Open Space process. These projects met the original brief of the work to develop and bring to life the core values of Nokia – they were the Values in action, being renewed and expressed in everyday actions and interactions.

Some examples of successful projects which delivered results included:

▌ 'One Nokia to the customer' (collaboration across functions to benefit customer experience).

▌ 'Relight the Fire' (refreshed articulation of the company's existing Values with what had been discovered collaboratively at the Summit).

▌ 'Positive performance management' (applying AI principles and elements to development and performance reviews). Today, Nokia's personal development process includes an appreciative coaching approach.

However, many of the other formalized initiatives started during the last day of the Summit died away. The consultants were clear with the Core Team and GEB beforehand that this could happen to as many as half of the initiatives from the Summit. This is a natural way of separating those projects which have genuine long-term energy and relevance and those which are little more than a manifestation of the energy of the event itself. Again, if people are to experience the Values in action they must be free to express what they, personally, find 'of value' in the way they volunteer into long-term action. Closing the Summit, Nokia's CEO spoke of this, stating that volunteerism and self-direction were at the heart of the ongoing process.

Nonetheless, it was felt that the challenge of normal workload pressure meant that some really good ideas didn't have enough chance to be realized. This experience has resulted in significant changes to how Ashridge Consulting now designs the final day of an AI Summit and what happens in the months that follow. There is a clear need to balance self-organized and self-directed action with sufficient structure and support to enable action to be sustained.

Informal outcomes

The generative, viral spread of learning at individual level has been extremely high, and has been a powerful enabler of localized, positive change – the most powerful outcome of the work. The Values in action and the appreciative, collaborative mindset from the Summit experience has found its way into many leaders' and teams' ways of working, processes, customer relationships and innovation processes throughout the Company. Subsequent AI-informed pieces of work have sprung up repeatedly since 2003 in places as far apart as the Far East, the United States and Latin America. Nokia has continued to use AI elements across HR and OD functions worldwide.

The original objective of the work was delivered in a lively and relevant output – a rethinking and re-articulation of the Corporate Values in today's world. More than an espousal or poster campaign, it is a genuine recommitment through localized, increasingly appreciative and affirming interactions and conversations. That, in itself, is an expression of what it means to be in Nokia.

REFLECTIONS AND LEARNING

Working with the informal, everyday interactions

Summits create a considerable amount of initial energy and buzz, but if they are either too early in a process of change, or are too 'stand alone' as a change intervention (as this one was in Nokia), the energy dissipates fast on return to 'business as usual'.

Projects led by Ashridge Consulting since have featured much more investment in developing 'positive deviancy' and 'radical incrementalism' at local level, early in the change process. This means working within the ordinary workplace – shops, call centres, offices – as opposed to taking people out of the workplace too soon to attend some extra-ordinary event. By focusing attention on the relationships, behaviours and choices being made daily between managers and staff, the consultants now support provocative action and conversation, leading to greater engagement and change.

Ashridge Consulting continue to use large group interventions such as AI Summits, but now locate those events in the middle of a change process which might be, in total, a two-year project (for an organization as large as Nokia). Designs of such work now allow for up to a year working informally and locally, creating change and successful empowerment experiences, before the Summit. Then a support system is put in place for the year after the Summit to give the initiatives and new relationships formed the best possible chance. Much of this work is done by internal change teams themselves, with coaching and support from the specialist consultants. This means that the organizational 'ground' (within the workplaces) is ready to receive the more radical and challenging projects that emerge at the Summit itself, as well as providing a 'fertile' environment for the informal shifts in behaviour that each individual Summit participant brings back with them.

Leaders need a 'good enough' structure in order to feel safe enough to 'play'

The AI 5D process has proved a useful framework and methodology. It provided a good enough holding structure to enable the Nokia executives to step into a highly emancipatory and participatory approach to change – containing their anxiety by providing a recognizable infrastructure. Without it, the inquiring, emergent aspects of the work would have been too different from the dominant project-based approaches to change.

As Barrett *et al* would put it, 'For the agent or idea to be persuasive, it must already present some ideas that members believe and see as legitimate. There must be some appealing principles that uphold current beliefs before it can pose a challenge to other beliefs.' (Barrett, Thomas and Hocevar, 1995).

Nevertheless, the challenge of living with emergent change as it actually starts to happen can be stressful for managers. Executives can struggle with their own feelings of wanting to be in control. This was most noticeable in the middle of the Summit, as has been noted earlier.

This is a paradoxical experience for them – because they are also aware that if they were 'in control' they would be limiting the degree of accountable, adult participation of others. These types of emancipatory, all-in-it-together change processes bring these paradoxes, often uncomfortably, close to the surface.

Therefore, in later projects Ashridge Consulting have insisted upon more in-depth coaching and learning for senior executives during the 'informal' first phase of the work, throughout a Summit and afterwards as they experience the increased 'empowerment' of the workforce, resulting in wonderful successes, and 'learning incidents' alike.

The introduction of AI tends to lead people to 'repress' negativity or problem-talk

The consultants were mindful of the compelling research of Dr Barbara Fredrickson of the University of Michigan (*et al*) which makes a direct link between the experience of embracing positive emotions with well-being, health and strength. Fredrickson and Losada (2005) assert that for 'human flourishing' (defined as 'to live within an optimal range of human functioning, one that connotes goodness, generativity, growth and resilience') we need to experience a 3:1 (approx) ratio of positive to negative interactions and emotions.

In addition, the research has shown that by focusing on the positive, Fredrickson's study groups demonstrated more flexible and complex behaviours, and dealt with paradoxes and dilemmas in a more sustainable way.

Based on this research and personal experience, the consultants therefore felt that AI was the right approach to Nokia's wish to reinvest in their values.

However, Fredrickson also found that without 'appropriate negativity' the experience became ungrounded and ineffectual. Consultants have to appreciate the full human experience. It is important to make a clear distinction between appreciative work (which embraces and supports human experience, possibility and growth, from a position of thorough inquiry in the present) and positive thinking (which projects forward utopian visions and requires people to ignore or repress negative feelings or experiences).

We find that when AI is brought into organizations as a kind of 'religion' for people to enrol into, it can have the impact of repressing appropriate challenge and negativity. We find that the most useful stance is to help people to explore all aspects of their experience, and the skill is in finding the most helpful time to encourage reframing (ie approaching the problem they are exploring from the 'opposite side') or letting go. What we try to avoid as AI practitioners is amplification or dramatization of problems, labels and critiques so that they 'grow' and become more stuck than before.

Repressed negativity did not prove to be a real difficulty in the Nokia work, as the dominant culture is one of rigorous critique and problem solving – common in technology and engineering companies. However, it is something that the consultants were constantly on the watch for.

AI itself can become an orthodoxy, or dogma, which is not congruent with social constructionist thinking

Tim Haynes, Director of Leadership and Organizational Development at GlaxoSmithKline, and recent participant in the Ashridge Masters in Organization Consulting, sums up very well some concerns about the emerging dogma within the AI community:

> AI itself creates some binary distinctions which I read as constructing notions of 'good' and 'bad'. For example, Watkins and Mohr (2001) develop Cooperrider and Srivastva's distinction between Paradigm 1 and Paradigm 2 action research assumptions to suggest there are two different metaphors for organization change which I would paraphrase as being to view organizations either (a) as 'problems to be solved' (a Newtonian perspective) or (b) as 'possibilities to be realized' (a constructionist perspective).
>
> I think AI strongly advocates the latter over the former – that it is 'good' to think of organizations as possibilities rather than as problems. This in itself creates a binary distinction which Gergen (1999), from a constructionist perspective, warns against – 'When we attempt to make firm distinctions, we crystallize the arbitrary and we create totalizing worlds.' Therefore AI is,

in my opinion, in danger of creating its own totalitarian monologue which privileges certain perspectives over others. (Haynes, 2006)

The consultants worked throughout the project to challenge and support each other in noticing those moments when it was appropriate to 'hold the line' in terms of both the appreciative stance and the methodology, and when it was appropriate to see, think, speak and act from a different stance.

SUMMARY

As the practice of AI develops, the challenge is to move beyond the seductive methodologies and compelling orthodoxy and to remain mindful of the risks of splitting and polarization. The authors of this chapter believe that social constructionism and the underpinning philosophy of appreciative, emancipatory inquiry has much to offer the world of organization change. As David Cooperrider himself acknowledges, there is much more to be learned and explored here, we have only just begun.

13

Case study: World Café

Arian Ward, Paul E Borawski and Juanita Brown

INTRODUCTION

This case study reviews a large-scale strategic change programme within the American Society for Quality using World Café. The concept of World Café is explored elsewhere in this book, but as an organizational process it complements Appreciative Inquiry as a conversational approach which has systems-wide applications.

THE ORGANIZATION

Headquartered in Milwaukee, Wisconsin, the American Society for Quality (ASQ) is the largest quality association in the world, with more than 100,000 members in 100+ countries on six continents.

ASQ has been at the forefront of the quality movement for 60 years.... By the end of the 1980s, the principles of quality had greatly influenced manufacturing and other industrial processes.... In the 1980s, ASQ members began to see how quality could be applied beyond the world of manufacturing.... Quality began to blossom into a much broader discipline aimed at leading, inspiring, and managing a broad range of businesses and activities, always with a focus on excellence.

Today manufacturing remains a core of ASQ's activities, but ASQ also has established itself as a champion of quality in education, healthcare, the service sector and government. (American Society for Quality, 2007a)

ASQ's new vision, role, and long-term objectives are the drivers and outcomes of the transformative journey described in this case study. The dramatic departure here is that ASQ is no longer just an association that serves quality professionals, as it has been for the past 60 years:

▌ ASQ's vision:

- By making quality a global priority, an organizational imperative, and a personal ethic, the American Society for Quality becomes the community for everyone who seeks quality concepts, technology, and tools to improve themselves and their world.

▌ Role and long-term objectives:

- To be stewards of the quality profession by providing member (customer) value

- To be stewards of the quality movement by providing increased society value from ASQ activities. (American Society for Quality, 2007b)

THE ORGANIZATION CHALLENGE

As ASQ began this transformative journey in 2002, they were faced with a host of challenges and opportunities from multiple sources within their strategic landscape – the marketplace, the world at large, and internal. ASQ knew they needed to navigate a new course through this rugged future landscape.

ASQ regularly engages in futuring and environmental scanning to help them chart this course. Futuring is a structured look ahead aimed at enhancing anticipatory skills. ASQ has used futuring for over 10 years as part of its strategic planning and repositioning for change.

ASQ's 2002 Futures Study was one of the primary drivers of the transformative journey described in this case study. Table 13.1 is a brief list of the key future forces identified in the last two studies (in order of relative expected impact on the future of quality). The complete 2005

Table 13.1 Key future forces

2002 future forces	2005 future forces
Quality must deliver bottom-line results.	Globalization
Management systems will increasingly absorb the quality function.	Innovation/Creativity/ Change
Quality will be everyone's job.	Outsourcing
The economic case for the broader application of quality will need to be proven.	Consumer sophistication
Global demand for products and services will create a global workforce.	Value creation
Declining trust and confidence in business leaders and organizations.	Changes in quality
Rising customer expectations.	

Futures Study is available on the ASQ website (American Society for Quality, 2007c).

The biggest difference in the findings of the two studies (other than different wording produced by different Futures groups) was the degree to which change and the accelerating rate of change will influence the future. This raises the importance of innovation and adaptation as needed future survival skills.

More near-term forces identified through market research and environmental scans include:

▌ Changes in the quality profession – The quality movement has strived to make quality a part of everyone's job. Particularly in manufacturing, they have succeeded in this to such an extent that the number of people in the formal role of 'quality professionals' has decreased. Globalization and outsourcing have resulted in quality jobs shifting to other locations or companies in which ASQ may have less of a presence.

▌ Increased competition – Increasing competition, fuelled by the internet, has squeezed sales and margins and weakened the market for many of the knowledge offerings of professional associations like ASQ.

▌ Changes in demographics – Changes in the demographics of ASQ's existing and potential markets require ASQ to rethink its value proposition and membership.

▌ Dot.com bust and economic downturn – Starting or renewing a membership in an association like ASQ is often a discretionary expense that is put off or avoided when times are tough.

▌ 9/11, terrorism, war – Beyond the obvious impact on our society's psyche and the economy, this also impacted travel, limiting the ability of associations like ASQ to rely as much on one of their biggest revenue producers – conferences, seminars and conventions.

Internally, ASQ faced the challenge of how to transform a successful, 60-year-old organization with ageing strategic processes and structures into a nimble organization capable of not only facing these external challenges, but turning them into opportunities.

SELECTING THE APPROACH

In his search for a fresh approach to strategy, ASQ's Executive Director and Chief Strategic Officer, Paul Borawski, contacted Juanita Brown, who had been developing new thinking around strategic futuring (Brown *et al*, 2005). Juanita and Paul explored the possibility that 'strategy as inquiry'– hosting strategic dialogues around ASQ's most important questions – might yield new insights and paths forward, especially in an uncertain environment. Paul believed ASQ members cared deeply about quality and he also wanted a way to unleash this spirit. That was when Juanita talked a bit about the World Café and introduced him to Arian, who had done a good deal of this kind of strategic dialogue work with Associations and other non-profits.

The dialogue approach to strategy that Juanita was referring to is something Arian calls Living Strategy™. Traditional approaches to strategy often seemed meant for static organizations in predictable environments. His response to this was Living Strategy (Table 13.2), which is basically:

▌ the dynamic story of the shared aspirations, strategic direction, and strategic outcomes of the association and the community it supports,

▌ emerging and continuously evolving

▌ from the collective knowledge of the community and

Table 13.2   Living Strategy

Traditional strategic planning	Living Strategy™
Strategic planning – assumes you can predict the future and develop successful plans based on those predictions.	Strategic thinking, questions, dialogue and stories – assumes you can't predict the future, but you can collectively prepare for what might emerge.
A linear process performed by a single elite group produces a static textual output.	Living Strategy continuously emerges out of ongoing, interwoven: • individual reflection and work; • group face-to-face and virtual interactions and collaborations; • dialogue across the whole community of organizational stakeholders. It lives as shared knowledge, not just information – compelling stories, images, and questions in stakeholders' minds and hearts, as well as in a repository accessible to all, about their shared aspirations, priorities, and inquiries into the future. It tries to understand the organization and its environment as an interconnected, whole system, where strategy serves to focus and align the interactions of the whole system towards a future collectively envisioned and evolved by those stakeholders.
Scheduled and time bound; eg once every 2 years looking out 3–5 years into the future.	Ongoing and dynamic, designed to change whenever change is indicated.

▌ from an expanding network of ongoing strategic conversations among all members of the community around the questions that matter most to them,

▌ all seamlessly interwoven into the 'fabric' of the current organization through a continuous process of reflection and renewal.

Arian was a co-creator of the World Café with Juanita and others back in January, 1995, and Living Strategy was developed from the same thinking, a desire to create an effective process for real organizations and real people to shape their common futures through powerful conversations around their most important questions. The World Café approach offers an emergent view which follows a simple yet powerful set of integrated Café design and hosting principles rather than a single 'recipe' or form (Figure 13.1). Café hosts then contribute their experiences in applying these Café principles back into the collective knowledge bank of the community.

Continuous learning and discovery based on the World Café community's collective experience in real-life situations over more than a decade has created a vibrant, living approach to engaging 'conversations that matter' as the heart of whole systems change. The Café approach to large-group dialogue is rapidly spreading across all continents and is being used in a growing number of corporate, community, government, health, education, NGO and multi-stakeholder settings. (See www.theworldcafe.com)

AIMS FOR THE CHANGE

Since ASQ was already aware of the need to change in order to deal with the challenges and opportunities they faced now and in the future,

Figure 13.1 Sense response diagram

the big questions for them were 'Change to what?' and 'How?' Paul recognized that to begin this transformative journey they needed a map of where to go. Here is how he framed the situation ASQ was facing at the start of this journey. 'Like many other associations, the end of the 1990s saw declines in membership and revenue. By early 2002, ASQ's stage was set for change. A six-year planning cycle was coming to an end, and ASQ decided it would refresh its view of the future through a new Futures Study and alternative approaches to setting strategy.'

After Paul and ASQ president at that time, Ken Case, engaged Arian to help them develop this new direction, they co-created an approach to Living Strategy for ASQ that was specifically tailored to the situation, needs and 'style' of ASQ. Figure 13.2 encapsulates the ultimate aims for this effort: to develop a 'Sense and Respond System' that would enable ASQ to evolve its Living Strategy from ongoing strategic dialogues among all stakeholders and to weave this into the fabric of the organization through its people, structures, processes and culture – to make it truly 'live' within the minds and hearts of everyone in the association.

DESCRIPTION

The ASQ Strategic Planning Committee began with the assumption that they didn't know what strategy was needed to set a truly new direction for ASQ. They also assumed that not only did they not know the answers, but they didn't yet know the right questions to ask.

Out of a series of initial conversations emerged key questions that would guide the inquiry. The heart of the strategy meeting was a connected series of Café dialogues around these strategic questions, such as:

▌ Who do we want to serve?

▌ What means the most to us?

▌ What are the few Big Questions that, if answered, would make the biggest difference in realizing our vision?

▌ What about our current reality gets in the way of making all this happen?

One of Paul's observations on that first strategy meeting in August 2002 was, 'I think if anybody who knew us had listened to what we planned

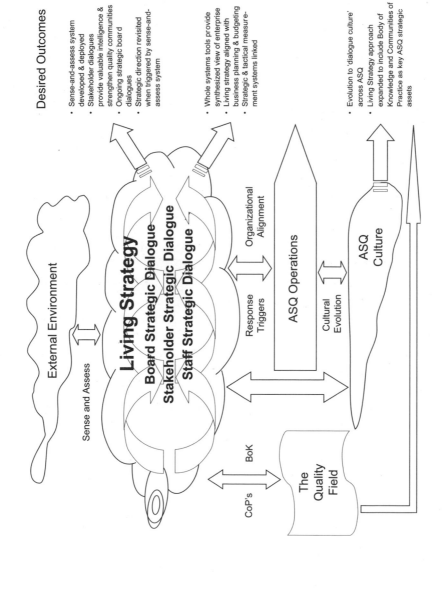

Desired Outcomes

- Sense-and-assess system developed & deployed
- Stakeholder dialogues provide valuable intelligence & strengthen quality communities
- Ongoing strategic board dialogues
- Strategic direction revisited when triggered by sense-and-assess system

- Whole systems tools provide synthesized view of enterprise
- Living strategy aligned with business planning & budgeting
- Strategic & tactical measurement systems linked

- Evolution to 'dialogue culture' across ASQ
- Living Strategy approach expanded to include Body of Knowledge and Communities of Practice as key ASQ strategic assets

External Environment

Sense and Assess

Living Strategy

Board Strategic Dialogue

Stakeholder Strategic Dialogue

Staff Strategic Dialogue

Organizational Alignment

Response Triggers

ASQ Operations

Cultural Evolution

ASQ Culture

CoP's

BoK

The Quality Field

Figure 13.2 World Café principles

to do with Cafés they would have laughed and said not to do it, that it wouldn't work. But you should have seen the room come to life with the first set of Café questions! Paul commented that 'this session turned ASQ strategically inside out. The two-day direction-setting session had not produced a one-page plan, as was customary. Instead, it left us with key questions that called for further exploration. So the whole thing started to blossom into realizing that many more voices (and a wider web of conversations) were needed to discover the answers to the key strategic questions raised at that initial session.'

Immediately after this meeting, the team began to broaden the conversation by engaging the full board in a virtual Café dialogue around the initial strategic direction and questions from the first strategy session. Through this series of virtual conversations, the full board was brought into the strategic direction-setting process in a meaningful way for the first time. The aim was to connect and cross-pollinate the diverse perspectives shared by various board members.

This set the stage for face-to-face Café dialogues around ASQ's strategic direction with the full board at the November board meeting. Rather than the typical 20-minute review with little discussion and quick approval of the strategic plan, the board engaged in a full six hours of Café conversations around the strategic direction as well as the core questions proposed in the summer meeting and further explored in the varied virtual Café conversations.

As a result of engaging in this and subsequent strategic dialogues, ASQ has continued to evolve its strategic direction-setting process to one that is truly 'alive'. It has become an expanding web of 'Living Strategy Cafés' (over 120 cafés, so far), spreading out from a small group of people, the Strategic Planning Committee, to a larger group, the board, and to many groups of other stakeholders. Strategic questions and stories act as the connectors between these conversations as well as the collective intelligence that emerges from them. Board and staff members act as the hosts of the conversations.

This reveals the deeper living network pattern of the World Café in action. As Ken Case (now an ASQ past president) describes this living process, it's 'an ongoing dialogue spreading in waves. The result is like a ripple effect, as when you throw a rock out in the pond and you see the little ripples going out. And if you notice, those ripples come back too. The more you do this and the better you do this, you start getting these ideas coming back. And there are some real pearls in those ideas that work their way back from some of those outer constituencies all the way to the board. That's the beautiful dynamics of this approach.'

In 2005, ASQ stepped back and took a hard look at the strategic progress they were making. It still wasn't yet what they were hoping to achieve from their Living Strategy. When they looked for the root causes of this, one of their key shared insights was that they weren't engaging one of their most important stakeholders in these strategic dialogues and resultant change efforts.

These were the 'Member Leaders' – the thousands of unpaid volunteers who are on the front lines of the association, interacting with members and helping to deliver the value they are seeking from their membership in the association. So a series of Member Leader gatherings were convened, beginning in Fall 2005 and continuing in the Spring of 2006 and 2007, with another planned for Fall, 2007.

Here is how ASQ staff writer John Ryan described the Fall 2005 gathering:

ASQ's Member Value Leadership Summit... made great strides toward establishing a renewed sense of community among the ASQ leadership and identified immediate and long-term opportunities for collaboration and improved cooperation....

'This is the first time such a wide representation of the ASQ Member Leadership – across all levels of the member organization – has gathered in one place,' said ASQ President Jerry Mairani....

Some 170 leaders representing a cross-section of the Society attended the event.... Participants were encouraged to think about out-of-the-box ways to change ASQ in order to enhance the value of the membership experience. The work at the summit involved intensive cross-fertilization of ideas using... café dialogues.

The Café dialogue format for the summit resulted in a high level of energy and engagement and prompted the sharing of many diverse viewpoints and disagreements. But over the course of the summit, a somewhat disjointed group began to meld into a more cohesive community, and numerous ideas emerged for shaping the ASQ of the future....

Participants closed the summit by signing a pledge of commitment to get to know each other better and work together more effectively as the ASQ leader community. (American Society for Quality, 2007d)

The Spring 2006 and 2007 Member Leader gatherings were even more successful, as word of the wonderful experience participants had at the Summit spread and the sense of trust and respect built through the rich Café interactions at the Fall Summit enabled deeper connections and dialogue at subsequent gatherings.

Many more stories and images of these amazing events are available on the ASQ community website (American Society for Quality, 2007e).

The overwhelming success of these first three Member Leader gatherings has led to a number of new initiatives as well as a commitment to continue this process of bringing Member Leaders together on a regular basis for rich dialogue and commitments to take action.

OUTCOMES

As an organizational anthropologist, Arian usually looks first at intangible outcomes, as most reflective of whole systems change. They include changes in people's mindsets and behaviours such as: the general 'mood' of the organization and its different parts; how engaged are people in the process of change and in day-to-day operations; how negative or positive is the scuttlebutt flowing through the informal network; how effectively do people engage in meaningful dialogue and collaborative action; how aligned are people around the strategic intent of the organization; how far-reaching and deep are these changes; and so on.

There are encouraging signs in how effectively the behaviours and attitudes which are needed to support ASQ's Living Strategy are becoming embedded into the psyche and actions of the organization:

▍ ASQ has made tremendous strides in developing a culture of dialogue across the organization. All board meetings, some staff meetings, all Member Leader gatherings, and even some member events feature or centre around conversations.

▍ All key ASQ stakeholders have at least begun to engage in meaningful conversations.

▍ These conversations have contributed to the development of more trust-based relationships which are necessary to allow ASQ leaders to take on changes that had been previously been impossible.

▍ Back-room politicking has diminished significantly; there are still heated discussions around contentious issues, but these are focused on the issues rather than the personalities.

Like many large-scale changes, tangible results were longer term in coming. In the first 2–3 years little change was evident in the three key measures of the association – member recruitment, member retention, and revenue. But the last year has seen an end to the multi-year decline in membership and revenue. So even the tangible outcomes are beginning to look like an overall success!

This success is summed up by Paul Borawski, the Executive Director and Chief Strategic Officer of ASQ:

> Living Strategy, and at its heart – Café conversations, – is everything I hoped for. It responds to the nagging limitations of my past experiences. It engages the board in strategic discussion. It enables strategic change.... Living Strategy has rekindled my hope, and has enlivened the board's relationship with each other and with staff. And probably most important – Living Strategy has enabled change.

REFLECTIONS

Paul Borawski:

> If you want to tap the wisdom of your board, then start asking them important questions and providing them time to delve into those questions. Don't be surprised when their response is to dig in.... And don't be surprised when from the diversity of their talents and experience comes a diversity of opinion and even conflict. Are you ready to guide a leadership body through conflict? Is your objective consensus or evolutionary transformation? Because real transformation almost never comes through consensus; change is just too difficult and painful for some to embrace up front....
>
> If you take the struggles of a few as a sign of trouble you'll be missing the shift toward greater involvement, greater exposure, and greater accountability. There's far less room to sit on the sideline. It's not for everybody. But you'll be rewarded by wisdom and creativity you knew were there that simply were never tapped before. Just make sure you're ready to use them.
>
> I was also surprised by the resistance of some of our Member Leaders. We clearly needed to involve them earlier in this process.
>
> One of my significant points of learning over the past few years is about systems thinking. Most of us are taught concepts and processes and that's great for isolating ideas for learning. But in the real world, concepts and processes do not stand in isolation. The concepts and processes we learn interact with other concepts and processes; there are interdependencies that create both expected and unexpected consequences. The world is complex. Systems thinking offers tools, albeit young tools, to begin to work with this complexity.
>
> Transformational change is not easily managed. It's reinvention on the run and it's challenging. Keep all the balls in the air, and change at the same time. Find the capacity within. And, when 'business as usual' requires attention, guess what suffers: strategy. But that doesn't mean the transformation has

to stop, since cultural transformation can continue in our everyday work, even if strategic transformation has to wait. So we need to create enough momentum for change in our day-to-day operations to sustain us in those times.

Other lessons:

▌ Get some agreement with your leadership that strategic redirection will require resources to succeed.

▌ Be prepared to learn and adapt. As the change starts, be watchful of the early signs and marketplace response. Don't expect all your changes to work, and be ready to adapt when they don't.

▌ There can be no solace in inaction. Boards and other leaders need to understand that there's as much accountability in not changing as there is in changing.

▌ Someone has to push, relentlessly. As the change process begins to unfold you'll find it's a bit like rolling a large rock uphill. Without someone's unrelenting, untiring efforts to roll the rock and place some stakes in the ground so it doesn't roll back, you won't make any progress.

Arian Ward:

I have no doubt that the key to whole systems change is strategic dialogue among all key stakeholders around the things that matter most to them. I've tried many other conversational techniques but the World Café is the best means I've found of doing this. I believe it's because it's so flexible, being based on a set of design principles that can be applied to almost any context rather than a prescribed process or 'form'. It's also a powerful set of principles to use to help guide the overall systems change.

Café dialogues were a tremendous two-way link between the association and members, customers, and other key stakeholders, providing high value to both the association in terms of market intelligence and to the stakeholders in terms of a deeper understanding of what's happening within the association and a stronger voice in what and how it delivers value to them.

An important lesson is to make these an ongoing part of normal operations and to spread them throughout the organization by teaching Member Leaders how to host these Café dialogues. We tried a little of this train-the-trainer approach, but could have carried it further. To complement the very successful Member Leader gatherings, we need a more local, personalized approach to helping them learn from each other, especially how to foster greater member loyalty and participation.

The initial gains made in the mindset and behaviours of all the Member Leaders and staff involved in the initial years of Living Strategy have been dramatic. Making Cafés and other types of dialogue a standard part of all board meetings was a key part of this. But the further we get from those initial efforts, the harder it is to engage the minds and passions of people who weren't involved initially. We continue to struggle with a universal problem among volunteer-led organizations: How do you maintain continuity and momentum when your volunteer leaders keep changing every year or two? The only solutions we know of for this are to keep reinforcing the same cultural behaviours so the continuity is carried in the culture rather than in the individuals, to keep orienting the newcomers to the underlying concepts, strategies, and techniques behind all of this, and to stay engaged in dialogue, whether it's in Cafés or some other form – keep them talking about questions that matter.

Juanita Brown:

We have learned from the ASQ case that collective processes that help an organization access its mutual intelligence in the face of uncertainty will be critical for leaders wishing to navigate the turbulent waters that lie ahead. This case study shows one important way in which an organization can exercise 'conversational leadership' in strategic, systemic, and practical ways. While requiring artistry and care in their introduction and implementation, we've discovered that World Café and other complementary approaches to hosting and convening strategic dialogues around an organization's most important questions form an essential part of the core leadership process for creating value and co-evolving positive futures in today's world.

14

Case study: Applying Appreciative Inquiry to deliver strategic change: Orbseal Technology Center

Jacqueline M Stavros and Joe R Sprangel Jr

INTRODUCTION

In this chapter, the authors share a story of how an Appreciative Inquiry (AI) approach to create positive change was applied to an emergent strategic planning framework called SOAR, based on its Strengths, Opportunities, Aspirations and measurable Results. SOAR is an innovative, strength-based approach to strategic planning that invites the whole system (stakeholders) into the process to propel an organization forward to its most preferred future with measurable results. This approach integrates AI with a strategic planning framework to create a transformation that inspires organizations' members to SOAR!

The initiative began in 2004 when Orbseal Technology Center (OTC) was relocated to Michigan (the company was part of a $60 million organization). In 2006, the ongoing success resulted in Orbseal being purchased by a $12 billion German organization. OTC was fully absorbed and the entire staff retained during the acquisition because of the positive results this division had with its internal and external stakeholders, especially with their US customer base. OTC is an American branch of the German organization that continues to use the guiding principles of AI and the SOAR framework in both its strategic thinking and daily operations. We will begin to look at the role of strategic management in helping OTC develop strategic change actions. The expectation is that these actions will lead to transformational change through a blend of AI approach and SOAR.

THE ORGANIZATION

In 1983 Orbseal began to manufacture adhesives and sealants for the automotive industry. In 1997, the Orbseal Technology Center was opened to staff personnel in Sales, Research and Development, and Design Engineering. This division was in a separate state from the corporate headquarters. OTC's ultimate goal from the collaborated efforts was to drive business and provide revenue growth for the organization. The program manager in charge of this effort decided that AI and the SOAR framework would help guide his team to create a division that would lead the organization to the top of its industry. He expressed the following to his team:

> Our organization made an investment to move this office from Richmond, Missouri, to be right next to its key customers in Detroit, Michigan, with the hope of creating a collaborative environment to drive business and provide growth for our organization. There is no guarantee that we will have business tomorrow, and it won't simply be waiting on our doorstep. It's our responsibility to create our future!
>
> We must realize it is a privilege to be the supplier of choice and it is our responsibility at the OTC to be the best at what we do. Blending the AI approach and SOAR framework that I learned in graduate school, I want us to do an inquiry as to our personal and organizational values and discover what we do best. Then, we will create a guiding vision and mission statement for the OTC, and align it with corporate vision and mission. Let's imagine the best possible future. OTC will then have a documented direction and purpose. We will wrap up this process with the discovery of what we do best and identify our unique value offering (UVO). This will allow us to dive deeper into our core strengths, and allow us to design strategic goals and objectives for a preferred future. We need to be innovative and inspire others into action. Are you in?

The OTC changed the language of the original AI 4D model:

Discovery → Dream → Design → Destiny

to a language that the organizational members were more comfortable with, resulting in a strength-based strategic planning framework (Strategic Impact 4-I Framework):

Inquire → Imagine → Innovate → Inspire (inspired action is key to execution of strategy by those involved in the process)

built on a foundation of Relational Awareness.

The programme manager received unanimous support for this challenge. The executive vice president (EVP) for the division flew in from corporate headquarters to be part of this strategic planning session. Typically, strategic planning was top-down in this organization and this bottom-up, whole system approach made the EVP curious and supportive. He shared this aspiration with his team: 'Today, we are part of a team that has been responsible for approximately $60 million in annual revenues. Tomorrow let us be the team that leads Orbseal to the top of our industry. Thank you for your investment of time and commitment to the team!'

THE ORGANIZATION CHALLENGE

OTC used a traditional top-down non-inclusive approach to strategic planning. This meant that the current strategic planning process involved only upper management and a core executive team. At OTC, during the first 90 days they waited to hear from headquarters as to what should be the strategy – the game plan. Then, the next 90 days, there was conflict among the three departments that had relocated and they were reorganized as OTC. The program manager clearly stated his challenges as:

| No one knew what the OTC purpose (mission) was and where we were going (vision).

| There was a lack of understanding on what the strategic goals were and who was responsible for creating these goals.

I No alignment between the strategy of OTC and Orbseal.

I The 45 employees of OTC were hungry for strategic direction.

The climate was very reactive, with a 'wait and see' attitude. Each department worked in a silo and was not sharing information. The programme manager also identified significant external challenges:

I intense competition nationally and internationally;

I customer market driven by cost and quality;

I customer market required 'give-backs' – an annual percentage of sales revenue.

There were two compounding factors: 1) the role of decision-making appeared centralized and 2) conflict emerged between the three managers in the OTC division.

THE ROLE OF DECISION MAKING

Twenty years of research by Nutt (1999) shows that organizations fail with half of their decisions. He found three common mistakes made in the decision process used by organizations, namely 1) effective practices are commonly understood yet not typically used, 2) decision makers take short cuts because of perceived pressure, and 3) failure to set an effective problem-solving environment. The research showed a common understanding of the need of employee participation, yet this method was used in only one out of five decisions.

As presented earlier in this chapter, the programme manager's decision to be proactive in regard to creating a strategic plan for OTC ultimately would lead to effective integration into the overall strategic plans for the organization. The next part of this chapter explains the selected approach and provides additional support that integrating AI into the strategic planning actions of the organization can lead to an improved performance and positive shifts in organization culture, climate and conversations.

SELECTING THE APPROACH
(WHY AI AND SOAR FRAMEWORK)

This part of the chapter looks at the viewpoints of Prahalad, Mintzberg, Hamel, and Markides as well as several strategic frameworks to validate SOAR.

Strategy perspective of influential management thinkers

Hamel and Prahalad (1996) posed the following questions prior to a meeting of the Strategic Management Society:

> How to create an organization that really, truly lives in the future, and then interprets today's decision in that context? How does one unleash corporate imagination? How does one turn technicians into dreamers? How does one turn planners into strategizers? Is there no recourse except to sit back and wait for the visionary to emerge? Planning may be discredited, and strategists on the run, but managers must not shirk from the responsibility of leading their organizations to the future (1996: 242).

A recent strategy perspective was presented by McCarthy (2000) as an outcome of a crosstalk interview with Henry Mintzberg who states:

> Certainly leaders make a difference. There is no question about it. But leaders often make a difference because they stimulate others, not because they come in with grand strategy. But what we're getting now, very dangerously, is what I call a dramatic style of managing: the great merger; the great downsizing; the massive, brilliant new strategy. Most of this is junk and fails utterly, but not until it fools the stock analysts for a few years (2000: 34).

Commentary on the Mintzberg interview with McCarthy was provided by Markides, who responded by stating that anyone in the organization can conceive new strategic ideas. The use of a democratic participative approach in which thousands of employees are asked to provide input to the strategic plan allows for greater potential of innovative suggestions than those brought forward by a handful of senior executives.

Strategic planning is typically a top-down centralized process or a team is assigned to determine the future of the corporation by assessing internal and external variables often using a SWOT format to analyse strengths, weakness, opportunities, and threats. SWOT is a common strategic planning tool that has served to maintain the status quo of business (de Kluyver and Pearce, 2006). We propose the use of an emerging framework that leverages, yet evolves beyond, the classical tool of SWOT:

Traditional SWOT Model:

Strengths → Weaknesses → Opportunities → Threats

Transform into SOAR:

Strengths → Opportunities → Aspirations → Results (List the measurable results desired by the participants. Focus on one or two key metrics in finance, operations, marketing, and learning & growth.)

OTC selected SOAR because they wanted to achieve strategic impact. The programme manager believed that the SOAR framework would help them search for the best in the division and organization as a whole – that which gives it life. He wanted his team to learn the art and practice of asking unconditional positive questions to heighten the positive potential and move the team forward into its preferred future. He felt this approach would bring responsibility and ownership to participants who were allowed to have valued input into the combined strengths and opportunities, resulting in the co-creation of strategy and results. He appreciated the flexibility of language change from 4Ds (Discovery, Dream, Design, and Destiny) to 4Is (Inquiry, Imagine, Innovate, and Inspiration), making it easier for the team to tap into information and knowledge at the core of their conversations – creative conversations for strategic change.

Review of strategic frameworks

Stakeholder theory and involvement (Figure 14.1) are pertinent to the design of an effective framework for strategy development (de Kluyver & Pearce, 2006). Jones, Felps and Bigley (2007) state:

> Stakeholder theorists view the corporation as a collection of internal and external groups (eg, shareholders, employees, customers, suppliers, creditors, and neighboring communities) – that is, 'stakeholders,' originally defined as 'those who are affected by and/or can affect the achievement of the firm's objectives' (Freeman, 1984a). Relationships with stakeholders can be wrought with tension when organizational self-interest and stakeholder well-being are in conflict. Moral concerns can be a barrier to positive relationships

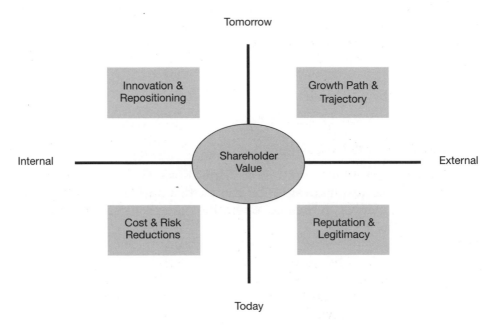

Figure 14.1 Key dimensions of shareholder value

Source: Hart and Milstein (2003: 57)

with any or many of the stakeholder groups; the sense that the organization is dealing legitimately with stakeholders is considered by many stakeholder scholars as 'a fundamentally moral phenomenon' (Jones *et al*, 2007: 141).

Freeman (1984b) suggests that organizations should consider a strategic management process that includes not only those groups who can affect it, but also those who are affected by its operations. Hart and Sharma (2004) developed the concept of 'radical transactiveness', focusing on 'gaining access to stakeholders previously considered extreme or fringe for the express purpose of managing disruptive change and creating competitive advantage' (2004: 9), engaging stakeholders in a two-way dialogue in which each influences and is influenced by the other. O'Driscoll, Pierce and Coghlan (2006), in investigating 'the psychology of ownership', state, 'Because participation in decision making provides increased opportunities for employees to exercise control and to voice concerns, they are more likely to experience procedural justice under participatory conditions' (Roberson, Moye and Locke, 1999). The AI approach and SOAR framework allow for both of these positive conditions and conversations to exist.

The programme manager wanted a strategic planning approach that was inclusive and allowed for breakthrough innovation. He also wanted the 45 people of OTC to get engaged in both the future and the everyday operation of the division. The following section offers a description of the project that moved OTC towards a most preferred future. This framework resolves the concerns of the leading strategic management literature and builds upon the application of applying AI as an effective strategic planning practice.

DESCRIPTION OF THE PROJECT EXPERIENCE

The SOAR (Strengths, Opportunities, Aspirations, and Results) framework will be presented in this section. First, the basics of the framework will be reviewed. Second, the OTC example will demonstrate the effectiveness of this approach.

The SOAR framework

The SOAR framework for strategic inquiry and decision making was designed to bring a stakeholder dialogue into the strategic planning process. Originally, Stavros, Cooperrider and Kelley (2003) provided the language and a framework to guide the strategic planning process to focus on how it may leverage its strengths to embrace opportunities and achieve aspirations. The SOAR framework goes beyond the SWOT model to link the internal strengths and external opportunities to the vision and mission of the organization to create strategic initiatives, strategy, tactical plans, and measurable results, as shown in Figure 14.2.

SOAR accelerates the organization's strategic planning efforts by focusing directly on those elements that will give life energy to the organization's future. An organization's life energy is located in the people. It is made explicit by dialogue between and among these groups of stakeholders (Holman, Devane and Cady, 2007). The SOAR approach to strategy development and formulation starts with an inquiry into strengths and opportunities. In this case, inquiry is orchestrated though an appreciative dialogue process (Cooperrider and Srivastva, 1987; Bushe, 1995). Effective inquiry for strategic planning includes explicit consideration of the purpose of the organization – its mission, the customers it serves, and the stakeholders it impacts. This inquiry enables participants to examine, clarify, and consciously evolve

Figure 14.2 SOAR: what we do and how we do it

Source: Stavros, Cooperrider and Kelley (2006)

their truly desired purpose and commitment to themselves and the organization.

The Imagine phase is where strengths and opportunities are collectively explored and possibly new ones identified through dialogue between stakeholders to set long-term goals and create strategies. This phase also identifies the shared value set, vision and mission of the organization through opportunities for stakeholders to create effective strategy formulation (de Kluyver and Pearce, 2006). The innovation phase is a call for aspirations and to co-construct the most preferred future. With these transformational factors taken into consideration, organizations are able to create a new future and sustain a sense of commitment and urgency over a long period of time (Hamel and Prahalad, 1989). This phase also involves design of strategies and tactics to support the new business model. Finally, the implementation phase is where employees are inspired through authentic recognition and reward to act on the shared plans and achieve measurable results.

The OTC experience – discovering the positive core

On 17 June 2004, Jackie Stavros and the programme manager met with the 45-person OTC team and the executive vice-president from corporate headquarters. The one-day event focused on discovering the positive core and the dream of what the OTC can be. The deliverables for the one-day event were to:

▌ Understand and align personal and OTC values (later to align with corporate values).

▌ Identify core strengths for further inquiry to create distinctive competencies.

▌ Identify possible opportunities for growth and innovation.

▌ Create a vision and mission statement.

From the above deliverables another inquiry was scheduled to include the newly created values, vision and mission and to take a deep dive into understanding how the core strengths can become distinctive competencies that allow the organization to achieve its strategic initiatives and go after new opportunities. The agenda for the day is shown in Table 14.1.

Inquiry into organizational strengths and opportunities

The SOAR framework (Figure 14.3) was presented and how it has been used by other organizations. By focusing on Strengths and Opportunities, organizations can reach their Aspirations (desired outcomes) to achieve measurable Results by:

▌ inquiring into strengths and opportunities;

▌ imagining the best pathway to sustainable growth;

▌ innovating to create the initiatives, strategies, structure, systems and plans; and

▌ inspiring action-oriented activities that achieve results.

After a review of the framework (for more information on how SOAR works, when and where it has been used, and an expanded table of

Table 14.1 Discovering the strategic core of the Orbseal Technology Center

Times	Events
10:00am: 11:30–1:00pm:	Welcome and Introductions – Overview of AI & SOAR Discover the Strategic Core of Orbseal 1:1 Interviews (box lunches served)
1:00–1:15pm	Debrief
1:15–2:00pm:	Identify: Values → Vision → Mission → Strategic Goals & Objectives
1:30–3:00pm:	Identification of Team Values (15 → 10 → narrow → 5) Discover Strategic Core → List Five Topic Areas (Team's Strengths and Opportunities) and create a Vision Statement that is both in a creative and narrative format
3:00–3:30pm:	Report Outs: Top Five Values Five Topic Areas A skit and a vision statement
3:30–4:00pm:	Strategic Inquiry with Appreciative Intent – Next Steps
4:00–4:30pm:	Create the Team's Mission Statement
4:30–5:00pm:	Report Out & Alignment Discussion
Next Steps:	Deep Inquiry into Core Competencies – each person to be interviewed by Programme Manager Create Market Opportunities and Strategy based on secondary inquiry Define Strategic Goals and Objectives Create Action Plans

applications across several industries, please refer to the new *Change Handbook* by Peggy Holman, Tom Devane and Steve Cady (2007)), the OTC team began the inquiry with the following statement and questions.

Figure 14.3 SOAR framework

Source: Stavros, Cooperrider and Kelley (2006)

Imagine – the most preferred future – what are the aspirations?

In this phase, team members began to imagine what the future might be. The SOAR approach allowed for passionate thinking, creativity, and positive imaging. The Imagine phase enabled them to co-create organizational values, a vision of the preferred future, and to identify strengths, product/service innovations, potential market opportunities, and aspirations. The results were energizing and fun.

What really connected the group was that for each top five values listed per team, three of the five values were identical across all four teams. They worked together to create a unifying set of values and vision:

▌ OTC's Values: dedication, flexibility, creativity, innovation, team spirit, and continuous communications;

▌ OTC's Vision: to be a diverse and global leader providing best-in-class engineering, NVH (noise, vibration and harshness), sealant, and adhesive solutions with unsurpassed sales and service.

The group also identified key strengths to explore in detail: adaptive, dedicated, positive working environment, and strong product core. A team member shared with the group what he believed was unique about the SOAR approach to visioning in the Imagine phase: 'I'm only an administrative professional with OTC. The opportunity to allow me to participate in the creation of a strategic vision and to openly let me share what I see and believe makes me feel part of a team! It was nice to hear that others have aspirations like mine. I feel connected to this team and empowered to make a positive impact.'

Innovate – what should be the strategic direction?

During this phase participants were asked to design the future by creating the ideal organization needed to reach its dream. The OTC team had in-depth dialogues about the possible strategic initiatives, strategies, best structure, and processes. Everyone had a voice and was part of the process. OTC created two possibility statements that they merged into one macro mission statement to achieve a present purpose:

> We are hardworking, flexible employees who design, develop, sell and service cost effective and innovative engineering, NVH, sealant and adhesive solutions that are manufacturable, profitable, and add value to our customers.
> We provide a safe positive work environment that is conducive to creativity that attracts and retains top quality employees.

With this adopted mission statement for its team, there is a collaborative work environment across the organization.

Inspire (also noted as Implementation) – move to action with energy

Inspired action can deliver the organization to its envisioned future. This phase involved shared discussions on the best way to deliver and sustain the organization's collective sense of purpose – the mission statement. For OTC, this meant beginning another strategic cycle. The EVP returned to headquarters with an objective of completing this SOAR approach with the 400 employees at the corporate office. He stated: 'The process went above my expectations because the three divisions became boundaryless and came together to co-create the future. Everyone was heard and everyone has a stake.'

A second interview guide was created to fully explore key strengths and opportunities that would support the strategic plan. These core topics were explored by all members:

Adaptable → highly adaptable to change and challenges
Dedicated → dedicated to exceeding internal and external customer satisfaction
Positive Work Environment → harmony and sharing among employees
Strong Product Core → strong foundation of optimized sealants and adhesives

After the second inquiry (this took almost six weeks), the team produced a strategic and tactical plan with action-oriented activities that would meet the organizational strategic initiatives (the objectives and goals). The OTC team created its strategic action plan to best move forward yet stay in alignment with the corporate strategic plan.

THE OUTCOMES

The programme manager felt the AI and SOAR framework allowed for:

▎ strengths and opportunities to be co-created outside of a box;

▎ creation, buy-in and ownership of the plan and the future;

▎ fresh focus on strengths and opportunities that could be transformed into aspiration and realities;

▎ a strategy plan with initiatives identified to drive performance and measurable results;

▎ connection in the room – communications were continuous and open.

The programme manager stated: 'people commit to what they help create and we are living our values, working within our mission and reaching for the vision!'

Ongoing AI-related projects beyond OTC's original scope are:

∎ Connect the strategic plan to a balanced scorecard.

∎ Continuous improvement and learning with positive valuation.

∎ Team spirit is alive and moving forward with both strategic intentions and positive intentions.

∎ Participants had a positive experience and want to expand this to corporate level.

REFLECTIONS AND LEARNING

The SOAR framework is a search for life for the organization and what gives life; it contains the whole of the organization. According to Rainey (2005), 'exploring the life-giving forces of the firm allows for knowledge to be validated and used productively' (2005: 211). This framework has use not only at the strategic business unit level (OTC), but also at the corporate and functional level. Beyond achieving measurable results, OTC members have learned to:

∎ identify the positive core of the organization (strengths and opportunities);

∎ obtain clarity of values, vision, and mission to align with strategic initiatives, strategies, and action plans (aspirations);

∎ plan, design, and facilitate a whole-system strategic planning session;

∎ identify measurements that drive performance (results).

The most important part of any strategic planning process relates to the question of sustainability of the designed path/course. Sustainability is best understood to have three components: confidence, momentum, and a balance of anticipation and responsiveness to a changing environment.

First, confidence is a capacity for heightened positive perception of strengths. This is what the SOAR framework achieves. In the first phase of SOAR the inquiry into the possible is all about the identification and mapping of strengths and magnification of opportunities. It is about the belief that the vision and tasks before the group can be realized. The people who are OTC believe and are achieving with confidence their desired future.

Second, momentum sustains confidence. Leach and Moon (2004) define momentum as the impetus gained by a moving object. Momentum can be defined as the fuel in the tank that drives strategy into action. A way to nurture momentum is to make the search for strengths, innovations and opportunities an everyday expectation and occurrence. People at OTC are doing just that in the way they approach customer service initiatives and in the designing of new products and services. They also want to include more stakeholders in the next planning process, such as suppliers and customers.

Finally, effective sustainability depends on being able to anticipate the future and be responsive to a changing environment. OTC has learned that just as important as it is to execute their strategy is to nurture a culture of strategic learning and leadership where anyone can creatively balance anticipating future events while responding to today's events. One of the repeated benefits of the SOAR framework is that organization members continue to discover strengths, seize opportunities, articulate aspirations and assess results. These are the nutrients organizations need to feed the kind of learning that is relevant and adaptable.

The last section provided the basics of the SOAR framework and the successful application of it at OTC to allow a group of committed stakeholders to proactively improve their situation versus waiting for corporate to do something – good or bad. By focusing on strengths and opportunities, organizations like OTC can reach their aspirations (desired outcomes) with measurable results. This will be accomplished by creating a critical mass focused on attaining the values, vision and mission of the organization. The final challenge is the need to develop systems to ensure that managers are supportive and accountable for creating an environment of positive strategic change. In order to continue the progress, a continuous dialogue must exist between and among organization stakeholders on who are we, where are we going, and how can we best get there. Of utmost importance when done correctly, this will result in a competitive advantage for the organization and an improved environment for all stakeholders.

INTERVIEW GUIDE 1: DISCOVERING THE STRATEGIC CORE OF ORBSEAL TECHNOLOGY CENTER

Our ultimate goal from the collaborated efforts at the OTC is to drive business and provide revenue growth for our organization. There is no guarantee that we will have business tomorrow, and it won't simply be waiting on our doorstep. We must realize it is a privilege to be the supplier of choice and it is our responsibility at the OTC to be the best at what we do. Today, we shall identify both our personal and organizational values and discover what we do best at the OTC. Then, we will create a guiding vision and mission statement for the OTC, and align it with corporate vision and mission. OTC will then have a documented direction and purpose. We will wrap up this workshop with the discovery of what we do best and our unique value offering (UVO). This will allow us to dive deeper into our core strengths, and allow us to create opportunities and design strategic goals and objectives for a preferred future.

Today, we are part of a team that has been responsible for approximately $60 million in annual revenues. Tomorrow let us be the team that leads Orbseal to the top of our industry.

Thank you for your time and commitment to the team!

∎ Why did you join Orbseal? How did you come to work for the Orbseal Technology Center (OTC)? How long have you been with the organization? What is your role and contribution(s)?

∎ Describe a peak experience or high point during your employment with the OTC. This would be a time when you felt most alive and engaged.

∎ What is it that you value about yourself, the nature of your work, the sales team, the R&D team, design engineering, and OTC?

∎ When OTC is at its best, what are the core factors (our strengths) that give life to our center, without which the OTC would cease to exist?

∎ Where do you see Orbseal in the next five years? What business segment(s), technical product(s), or process innovation(s) has been successfully created and launched? What opportunities have we seized? And, how did OTC help to get us there?

∎ What wishes or hopes do you have to strengthen the core of our division or that of the organization?

Appendix: Resource list

AI COMMONS

AI Commons is a worldwide portal devoted to the sharing of academic resources and practical tools on Appreciative Inquiry and the rapidly growing discipline of positive change. This site is a resource for leaders of change, scholars, students and business managers – and is hosted by Case Western Reserve University's Weatherhead School of Management.
http://appreciativeinquiry.cwru.edu

AI CONSULTING

AI Consulting, LLC offers a collaborative, strength-based approach to strategic change and transformation. At the heart of our practice is Appreciative Inquiry (AI), an approach that draws on the strengths and values of an organization in order to implement its change agenda and achieve its highest goals. AI Consulting has the greatest concentration of AI expertise and its consultants span the globe. Among them are the thought leaders, authors, and founders of AI. Anne Radford is one of AIC's founders together with David Cooperrider, Diana Whitney, Bernard Mohr and Jane Magruder Watkins.
http://www.aiconsulting.org/

AI DISCUSSION LIST

AI Discussion List is sponsored by the David Eccles School of Business, University of Utah, United States. A place to ask for advice, contribute views and keep up to date with research results and articles published around the world. To register, go to:
http://lists.business.utah.edu/mailman/listinfo/ailist

AI (APPRECIATIVE INQUIRY) PRACTITIONER

The *AI (Appreciative Inquiry) Practitioner* is for people interested in making the world a better place using Appreciative Inquiry and strength-based change approaches. The publication highlights emerging issues and leading examples of positive change from around the world. Guest editors bring their passion to special AIP issues, adding their experience and widening the knowledge in this field of change. The journal is published quarterly: in February, May, August and November. Anne Radford is the publisher and editor-in-chief.
http://www.aipractitioner.com editor@aipractitioner.com

ANNE RADFORD

The website lists public AI workshops where leaders, managers and consultants learn to use AI as a way of thinking as well as a methodology. Anne Radford together with colleagues also brings the strength-based perspective to workshops on topics such as Appreciative Leadership or Innovation. The AI Dialogues sponsored by the *AI Practitioner* provide discussion days where practitioners together with business leaders focus on case studies or emerging OD issues.
http://www.ARadford.co.uk

EUROPEAN NETWORK AROUND APPRECIATIVE INQUIRY

European network around Appreciative Inquiry and strength based change is a group of individuals from different countries in Europe who have started to meet with the dream of growing a network of professionals to share ideas and to collaborate. Registration does not imply any costs or commitments but will keep you informed about

what is going on in the network. For more information go to:
http://www.networkplace.eu

To register for the network, go to:
http://www.webforum.com/form/leander/form.asp?sid=582015205

FUTURE SEARCH NETWORK

Future Search Network is a collaboration of hundreds of volunteers worldwide providing future search conferences as a public service. It serves communities, non-governmental organizations and other non-profits for whatever people can afford. Its mission is to help communities everywhere become more open, supportive, equitable and sustainable. It also works with for-profit organizations who share these values, charging standard fees. Future Search Network is based on principles of service, colleagueship and learning. They can be found at:
http://www.futuresearch.net/

JEMSTONE CONSULTANCY LTD

Jemstone Consultancy offers approaches to organizational change based on Appreciative Inquiry, Positive Psychology, systemic consulting and story, such as strengths-based coaching, appreciative consultancy and positive team building. The Appreciating Change website introduces these services and a free subscription via RSS to the new *Jemstone Tidbits* weblog newsletter: http://www.appreciatingchange.co.uk
　　The Jemstone site offers free access to a range of papers and presentations on Appreciative Inquiry and related topics. You can also download back copies of the newsletter *Jemstone Tidbits* that provides ideas, news, and stories relevant to organizational change and development.
http://www.jemstoneconsultancy.co.uk

NTL INSTITUTE

Founded in 1947, the NTL Institute, based in Alexandria, Virginia, with a facility in Bethel, Maine, is a not-for-profit educational company of members and staff whose purpose is to advance the field of applied behavioural sciences and to develop change agents for effective

leadership for organizations of all varieties. Included in its programmes in the United States are its AI programmes and a practicum. A few of its behavioural programmes are offered in the UK.
http://www.ntl.org

OPEN SPACE WORLD

This website contains helpful information about Open Space together with stories about how the approach has been used. It also contains useful web links to other relevant material. It can be found at:
http://www.openspaceworld.org/cgi/wiki.cgi

OPM

Founded in 1989, OPM is a not-for-profit consulting organization which provides advice and consulting to UK organizations on leadership, change and policy. The organization is based in London and has been working with conversation methods with clients in health, local and central government, including using Future Search, World Café and Appreciative Inquiry. For details about OPM's work or to access its free newsletter visit:
http://www.opm.co.uk

TAOS INSTITUTE

The Taos Institute is a community of scholars and practitioners concerned with the social processes essential for the construction of reason, knowledge and human value. The Institute focuses on creating promising futures through social construction. Founders include Ken Gergen, Harlene Anderson and Sheila McNamee – authors of key texts on social constructionism. On their website there is information on their newsletter, workshops and PhD programme in the Social Sciences at Tilburg University in the Netherlands.
http://www.taosinstitute.net

WORLD CAFÉ COMMUNITY

The World Café Community is a network of Café practitioners. The website includes stories, practical advice and guidance and has a discussion forum for sharing ideas and experiences.
http://www.theworldcafe.com/

References

AI Commons [accessed 1 March 2007] [Online] http://appreciative inquiry.case.edu/

AI Commons [accessed 1 March 2007] *AI Practitioner* [Online] http://www.aipractitioner.com

AI Practitioner (2005) Special Issue on Empowerment and Leadership, November, pp 37

Amason, A (1996) Distinguishing the effects of functional and dysfunctional conflict on strategic decision making: resolving a paradox for top management teams. *Academy of Management Journal*, **39**, pp 123–48

American Society for Quality (2007a) [accessed 13 March 2007] http://www.asq.org/about-asq/who-we-are/history.html

American Society for Quality (2007b) [accessed 13 March 2007] http://www.asq.org/strategy/visionroleobj.html

American Society for Quality (2007c) [accessed 13 March 2007] http://www.asq.org/strategy/pdf/asq_futures_study_2005_brochure.pdf

American Society for Quality (2007d) [accessed 13 March 2007] http://www.asq.org/media-room/news/2005/10/31-leadership-summit.html

American Society for Quality (2007e) [accessed 13 March 2007] http://asqgroups.asq.org/summit/Updates/4-29-2006_Member_Leader_Interchange.pdf

Art of Hosting [accessed 6 February 2007] http://www.artofhosting.org/theart/

Astley, W and Van de Ven, A (1983) Central perspectives and debates in organization theory. *Administrative Science Quarterly*, **28**, pp 245–73

Baker, A, Jensen P and Kolb D (2002) *Conversational Learning – An experiential approach to knowledge creation*. Quorum Books, London

Baldwin, C (1998) *Calling the Circle*, Bantam Books, London

Bansal, P (2002) The corporate challenges of sustainable development. *Academy of Management Executive*, **16**, pp 122–31

Barnett Pearce, W and Pearce, K A (1998) Transcendent storytelling: abilities for systemic practitioners and their clients. *Human Systems*, **9**, pp 167–85

Barrett, F J and Fry, R (2005) *Appreciative Inquiry: A positive approach to building cooperative capacity*, Taos Institute Publications, Chagrin Falls, OH

Barrett, F J, Thomas, G F and Hocevar, S P (1995) The central role of discourse in large scale change: a social construction perspective. *Journal of Applied Behavioral Science*, **31** (3), pp 352–72

Berger, P and Luckmann, T (1966) *The Social Construction of Reality: A treatise in the sociology of knowledge*. Anchor Books, Garden City NY

Bion, W R (2000) *Experiences in Groups*, Brunner-Routledge, London

Bohm, D (1996) *On Dialogue*, Routledge, London

Brown J, Isaacs D and the World Café community (2005) *The World Café: Shaping our futures through conversations that matter*, Berrett-Koehler, San Francisco

Bruner, J (1987) Life as narrative, *Social Research*, **54** (1), pp 1–17

Burnes, B (2000) *Managing Change: A strategic approach to organisational dynamics*, 3rd edn, Pearson Educational, London

Bushe, G (1995) Advances in appreciative inquiry as an organization development intervention, in *Appreciative Inquiry: Foundations in positive organization development*, pp 179–208

Cecchin, G (1987) Hypothesising, circularity and neutrality revisited, an invitation to curiosity, *Family Process*, **26** (4), pp 405–13

Collins, D (1998) *Organisational Change: Sociological perspectives*, Routledge, London

Conner, D R and Clutterbuck, D (1997) *Managing at the Speed of Change: How resilient managers succeed where others fail*, John Wiley & Sons, London

Cooperrider, D and Srivastva, S (1987) Appreciative inquiry in organizational life, in *Research in Organizational Change and Development: Volume 1*, ed R Woodman and W Pasmore, pp 129–69, JAI Press, Greenwich, CT

Cooperrider, D and Whitney, D (2001) A positive revolution in change: Appreciative Inquiry, in *Appreciative Inquiry: An emerging direction for organisational development*, ed D Cooperrider, P Sorensen, T Yaeger and D Whitney, pp 9–31, Stipes Publishing, Champaign, IL

Cooperrider, D and Whitney, D (2005) *Appreciative Inquiry: A positive revolution in change*, Berrett-Koehler, San Francisco

Cooperrider, D, Whitney, D and Stavros, J M (2005) *Appreciative Inquiry Handbook: The first in a series of AI workbook for leaders of change*, Berrett-Koehler, San Francisco

Dean, J and Sharfman, M (1996) Does decision process matter? A study of strategic decision-making effectiveness, *Academy of Management Journal*, **39**, pp 368–96

Dechant, K and Altman, B (1994) Environmental leadership: from compliance to competitive advantage, *Academy of Management Executive*, **8**, pp 7–20

Descartes, R (1890) *The Principles of Psychology*, Harvard University Press, Cambridge, MA, 1981. Originally published in 1890

Ellinor, L and Gerard, G (1998) *Dialogue: Rediscover the transforming power of conversation*, John Wiley, Chichester

Flaherty, J (2004) *Coaching: Evoking excellence in others*, Butterworth-Heinemann, London

Fredrickson, B (1998) What good are positive emotions? *Review of General Psychology*, **2** (3), pp 300–19

Fredrickson, B and Branigan, C (2005) Positive emotions broaden the scope of attention and thought-action repertoires, *Cognition and Emotion*, **19** (3), pp 313–32

Fredrickson, B and Losada, M (2005) Positive affect and the complex dynamics of human flourishing, *American Psychologist*, **60** (7), pp 678–86

Freeman, R (1984a) The social responsibility of business is to increase its profits, *The New York Times*, 13 September, pp 32–33, 122–26

Freeman, R (1984b) *Strategic Management: A stakeholder approach*, Pitman, Boston

French, W and Bell, C (1999) *Organisational Development: Behavioural science interventions for organisational improvement*, 6th edn, Prentice Hall, New Jersey

Gergen, K (1993) *Toward Transformation in Social Knowledge*, Sage, London

Gergen, K (1999) *An Invitation to Social Construction*, Sage, London

Gergen, K (2001) Qualitative inquiry: tensions and transformations, in *Handbook of Qualitative Research*, 2nd edn, ed N Denzin and Y Lincoln, Sage, London

Gilmour, D and Sutton-Cegarra, B (2005) Enabling the Easy Business transformation in Castrol Marine, *AI Practitioner*, Special Issue on Empowerment and Leadership, November, p 35

Hamel, G and Prahalad, C (1989) Strategic intent, *Harvard Business Review*, May/June, pp 63–76

Hamel, G and Prahalad, C (1996) Competing in the new economy: managing out of bounds, *Strategic Management Journal*, **17**, pp 237–42

Harman, W (1999) Shifting context for executive behaviour: signs of change and revaluation, in *Appreciative Management and Leadership*, ed S Srivastva and D Cooperrider, Williams Custom Publishing, Ohio

Hart, S and Milstein, M (2003) Creating sustainable value, *Academy of Management Executive*, **17**, pp 56–67

Hart, S and Sharma, S (2004) Engaging fringe stakeholders for competitive imagination, *Academy of Management Executive*, **18**, pp 7–18

Hawes, S (1993) *Reflexivity and collaboration in the supervisory process: a role for feminist post-structural theories in the training of professional psychologists*, Conference draft for the National Council of Schools Professional Psychologist Conference, La Jolla, California

Haynes, T (2006) *Social Construction and AI*, Ashridge Masters (MSc) in Organisation Consulting: Assignment 6, unpublished copy available from Ashridge Business School Library Collection with author's permission

Hitt, M and Tyler, B (1991) Strategic decision models: integrating different perspectives, *Strategic Management Journal*, **12**, pp 327–51

Holman, P, Devane, T and Cady, S (2007) *The Change Handbook*, Berrett-Koehler, San Francisco

Isaacs, W (1999) *Dialogue and the Art of Thinking Together*, Doubleday, New York

Jones, T, Felps, W and Bigley, G (2007) Ethical theory and stakeholder-related decisions: the role of stakeholder culture, *Academy of Management Review*, **32**, pp 137–55

de Kluyver, C and Pearce, J (2006) *Strategy: A view from the top*, Prentice Hall, Upper Saddle River, NJ

Lang, P, Little, M and Cronen, V (1990) The systemic professional domains of action and the question of neutrality, *Human Systems*, **1**, pp 39–55

Leach, J and Moon, J (2004) *Pitch Perfect*, Wiley Publishers, Hoboken, NJ

Martin, P (2006) *Making Happy People: The nature of happiness and its origins in childhood*, Harper, London

Maturana, H and Varela, F (1987) *The Tree of Knowledge*, New Science Library, Boston and London

McCarthy, D (2000) View from the top: Henry Mintzberg on strategy and management, *Academy of Management Executive*, **14**, pp 31–42.

McCarthy, D, Maier, S and Seligman, M (1976) View from the top: Henry Mintzberg on strategy and management, *Academy of Management Executive*, **14**, pp 31–42

Maier, S F and Seligman, M E P (1976) Learned helplessness: theory and evidence, *Journal of Experimental Psychology: General*, **105**, pp 3–46

Mead, G H (1934) *Mind, Self and Society: From the standpoint of a social behaviouralist*, Chicago University Press, Chicago

Micklethwait, J and Wooldridge, A (2003) *The Company: A short history of a revolutionary idea*, Phoenix, London

Morgan, G (1997) *Images of Organization*, Sage, California

New Economic Foundation [accessed 3 January 2007] Participation works! 21 techniques of community participation for the 21st century. [Online] http://www.neweconomics.org/gen/z_sys_publication detail.aspx?pid=16

Nokia (2007) [accessed 2 January 2007] http://www.Nokia.com

Nutt, P (1999) Surprising but true: half the decisions in organizations fail, *Academy of Management Executive*, **13**, pp 75–90

O'Driscoll, M, Pierce, J, and Coghlan, A (2006) The psychology of ownership: work environment structure, organizational commitment, and citizenship behaviors, *Group & Organization Management*, **31**, pp 388–416

Oliver, C (1996) Systemic eloquence, *Human Systems*, **7**, pp 247–64

Oliver, C and Brittain, G (1999) *Language: Generosity, authority, morality, enquiry*, private paper

Oliver, C and Brittain, G (2001) Situated knowledge management, *Career Development International*, **6** (7), full text

Owen, H (1997) *Open Space Technology: A user's guide*, 2nd edn, Berrett-Koehler, San Francisco

Papesh, M E [accessed 22 September 2006] Fredrick Winslow Taylor [Online] http://www.stfrancis.edu/ba/ghkickul/stuwebs/bbios/biography/fwtaylor.htm

Pascal, R, Millemann, M and Gioja, L (2000) *Surfing the Edge of Chaos: The laws of nature and the new laws of business*, Three Rivers Press, New York

Passmore, J (2003) Professional standards research: appreciative inquiry, *People Management*, December

Pavlov, I (1927) *Conditioned reflexes*, Oxford University Press, Oxford

Penn, P (1985) Feed-forward: future questions, future maps, *Family Process*, **24** (3), pp 299–310

Porter, M (1980) *Competitive Strategy*, The Free Press, New York

Rainey, M (2005) An appreciative inquiry into the factors of culture continuity during leadership transitions: a case study of Leadshare, Canada, in *Appreciative Inquiry: Foundations in positive organization development*, ed D Cooperrider, P Sorensen, T Yaeger and D Whitney, pp 209–19, reprinted from *OD practitioner* (1996), **28**, pp 34–41

Roberson, Q, Moye, N and Locke, E (1999) Identifying a missing link between participation and satisfaction: the mediating role of procedural justice perceptions, *Journal of Applied Psychology*, **84**, pp 585–93

Rose, M (1988) *Industrial Behaviour*, Penguin, Harmondsworth

Schein, E (1988) *Process Consultation: Its role in organisation development*. Addison-Wesley, Wokingham

Schweiger, D, Sandberg, W and Ragan, J (1986) Group approaches for improving strategic decision making: a comparative analysis of dialectical inquiry, devil's advocacy, and consensus approaches to strategic decision making, *Academy of Management Journal*, **29**, 51–71

Schweitzer, A (1969) *The Teaching of Reverence for Life*, Holt, New York

Scott, S (2002) *Fierce Conversations: It's not what you think it's what you say*, Piatkus, London

Seligman, M E P (1996) *The Optimistic Child*, Houghton-Mifflin, New York

Seligman, M E P (2003) *Authentic Happiness: Using the new positive psychology realise your potential for lasting fulfilment*, Nicholas Brealey, London

Seligman, M E P (2006) *Learned Happiness: How to change your mind and your life*, Vintage, New York

Shaw, P (2002) *Changing Conversations in Organisations – a complexity approach to change*, Routledge, London

Sidman, M (1989) *Coercion and its Fallout*, Authors Cooperative, Boston

Slater, S and Lovett, D (1999) *Corporate Turnround*, Penguin Business Books, London

Stavros, J, Cooperrider, D and Kelley, D (2003) Strategic Inquiry: Appreciative Intent: Inspiration to SOAR. *AI Practitioner*, November, 2–19

Stavros, J and Torres, C (2006) *Unleashing the Power of Appreciative Inquiry in Daily Living*, Taos Institute Publishing, Chagrin Falls, OH

Steinbock, S (2001) *The Nokia Revolution – The story of an extraordinary company that transformed an industry*, Amacom Books, New York

Stone, D, Patton, B, Heen, S and Fisher, R (1999) *Difficult Conversations: How to discuss what matters most*, Penguin, London

Streatfield, P J (2001) *The Paradox of Control in Organizations*, Routledge, London

Suntop Media Thinkers 50 [accessed 9 January 2007] *Suntop Media Thinkers 50. The Thinkers Top 50* [Online] http://www.thinkers50.com

Swarthmore Bulletin (2002, 1 June) [accessed 27 January 2007] http://www.swarthmore.edu

Taylor, F (1912) Scientific management, reproduced in Pugh, D (1997) *Organisational Theory: Selected readings*, 4th edn, Penguin, London

Thomas, H, Pollack, T and Gorman, P (1999) Global strategic analyses: frameworks and approaches, *Academy of Management Executive*, **13**, 70–82

Thompson, A and Strickland, A (2005) *Crafting and Executing Strategy*, McGraw-Hill, New York

Tomm, K (1987) *Interventive interviewing part III, Intending to ask circular, linear, strategic and reflexive questions*, Draft May 1987

Voltaire, F M (1759) *Candide, ou l'Optimisme*. Paris, France: Editions de la Sirene (reprint 1913)

Wallas, G (1926) *The Art of Thought*, Harcourt Brace, New York

Ward, A (2007) *Living Strategy*, Community Frontiers, Boulder Creek, CA, http://communityfrontiers.com/living.htm

Watkins, J M and Mohr, B J (2001) *Appreciative Inquiry – Change at the speed of Imagination*, Jossey-Bass/Pfeiffer, San Francisco

Weisbord, M and Janoff, S (2000) *Future Search – An action guide to finding common ground in organisations and communities*, Berrett-Koehler, San Francisco

Welch, J and Byrne, J (2001) *Jack: Straight from the gut*, Warner Books, New York

Wheatley, M (1999) *Leadership and the New Science – Discovering order in a chaotic world*, Berrett-Koehler, San Francisco

Wheatley, M (2002) *Turning to One Another*, Berrett-Koehler, San Francisco

Whitney, D and Fry, R (2006) Interviews with Diana Whitney and with Ron Fry. Getting started: secrets to initiating and contracting for successful large inquiries, *AI Practitioner*, May, pp 6–9

Whitney, D and Cooperrider, D (2000) The Appreciative Inquiry Summit: An emerging methodology for whole system positive change, *OD Practitioner*, **32**, pp 13–26

Whitney D and Trosten-Bloom, A (2003) *The Power of Appreciative Inquiry: A practical guide to positive change*, Berrett-Koehler, San Francisco

Whitney, D, Cooperrider, D, Kaplan, B S and Trosten-Bloom, A (2001) *Encyclopedia of Positive Question*, Berrett-Koehler, San Francisco

Wikipedia [accessed 3 March 2007] http://en.wikipedia.org/wiki/René_Descartes#Dualism

The World Café (2007) http://www.theworldcafe.com

Zeldin, T (1998) *Conversation – How talk can change your life*, The Harvill Press, London

Index

ALSO AVAILABLE FROM KOGAN PAGE

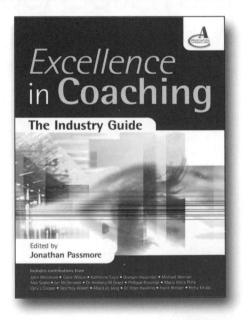